JN043911

香川県の教員採用試験過去問シリーズ⑤

2025年度版

# 香川県の英語科

# 過去問

協同教育研究会 編

協同出版

本書には，香川県の教員採用試験の過去問題を収録しています。各問題ごとに，以下のように5段階表記で，難易度，頻出度を示しています。

## 難　易　度

| | |
|---|---|
| 非常に難しい | ☆☆☆☆☆ |
| やや難しい | ☆☆☆☆ |
| 普通の難易度 | ☆☆☆ |
| やや易しい | ☆☆ |
| 非常に易しい | ☆ |

## 頻　出　度

| | |
|---|---|
| ◎ | ほとんど出題されない |
| ◎◎ | あまり出題されない |
| ◎◎◎ | 普通の頻出度 |
| ◎◎◎◎ | よく出題される |
| ◎◎◎◎◎ | 非常によく出題される |

**※本書の過去問題における資料，法令文等の取り扱いについて**

本書の過去問題で使用されている資料や法令文の表記や基準は，出題された当時の内容に準拠しているため，解答・解説も当時のものを使用しています。ご了承ください。

## はじめに～「過去問」シリーズ利用に際して～

教育を取り巻く環境は変化しつつあり，日本の公教育そのものも，教員免許更新制の廃止やGIGAスクール構想の実現などの改革が進められています。また，現行の学習指導要領では「主体的・対話的で深い学び」を実現するため，指導方法や指導体制の工夫改善により，「個に応じた指導」の充実を図るとともに，コンピュータや情報通信ネットワーク等の情報手段を活用するために必要な環境を整えることが示されています。

一方で，いじめや体罰，不登校，暴力行為など，教育現場の問題もあいかわらず取り沙汰されており，教員に求められるスキルは，今後さらに高いものになっていくことが予想されます。

本書の基本構成としては，出題傾向と対策，過去5年間の出題傾向分析表，過去問題，解答および解説を掲載しています。各自治体や教科によって掲載年数をはじめ，「チェックテスト」や「問題演習」を掲載するなど，内容が異なります。

また原則的には一般受験を対象としております。特別選考等については対応していない場合があります。なお，実際に配布された問題の順番や構成を，編集の都合上，変更している場合があります。あらかじめご了承ください。

最後に，この「過去問」シリーズは，「参考書」シリーズとの併用を前提に編集されております。参考書で要点整理を行い，過去問で実力試しを行う，セットでの活用をおすすめいたします。

みなさまが，この書籍を徹底的に活用し，教員採用試験の合格を勝ち取って，教壇に立っていただければ，それはわたくしたちにとって最上の喜びです。

協同教育研究会

# CONTENTS

# 第１部

# 香川県の
# 英語科
# 出題傾向分析

# 香川県の英語科　傾向と対策

## 中学校

2024年度の出題は，2023年度に引き続きリスニング1題，学習指導要領に関する問題1題，文法・語法3題，長文読解問題1題，英作文3題の合計9題である。配点は，大問1から順に，23点，10点，3点，8点，8点，8点，22点，9点，9点で100点満点である。

リスニング問題は，対話文を聞いて質問に答えるもの，長めの対話文を聞いて質問に答えるもの，文章を聞いて質問に答えるものという3部構成になっていて，ここ数年大幅な変更点はない。全体にリスニング問題としては標準レベルで，特にPart2，Part3で着実に得点するためには，実用英語検定2級程度以上のレベルで学習を重ねておくことが必要である。Part3については，表を日本語で完成させて答える記述式の問題であった。あらかじめ問題文に目を通し，どのような内容を聞き取ればよいのかを把握した上で，メモを取りながら音声を聞くとよい。

文法・語法問題は，空所補充，連立完成の形式で出題されている。難易度は高校教科書から大学入試レベルである。基本的な問題も含まれているので，標準レベルの大学入試対策用の文法問題集を1冊仕上げておけば対応できるだろう。また，「文化祭」，「生徒会」，「指導案」など学校で使用される語彙問題と教室で教師が生徒に出す指示文も例年通り出題された。英語による授業を想定し，基本的な表現を覚えておくことが必要である。

学習指導要領に関する問題は，中学校学習指導要領の一部の空所補充は例年通りであった。改訂の趣旨や要点を踏まえて，新旧の学習指導要領を比較し，細かいところまで読み込んでおく必要がある。小学校，中学校，高等学校の連携について重視される傾向にあるため，時間があれば，異校種の学習指導要領にも目を通しておくことが望ましい。

長文読解問題のテーマは，最近の社会問題，教育問題などが取り上げられており，英語に関する知識ばかりではなく，社会全般に広く関心を持って知識を身につけておく姿勢が必要である。特に西欧と日本の文化比較や，科学，教育，福祉分野等の問題について日本語，英語にかかわらず常に情報を取り入れておくことが大切である。長文読解問題は総合的に出題される形式がほとんどなので，過去問題を解いて苦手な形式のものがあれば重点的に補強しておくことが効果的である。

英作文については，2024年度は，和文英訳が3つと，「中学生は制服を着用すべきだ」というテーマで，聞き手に伝わりやすい文を参考例として書くという設定の自由英作文が出題されている。「生徒の参考例になるように」と但し書きがあるよう，平易な表現であっても文法的なミスをしないこと，中学生が理解できる語彙や言い回しであることに注意が必要である。様々な社会問題や，教育，授業の実践などについての自分なりの考えをしっかり持って表現できるようにしておくことが必要である。

**高等学校**

2024年度の出題は，リスニング1題，学習指導要領に関する問題1題，文法・語法3題，長文読解問題1題，英作文2題の合計8題である。配点は，大問1から順に，23点，8点，8点，8点，8点，29点，8点，8点で100点満点である。

中高共通問題については，中学校を参照のこと。

学習指導要領に関する出題形式は，記述式中心であるが，年度により内容についての選択式問題もあった。細かい内容が問われているので，本文を熟読して用語をきちんと頭に入れておくことが必要である。学習指導要領解説を参照しながらすみずみまで精読しておくこと。

長文読解問題のテーマは，中学校と同様，例年幅広いテーマから出題されているので，最近の社会問題に対する問題意識を保持し，語彙も習得しておくことが重要である。

和文英訳については，エッセイの一部を英訳する形式が頻出である。エッセイや論説文など課題文の一部を英訳する場合は，日本語にとらわれすぎず本文の趣旨を正しく読み取り，自然な英文を作れるよう学習しておきたい。

自由英作文のトピックは「翻訳アプリがあれば英語の勉強は必要ない」で，これに対する意見をまとめる。40語でまとめるには，かなり大きな話題なので，十分に書く事柄を絞ることが必要である。教育や日常の問題について自分自身の考えを書くという解答形式については，とっさに考えをまとめるのは難しい場合がある。日頃から教員としての立場での自分の信念や姿勢をしっかり持つとともに，日常の様々な事象に対する問題意識を高めておくこと，試しにいろいろなトピックで書いてみることが必要である。

# 過去5年間の出題傾向分析

中学＝●　高校＝▲　中高共通＝◎

| 分類 | 設問形式 | 2020年度 | 2021年度 | 2022年度 | 2023年度 | 2024年度 |
|---|---|---|---|---|---|---|
| リスニング | 内容把握 | ◎ | ◎ | ◎ | ◎ | ◎ |
| 発音・アクセント | 発音 | | | | | |
| | アクセント | | | | | |
| | 文強勢 | | | | | |
| 文法・語法 | 空所補充 | ◎ | ◎ | ◎ | ●▲ | ●▲ |
| | 正誤判断 | ◎ | | | | |
| | 一致語句 | | | | | |
| | 連立完成 | ◎ | ◎ | ◎ | ●▲ | ●▲ |
| | その他 | | | ● | ● | ●▲ |
| 会話文 | 短文会話 | | | | | |
| | 長文会話 | | | | | |
| 文章読解 | 空所補充 | ●▲ | | ●▲ | ●▲ | ●▲ |
| | 内容一致文 | ●▲ | | ●▲ | ● | ●▲ |
| | 内容一致語句 | | | ▲ | ▲ | ●▲ |
| | 内容記述 | ●▲ | | ▲ | ▲ | ▲ |
| | 英文和訳 | ●▲ | | ● | ●▲ | ▲ |
| | 英問英答 | | | | | |
| | その他 | ●▲ | | ▲ | ▲ | ▲ |
| 英作文 | 整序 | | | | | |
| | 和文英訳 | ●▲ | ◎ | ●▲ | ●▲ | ●▲ |
| | 自由英作 | ●▲ | | ●▲ | ●▲ | ●▲ |
| | その他 | ●▲ | | ●▲ | ●▲ | ●▲ |
| 学習指導要領 | | ◎ | | ●▲ | ●▲ | ●▲ |

# 第2部

# 香川県の
# 教員採用試験
# 実施問題

# 2024年度　実施問題

## 【中高共通】

【１】Listening Comprehension Section

Listening Comprehension Section is composed of three parts: PART 1, PART 2 and PART 3. In each part, you may take notes while listening.

【PART 1】

In this part, you will hear five conversations between two people. After listening to a conversation, you will hear a question about it. Read the four choices on your test paper, choose the best one to the question, and write it on your answer sheet. You will hear each conversation and question just one time.

No. 1

(M)　Excuse me, I'd like to buy a refrigerator.

(W)　This is the most popular model. It has a big vegetable compartment. You can keep various vegetables fresh.

Question: Where does this conversation most likely take place?

(A)　At a pharmacy.

(B)　At an appliance store.

(C)　At a plumbing company.

(D)　At a grocery store.

No.2

(W)　I've been hearing a lot about AI today. Do you know, anything about it?

(M)　Yeah, I saw on the news that some professional *shogi* players have been defeated by AI technology.

Question: What is implied in this conversation between the man and the woman?

(A) AI technology has surpassed the ability of professional *shogi* players.

(B) The man is a professional player and has appeared in the news.

(C) The woman is curious about *shogi* and wants to play it.

(D) All professional *shogi* players beat AI technology.

No.3

(M) Hi, how's it going? I heard you were sick last week.

(W) OK, thanks. I had a cold and a slight fever last week, so I canceled my part-time job to avoid close contact with others. I didn't want to make them sick too.

Question: Why did the woman take last week off from her part-time job?

(A) To avoid catching a cold from others.

(B) To help take care of the man.

(C) To obtain medicine at the hospital.

(D) To keep her cold from spreading to others.

No.4

(W) Hi, Mr. Rodgers. This is Mary Abbot from BFG Cleaning Services. Thank you for calling us yesterday. I'll tell you about the price estimate for cleaning your house. It'll cost you two hundred thirty dollars including tax.

(M) Oh, that isn't within our budget. Is there any way you could reduce the price to two hundred dollars?

Question: Which statement is true about this conversation?

(A) The woman is willing to offer a discount to the man.

(B) The woman requires the man to lower his price.

(C) The man has accepted the price offered by the woman.

(D) The man is not content with the estimated price.

No.5

(M) Hi, Kanako. I'm Tom, the host of the short-stay room for rent that you booked.

(W) Hello, Tom. Pleased to meet you. I have a question. I read about the room on the website. It said, “No Pets” and “No Parties.” Are there any other rules?

Question: What information does the woman want to get?

(A) How the woman should make a reservation.

(B) What the woman is not allowed to do.

(C) When the woman should check out.

(D) How the woman should contact the man.

【PART 2】

In this part, you will hear a conversation between a man and a woman. After that, you will be asked four questions. Read the four choices on your test paper, choose the best one to the question, and write it on your answer sheet. You will hear the conversation and the questions two times.

(M) May I come in?

(W) Yes! Oh, hello, Peter. How can I help you?

(M) Excuse me, Professor, but I'd like to ask you a few questions about the university study tour. I heard that you are organizing the tour. Is that right?

(W) Yes, I am. What would you like to know, Peter?

(M) How many days does the tour last?

(W) It's a three-day trip.

(M) How much does it cost?

(W) It costs 230 pounds.

(M) Will that cover everything?

(W) Not quite. It will cover your train trip to London, your Travelcard for traveling around London, and your hotel expenses. It will also cover any admission or event fees.

(M) What about food?

(W) Your breakfast and evening meal will be provided at the hotel. You will need to pay for lunch, though.

(M) I see. Can you tell me about the itinerary?

(W) Well, on the first day, we'll travel to London. We should arrive at the hotel by midday. We'll check in and then take the underground to the Science Museum. The museum has two excellent exhibitions about the environment.

(M) That sounds really interesting.

(W) On the second day, in the morning, we will go to the Thames Barrier and take a guided tour. We'll learn all about the history of the River Thames and about the river's environment and wildlife. In the afternoon, we'll visit the British Museum. On the third day, we will explore the city of London.

(M) My friend Rika from Japan wants to take the tour, too.

(W) Great! I'm sure you'll both enjoy yourselves and learn a lot.

Question No. 1: Who most likely is the man?

(A) The woman's coworker.

(B) The woman's friend.

(C) The woman's student.

(D) The woman's travel agent.

Question No. 2: How long does the study tour last?

(A) For two days.

(B) For three days.

(C) For four days.

(D) For five days.

Question No. 3: What extra cost will need to be paid?

(A) The entrance fees to the museums.

(B) Travelcard for traveling around London.

(C) Some meal expenses.

(D) The accommodation fees.

Question No. 4: Which is true about the tour plan?

(A) The participants will go to London by plane.

(B) The participants will make a presentation about the River Thames.
(C) The participants will learn about the history of their university.
(D) The participants will visit museums on this tour.

【PART 3】

In this part, you will hear one speech. Summarize the speech by writing the answers in Japanese on your answer sheet. You'll hear the speech two times.

Now, listen.

Honeybees are great dancers. But they don't just do it for fun. Dancing is their way of communicating. They dance to help each other find tasty flowers. That's because bees rely on flowers for food. Scientists studied honeybee dance moves.

What do bee dance moves look like? A bee starts dancing by taking a step. At the same time, it wiggles side to side. It shakes really fast. It keeps doing this while it moves around. Scientists call this the "waggle dance." These dance moves help other bees find food. The bee's position is important. It shows other bees which way to go. If the bee shakes a lot that means food is farther away. Less shaking means the food is closer. If the bee dances for a long time, that's good. It means the food is very tasty. Scientists found out how bees learn the waggle dance. The scientists recorded videos of bees in a lab. Then the scientists compared two groups of young bees. The bees were only 10 days old. In one group, young bees could watch older ones dance. These young bees were good dancers. In the other group, young bees could not watch older dancers. These young bees could not dance as well. Now scientists know how bees learn the waggle dance. They watch each other. This shows how good bees are at learning.

Bees are very good at communicating. But today, people are getting in the way. People use products called pesticides. These are poisons. They mainly kill things that eat the plants that we like to eat. But pesticides affect bees, too. One study looked at the effects on bees. After touching the poisons, bees were not the same. The waggle dance changed. The bees also started making more mistakes.

述べられている内容について，次の(　①　)～(　⑤　)にあてはまる日本語を，それぞれ書け。

| | |
|---|---|
| ミツバチのダンス | ミツバチはダンスでコミュニケーションをとっている。餌である花を探し出すためにダンスをしている。 |
| ダンスの意味 | ・ミツバチの（　①　）は他のハチが行くべき方向を示す。<br>・ハチの揺れが小さければ，餌が（　②　）ことを示す。<br>・ハチが長時間踊っていれば，餌が（　③　）ことを示す。 |
| 科学者の実験 | 科学者が２つのグループを比較した結果，ミツバチは（　④　）ことで，ダンスを学んでいることがわかった。 |
| ミツバチへの悪影響 | ミツバチが殺虫剤にふれると，ダンスが変わり，（　⑤　）が多くなった。 |

This is the end of the Listening Comprehension Section.

(☆☆☆◎◎◎)

【2】次の(1)～(4)の場面において，授業者は生徒に対して英語でどのように言うべきかを書け。

(1)　前回の授業を復習することを伝えるとき。

(2)　ワークシートに自分の考えを書くように指示するとき。

(3)　残り時間があと5分であることを伝えるとき。

(4)　聞き手から発表者に対して質問をするように指示するとき。

(☆☆☆◎◎◎)

【3】次の(1)～(4)の各組において，a)とb)がほぼ同じ意味になるように，b)の(　　)内にあてはまる最も適切な一語をそれぞれ書け。

(1)　a)　He is responsible for this project.

　　b)　He is (　　) charge (　　) this project.

(2)　a)　I have never seen such a beautiful sunset.

　　b)　This is the (　　) beautiful sunset I have (　　) seen.

(3)　a)　I'm sorry that I can't go with you.

b)　I (　　) I (　　) go with you.

(4)　a)　While he was staying in Japan, he studied electronics.

b)　(　　) his (　　) in Japan, he studied electronics.

(☆☆☆◎◎◎◎)

【4】次の(1)～(4)が，それぞれ日本語の意味に合う英文になるように，(　　)内にあてはまる最も適切な一語をそれぞれ書け。

(1)　それについてどう思いますか。

(　　) do you (　　) about it?

(2)　この橋は，今建設中です。

This bridge (　　) (　　)built now.

(3)　外出しようとしていたら，電話が鳴りました。

I was (　　)(　　) go out when the phone rang.

(4)　私は一日おきにジムに通っている。

I go to the gym (　　) (　　) day.

(☆☆☆◎◎◎◎)

## 【中学校】

【1】中学校学習指導要領(平成29年告示)の「第2章　第9節　外国語」に関して，次の(1)，(2)の問いに答えよ。

(1)　次の文は，「第1　目標」の一部を示そうとしたものである。文中の（　①　)，(　②　)にあてはまる語句を，それぞれ以下のア～エから一つ選んで，その記号を書け。

> 外国語によるコミュニケーションにおける(　①　)を働かせ，外国語による聞くこと，読むこと，話すこと，書くことの(　②　)を通して，簡単な情報や考えなどを理解したり表現したり伝え合ったりするコミュニケーションを図る資質・能力を次のとおり育成することを目指す。

①　ア　思考力・判断力　　イ　知識・技能　　ウ　感性・情緒
　　エ　見方・考え方

② ア　一連の過程　　　イ　言語活動　　　ウ　技能の活用
　エ　統合的な学習

(2) 次の文は，「第2　各言語の目標及び内容等　英語　1　目標　(3) 話すこと [やり取り]」を示そうとしたものである。文中の(　①　)〜(　③　)にあてはまる語句を，それぞれ以下のア〜エから一つ選んで，その記号を書け。

| |
|---|
| ア　関心のある事柄について，簡単な語句や文を用いて即興で(　①　)ことができるようにする。<br>イ　日常的な話題について，(　②　)や自分の考え，気持ちなどを整理し，簡単な語句や文を用いて伝えたり，相手からの質問に答えたりすることができるようにする。<br>ウ　社会的な話題に関して聞いたり読んだりしたことについて，考えたことや感じたこと，その理由などを，簡単な語句や文を用いて(　③　)ことができるようにする。 |

① ア　話す　　イ　伝える　　ウ　伝え合う　　エ　述べ合う
② ア　概要　　イ　要点　　ウ　情報　　エ　事実
③ ア　話す　　イ　伝える　　ウ　伝え合う　　エ　述べ合う

(☆☆☆◎◎◎)

【2】次の(1)〜(3)の日本語を英語で書け。

(1)　小テスト　　(2)　学期　　(3)　合唱コンクール

(☆☆◎◎◎)

【3】次の英文を読み，以下の(1)〜(6)の問いに答えよ。

According to a U.S. survey, Japanese became the most common language used in blog posts in the fourth quarter of 2006. It turned out that Japanese (　①　) for 37 percent of all blog posts, English for 36 percent, and Chinese for 8 percent. This figure is all the more remarkable when we think of the fact that Japanese is spoken by only 1.8 percent of the world's population.

Interestingly, Japan's blogging culture has evolved in a very different manner from ②<u>that</u> in other nations. According to a 2007 survey, 75 percent of Japanese blog content is about everyday events, which are mostly trivial matters. Writing a diary does not require any special skill, knowledge or experience, making it easier for many Japanese to start their own blogs. Another characteristic of Japanese blogs is the use of many photos, ③<u>which may be an extension of the diary-like desire to document everyday life</u>. What is more, Japanese bloggers often write anonymously. [ A ]

By contrast, many U.S. and European blogs are journalistic or opinion-oriented. The authors, using their real names, present information and perspectives that are not usually available in the mainstream media. Actually, about 40 percent of English-language bloggers said that their primary goal was to raise their own visibility as an authority in their respective fields. They usually write less often than Japanese bloggers but their postings are longer. [ B ]

But why is Japanese blogging culture so different from the rest of the world? Many experts believe that the answer is deeply embedded in traditions that date back hundreds of years. Japanese have long been using diaries as a medium for writing down things like changes of season and about nature. In the Heian period (794-1192), women expressed their personal feelings in kana characters and lifted the lid on court lifestyles and romances. [ C ]

Just as the use of kana made it easier for women in the Heian period to write diaries, the increasing availability of personal computers, digital cameras and other blog tools has transformed Weblogs — long regarded as a program for engineers and researchers — into a common medium used by modern Japanese women. [ D ]

Generally speaking, Japanese are good at adopting foreign cultures, blending them with their own traditions and then developing a distinctive mix of both. Since the term "Weblog", was first used in the United States a decade ago, the concept of blogging has become deeply rooted in Japanese society.

E

(1) 本文中の①の(　　)内にあてはまる最も適切な語を，次のア～エから一つ選んで，その記号を書け。

ア fell　イ accounted　ウ stood　エ allowed

(2) 下線部②のthatが示す具体的な内容を，次のア～エから一つ選んで，その記号を書け。

ア blog content　イ blogging culture　ウ a manner

エ the figure

(3) 下線部③について，その内容について最も適しているものを，次のア～エから一つ選んで，その記号を書け。

ア 専門分野において権威を示したいという願望の表れのようなもの。

イ 社会的な出来事に対する批評のようなもの。

ウ 日々の出来事を記録する日記の延長のようなもの。

エ 社会問題について調査・分析した報告のようなもの。

(4) 本文の内容と一致するグラフとして最も適切なものを一つ選んで，その記号を書け。

ア blog which photos are used in Japan

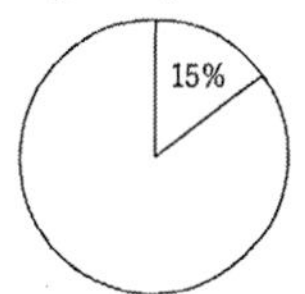


イ Japanese blog content in 2007

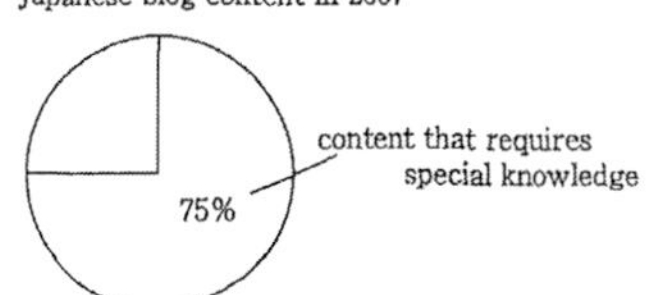


ウ U.S. and European blogger's purpose

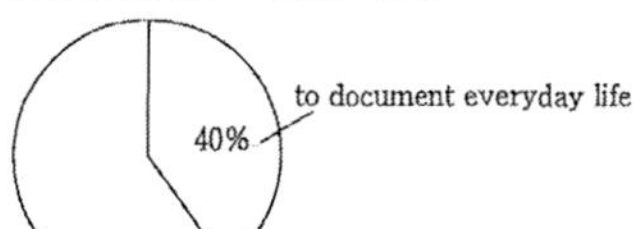


エ language usage among the world population

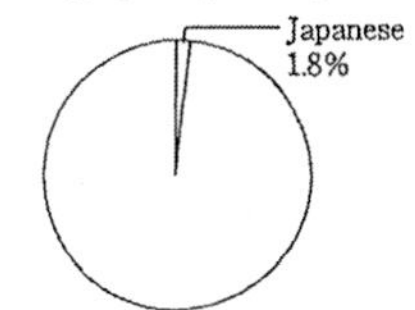


(5) 次のア，イの文は，本文中の A ～ E のいずれかに入る。最も適切な箇所を一つ選んで，その記号をそれぞれ書け。

ア In the same way Heian people developed kana from kanji introduced from China, Japan adopted the Internet, which developed in the United States, to create its own blogging style.

イ　This may be linked to present-day blogging culture.

(6)　本文の内容と一致するものを，次のア～オから二つ選んで，その記号を書け。

ア　More than one-third of blog posts until 2006 were shown to have been written in Japanese.

イ　Western bloggers make effective use of photographs to attract readers to the content.

ウ　More and more Japanese bloggers are using their real names in the blog posts.

エ　Japanese are said to have a remarkable ability to incorporate foreign cultures into their own traditions.

オ　Some English-language bloggers blog to make themselves renowned in their field.

(☆☆☆◎◎◎)

【4】次の(1)～(3)の日本語を英語に直して書け。

(1)　他者と意見を交流すると言語技能が向上する。

(2)　瀬戸内海は「世界の宝石」として知られている。

(3)　丸亀城は美しい石垣のある有名な城だ。

(☆☆☆◎◎◎)

【5】中学3年生の授業で「中学生は制服を着用すべきだ」というテーマのディベートをするために，聞き手に伝わりやすい文を書く指導を行う。賛成，反対の立場を明確にし，生徒の参考例となるよう，40語以上の英語で書け。ただし，ピリオドやクエスチョンマークなどは下線の間に記入し，語数には含めない。

(40語)

(☆☆☆◎◎◎◎)

## 【高等学校】

【1】次の文は高等学校学習指導要領(平成30年告示)「第2章　第8節　外国語　第2款　各科目　第1　英語コミュニケーションⅠ　1　目標」の一部を示そうとしたものである。次の①～④の(　　)内にあてはまる語句を書け。

> (4)　話すこと[発表]
> ア　日常的な話題について，使用する語句や文，事前の(　①　)などにおいて，多くの支援を活用すれば，基本的な語句や文を用いて，情報や(　②　)，気持ちなどを(　③　)性に注意して話して(　④　)ことができるようにする。

(☆☆☆◎◎◎)

【2】次の英文を読み，以下の(1)～(12)の問いに答えよ。

We may not realize it, but oil is an essential part of our everyday lives. Oil, which is usually called petroleum, is a valuable world resource because of the many useful products that are manufactured from it. 〔 ① 〕, petroleum is probably the most important substance we use in modern society, next to water. The process of manufacturing petroleum products begins when oil is first taken out of the ground.

When petroleum first comes out of the ground, it is called crude oil. This oil is impure. In other words, it is dirty and people need to clean, or 〔 ② 〕, it. First, the oil goes into a furnace to heat it. When the oil is heated, it separates into lighter and heavier parts. The lightest part of the oil becomes natural gas. We use natural gas to heat our homes. The heaviest part of the oil becomes asphalt. We use asphalt to pave roads and parking lots. In between the natural gas and the asphalt this process produces gasoline, kerosene, heating oil, and lubricating oil. We use lubricating oil to grease machines and other metal objects with moving parts, for example, sewing machines. 〔 ③ 〕, these are just a few of the 6,000 petroleum products, or petrochemicals, which are manufactured from crude oil. ④Petrochemicals are used in almost every area of our lives, including housing and clothing as well as medicine and transportation.

In the past, people's homes contained only natural materials, such as wool or cotton carpets, and wood furniture. Today, however, furniture, furniture fabrics, carpeting, paint, and wallpaper are all made from petroleum-based synthetics. We heat our homes with oil or natural gas 〔 ⑤ 〕 of wood. In the past 50 years, our clothes have been made from synthetic fibers such as rayon, nylon, polyester, Orlon, Dacron, and acetate. Today, clothing is even made from used plastic containers, which are also petrochemical products. The detergents we use to wash dishes and clean our clothes are petroleum-based products, 〔 ⑥ 〕 are children's toys, shampoo, lipstick, and hand lotion.

Petrochemicals have a wide variety of medical uses. Some of the drugs that our doctors prescribe are made of petrochemicals. For example, cold medicines that relieve our stuffy noses and drugs that help some people breathe more easily are petrochemical products.

The transportation industry is very dependent on petrochemicals. We all know that gasoline, kerosene, and diesel oil provide fuel for cars, motorcycles, trucks, airplanes, and ships. However, ⑦not everyone is aware that cars and trucks are made of petrochemicals, too. For instance, car and truck bodies are made of hundreds of pounds of polyester. Bumpers are no longer made of steel, and tires are synthetic, not real, rubber. Seat covers are vinyl. Traffic lights, road signs, and the painted lines on roads are all made of petrochemicals.

Although the world supply of petroleum is limited and will run out one day, for now we have an ⑧adequate supply to meet the world's needs. Petrochemical products will remain an essential part of our lives for many years to come.

(1) 本文中の①の〔　　〕内にあてはまる最も適切な語句を，次のア～エから一つ選んで，その記号を書け。

ア In fact　イ On the contrary　ウ Nevertheless
エ Meanwhile

(2) 本文中の②の〔　　〕内にあてはまる最も適切な語を，次のア～エから一つ選んで，その記号を書け。

ア retain　イ retreat　ウ resort　エ refine

(3) 本文中の③の〔　　〕内にあてはまる最も適切な語句を，次のア～エから一つ選んで，その記号を書け。

ア On the other hand　イ Accordingly　ウ For example
エ However

(4) 下線部④を日本語に直せ。

(5) 本文中の⑤の〔　　〕内にあてはまる最も適切な語句を，次のア～エから一つ選んで，その記号を書け。

ア regardless　イ in terms　ウ in spite　エ instead

(6) 本文中の⑥の〔　　〕内にあではまる最も適切な語を，次のア～エから一つ選んで，その記号を書け。

ア since　イ as　ウ unless　エ while

(7)　下線部⑦の内容として最も適切なものを，次のア～エから一つ選んで，その記号を書け。

ア　自動車やトラックが石油化学製品でできていることを，認識している人はほとんどいないこと。

イ　自動車やトラックが石油化学製品でできていることを，誰もが認識していること。

ウ　自動車やトラックが石油化学製品でできていることを，誰もが認識しているわけではないこと。

エ　自動車やトラックが石油化学製品でできていることを，認識している人はまったくいないこと。

(8)　下線部⑧について，この文脈で置き換えられる語として最も適切なものを，次のア～エから一つ選んで，その記号を書け。

ア　sufficient　　イ　small　　ウ　scarce　　エ　flexible

(9)　crude oilを熱することによって発生する物質でないものを，次のア～エから一つ選んで，その記号を書け。

ア　acetate　　イ　asphalt　　ウ　lubricating oil　　エ　natural gas

(10)　石油化学製品と医薬品の関係性とその具体例について，本文中でどのように書かれているか。日本語で書け。

(11)　次のア～ウが，本文の内容に合っていれば○，本文の内容に合っていなければ×を書け。

ア　Detergents are produced based on petroleum.

イ　Petroleum is used only as a fuel for vehicles.

ウ　Petroleum is utilized as a material for products.

(12)　この文章につけるタイトルとして最も適切なものを，次のア～エから一つ選んで，その記号を書け。

ア　The History of the Use of Oil

イ　The Way We Make Petrochemical Products

ウ　Oil as an Important World Resources

エ　Resources that Replace Natural Materials

(☆☆☆◎◎◎)

【3】次の文の下線部(1)，(2)を英語に直して書け。

eスポーツは新しいビジネス分野かもしれませんが，そのルーツは遠くさかのぼります。(1)最初のeスポーツ競技大会の1つは40年以上前に米国で開催されました。そのときプレーヤーたちは，日本の有名なゲームであるスペースインベーダーで最高得点を競い合いました。しかし，状況は変わりました。今ではeスポーツのプレーヤーやチームは，大きな競技大会で1対1の勝負をします。(2)何千人ものファンがスタジアムで試合をライブで観戦し，さらに何百万人もの人たちがライブ配信を見ています。

(☆☆☆◎◎◎)

【4】翻訳アプリがあれば英語の学習は必要ないという意見について，あなたはどのように考えるか。次の三つの条件を踏まえて英語で書け。

条件1　40語以上であること。ただし，ピリオドやクエスチョンマークなどは下線の間に記入し，語数には含めない。

条件2　自分の意見を述べること。

条件3　そのように考える理由を述べること。

(40語)

(☆☆☆◎◎◎)

# 解答・解説

## 【中高共通】

【1】PART 1　No.1　B　　No.2　A　　No.3　D　　No.4　D

No.5　B　　PART 2　No.1　C　　No.2　B　　No.3　C　　No.4　D

PART 3　①　位置　　②　より近い　　③　とてもおいしい

④　互いに見合う　　⑤　間違い

〈解説〉PART 1　No.1　男性が冷蔵庫を買いに来て，女性が人気機種の紹介をしているため，(B)の「家電用品店で」が正しい。　No.2　男性が「AI技術に負けた将棋の棋士もいる」と発言していることから，(A)がその内容に一致する。　No.3　女性は，自分が風邪をひいて，他の人との接触を避けるためにアルバイトを休んだと述べている。よって(D)の「風邪を他の人にうつさないようにするため」が正しい。

No.4　ハウスクリーニングの見積もりを女性が男性に告げると，男性が予算外であると返答しているため，(D)の「男性は見積もり額に満足していない」が正しい。　No.5　女性は借りようとしている部屋の規則を聞いているので，(B)の「女性がすることを許されていないこと」が正しい。　PART 2　No.1　男性の2回目の発話で，女性にProfessorと呼び掛けて大学の研修旅行のことを尋ねていることから女性は教授，男性は学生だと判断でき(C)が正しい。　No.2　女性の3回目の発話より，3日間であることがわかる。　No.3　女性の6回目の発話You will need to pay for lunch, though.より，昼食は別に支払う必要があることが読み取れ，(C)が正しい。　No.4　女性の7回目と8回目の発話で，科学博物館the Science Museumと大英博物館the British Museumを訪れることがわかり，(D)が正しい。　PART 3　①　第2段落8文目と9文目より，position「位置」が入る。　②　第2段落11文目より，closer「より近い」が入る。　③　第2段落12文目と13文目より，very tasty「とてもおいしい」が入る。　④　第2段落後ろから2文目They watch each other.が該当し，日本語にすると「互いに見合う」となる。

⑤　第3段落ではミツバチに対する殺虫剤の悪影響について述べられていて，最終文のmistakes「間違い」が入る。

【2】(1)　Let's review our previous lesson.　(2)　Write your opinion on your worksheet.　(3)　Five minutes left.　(4)　Ask your presenter a question.

〈解説〉(1)「復習する」はreview，「前回の」はpreviousやlastで表す。生徒への伝達のためLet's ～とする。　(2)「意見」はopinionで表す。生徒への指示のため命令形でよい。　(3)　残り時間を表す場合は時間＋leftで短く簡潔に述べる。　(4)「発表者」はpresenterで表す。(2)と同じく生徒への指示のため命令形を用いる。

【3】(1)　in，of　(2)　most，ever　(3)　wish，could　(4)　During，stay

〈解説〉(1)　be responsible for～は「～に責任がある，～の担当である」の意でin charge of～がほぼ同様の意味になる。　(2)「私が～した中で最も…なものである」という意味にするために，最初の空所には最上級のmost，次の空所にはeverを用いる。　(3)「あなたと一緒に行けなくて残念だ」という現実を示すa)の文に対し，仮定法を用いるのがb)の文になる。「～であればよいのに」と願望を表すwishを最初の空所に，仮定法過去のcouldを次の空所に入れる。　(4)　While～「～する間」の副詞節はDuring～で言い換えられる。次の空所は名詞のstay「滞在」を入れれば直前のhisとうまくつながる。

【4】(1)　What，think　(2)　is，being　(3)　about，to　(4)　every，other

〈解説〉(1)　日本語の「どう」にひきずられてHowを使わないように注意。「～をどう思いますか」はWhat do you think about～?で表す。

(2)　This bridgeが主語であり，「建設中」は現在進行形＋受動態でis being builtとする。　(3)「～しようとしている」はbe about to doで表す。

(4)「一日おきに」はevery other dayで表す。

## 【中学校】

【1】(1)　①　エ　②　イ　(2)　①　ウ　②　エ　③　エ

〈解説〉平成29年3月告示の中学校学習指導要領では，「外国語科」におけるコミュニケーション能力の育成が一層重視されるように改訂されたことに着目する。　(1)　目標については，最低限「外国語科」及び「英語科」の両方の目標を全文暗記し，できれば「読むこと」，「聞くこと」などの各領域の目標もおさえておきたい。　(2)　出題の「話すこと[やり取り]」の領域では，コミュニケーション能力の向上という観点から，「即興で」話すことがキーワードの一つとなっている。なお，「話すこと[やり取り]」は，「話すこと[発表]」とともに改訂時に新設された領域である。学習指導要領解説外国語編を参照しながら，具体的な内容を確認しておくこと。

【2】(1)　quiz　(2)　term　(3)　chorus contest

〈解説〉(1)　testは学期末などのある程度の節目の試験だが，いわゆる小テストはquizとなる。　(2)　学期はtermで表し，例えば「1学期」はthe first termとなる。　(3)「合唱」はchorusであるが，「コンクール」はフランス語由来の外来語であることに注意。英語ではcontest(もしくはcompetition)となる。

【3】(1)　イ　(2)　イ　(3)　ウ　(4)　エ　(5)　ア　E　イ　C　(6)　エ，オ

〈解説〉(1)　空所を含む文は「日本語はすべてのブログの投稿の37パーセントを占める」といった内容になることがわかる。選択肢でそのような意味を表すのはイでaccount for～で「～を占める」の意。

(2)　このthatは前に出てきた語句の繰り返しを避ける代名詞であり，blogging cultureの繰り返しを避けるためにここでは用いられている。

(3)　extension「延長」，diary-like desire to document「日記のように文章

を書きたいという願望」といった語句から，ウが適切だと判断できる。(4) エの内容が第1段落最終文と一致する。　(5) ア　挿入文は，アメリカで発展したインターネットを後から日本が取り入れて，日本独自のスタイルを確立したという内容であり，ほぼ同じ内容の空所Eの直前の文にスムーズにつながる。　イ　挿入文は「これは現在のブログ文化につながるかもしれない」という意味であるため，直前に昔の時代の内容が来ると判断できる。空所直前で昔の時代の内容が述べられているのは，平安時代の文化を述べている空所Cの直前のみである。
(6) エの内容が最終段落1文目，オの内容は第3段落3文目と一致する。

【4】(1)　Exchanging opinions with others improves language skills.
(2)　The Seto Inland Sea is known as the “Jewel of the World”.
(3)　Marugame Castle is a famous castle with beautiful stone walls.

〈解説〉(1)「他者と意見を交換すると」は動名詞を用いてExchanging opinions with othersとし，文全体の主語とする。動詞は他動詞improve「向上させる，上達させる」とし，目的語はlanguage skills「言語スキル」とする。　(2)「瀬戸内海」はThe Seto Inland Sea。香川県の地理的特徴を英語で説明できるようにしておくとよい。「…は～として知られている」は…is known as～で表す。　(3)「石垣」は「石の壁」stone wallsで表せる。「～のある」は「～を持つ」と言い換えてwithを用いればよい。

【5】(解答例)　I agree with this opinion. I have two reasons for this. First, we don’t have to worry about what to wear every morning. Second, we can feel a sense of belonging to our school and behave better in school uniforms. So, I believe school uniforms are necessary in our school life. (51 words)

〈解説〉初めに反対か賛成かを述べ，その根拠理由を順序立てて述べ，最後にまとめるという形式を生徒に示す。解答例では，「中学生は制服を着用すべきだ」というテーマに賛成の立場の意見を述べ，根拠理由として「毎朝何を着るか悩まなくてよい」,「学校への帰属意識を感じ,よりよいふるまいができる」という2つの理由を挙げている。その他の理由として,「通学用の私服を買う必要がなく経済的である」,「みな同じ服を着ることで公平さを保てる」,「どこの学校の生徒か一目でわかるため,防犯上役に立つ」なども考えられる。

## 【高等学校】

【1】① 準備　② 考え　③ 論理　④ 伝える

〈解説〉平成30年3月告示の高等学校学習指導要領では,従来の「話すこと」の領域が,「話すこと[発表]」と「話すこと[やり取り]」の2つの領域に分離された。出題の「話すこと[発表]」は,主にスピーチやプレゼンテーション,「話すこと[やり取り]」はディスカッションやディベートに関する資質・能力を育成するための領域である。なお,高等学校の英語科では,学年が進むにつれ「英語コミュニケーションⅠ→Ⅱ→Ⅲ」および「論理・表現Ⅰ→Ⅱ→Ⅲ」の科目へ進んでいく。高等学校学習指導要領外国語編・英語編(平成30年7月)の巻末資料には,これらの科目ごと・領域ごとの目標や言語活動が一覧表にまとめられている。大変役に立つ資料であるので,学習指導要領と併せて目を通しておきたい。

【2】(1) ア　(2) エ　(3) エ　(4) 石油化学製品は,医療や交通だけでなく,住居や衣類を含む私たちの生活のほとんど全ての分野で使われている。　(5) エ　(6) イ　(7) ウ　(8) ア　(9) ア　(10) 関係性…医師が処方する医薬品の中には,石油化学製品でできているものがある。　具体例…鼻づまりを和らげる風邪薬や呼吸を楽にする薬も石油化学製品である。　(11) ア ○　イ ×　ウ ○　(12) ウ

〈解説〉(1) 空所の前で「石油は貴重な世界の資源である」,空所の後で「石油は近代社会で水の次に重要な物質である」と両方ともその重要性が述べられている。よってアのin fact「実際のところ」が適切。そ

れ以外の選択肢はいずれも逆接の意味である。 (2) 空所の前で「原油はきれいにしなければならない」とあり，直前のorは「つまり」の意味なのでcleanと同じ意味であるrefine「精製する」が適切。
(3) 空所の後では「6,000もの石油化学製品の中の2，3個にすぎない」というマイナスの表現のため逆接のHoweverが入ると判断する。
(4) almost every areaは「ほとんど全ての分野」，including～は「～を含む」，A as well as Bは「BだけでなくAも」といった語句に注意して訳す。 (5) instead of～で「～の代わりに，～ではなく」の意味。
(6) as V＋Sと倒置の形で「～も同様である」の意で，空所を含む箇所は「子供のおもちゃ，シャンプー，口紅，ハンドローションも同様に石油ベースの製品である」という意味になる。 (7) not everyone is awareは部分否定の表現で「誰もが～を意識しているわけではない」の意味になりウが適切である。 (8) adequateは「適切な，十分な」の意味で選択肢の中ではアのsufficient「十分な」が同様の意味となる。
(9) crude oilを熱することについては第2段落で言及されている。熱した時に発生する物質の中でアのacetateは述べられていないためこれが正解となる。 (10) 医薬品との関係性については第4段落1・2文目，具体例は同段落3文目に述べられており，適切に日本語でそれぞれまとめればよい。 (11) ア 第3段落最終文に，洗剤も石油由来と述べられているため一致する。 イ 第2段落の下線部④の通り，石油の用途の広さが述べられているため，「石油は乗り物の燃料としてだけ使用される」は不一致。 ウ 第3段落以降で，車のタイヤやシートカバーなど，石油が各種製品の原料として使用されていることが述べられているため，一致する。 (12) 第1段落・最終段落で石油は世界の重要な資源で限りあるものであるというこの文章全体の要旨を表す記述が見られ，表題としてふさわしいのはウと判断できる。

【3】(1) One of the first e-sports tournaments was held in America over 40 years ago. (2) Thousands of fans watch the games live in stadiums, and millions of people watch live streams.

〈解説〉(1)「eスポーツ競技大会」はe-sports tournamentsで表す。「開催される」はholdの受動態heldを用いる。　(2)「～をライブ鑑賞する」はwatch～liveと表現する。「ライブ配信」はwatch live streamsとなる。

【4】(解答例)　Although some translation apps are improving rapidly, I believe that English learning is necessary. Learning English provide students valuable opportunities to realize different cultures, traditions, habits, histories, ways of thinking and so on. However, translation apps do not recognize these differences and subtle nuances to describe what we really mean. This is why I believe that learning English is very important for students. (63words)

〈解説〉「翻訳アプリがあれば英語の学習は必要ない」という意見について，解答例では「英語学習は必要である」ことを述べている。理由としては，生徒にとって，英語学習は異なる文化や伝統や習慣等を理解するための貴重な機会となるが，翻訳アプリはこうした違いや微妙なニュアンスの差を識別できないため，本当に自分が言いたいことを伝えられないことを挙げている。語数指示は「40語以上」となっているが，公式の解答用紙を見ると最大で66字まで書くことができるようになっている。50～60語数程度で自分の意見をまとめられるように準備しておくとよいだろう。

# 2023年度　実施問題

## 【中高共通】

【1】Listening Comprehension Section

Listening Comprehension Section is composed of three parts: PART 1, PART 2 and PART 3. In each part, you may take notes while listening.

【PART 1】

In this part, you will hear five conversations between two people. After listening to a conversation, you will hear a question about it. Read the four choices on your test paper, choose the best one to the question, and write it on your answer sheet. You will hear each conversation and question just one time.

No. 1

(W) Hi, I'm going to Heathrow airport by train tomorrow, and my plane leaves at five p.m. Check-in time begins at 3:40 p.m. What time do you think I should leave central London?

(M) For Heathrow? Well, it'll take about two hours. You'd better leave at noon because often there are delays on the train.

Question: What time does the woman's check-in start?

(A) At noon.
(B) At 2:00 p.m.
(C) At 3:40 p.m.
(D) At 5:00 p.m.

No. 2

(M) Sorry, I'm late. I got stuck in traffic on the bypass. There was a bad accident.

(W) No problem. I stopped driving to work because the roads were so congested and it was too stressful.

Question: Why did the woman stop driving to work?

(A) Because she was afraid of having an accident.

(B) Because she was frustrated with traffic jams.

(C) Because she always got carsick when driving.

(D) Because she was not very good at driving.

No. 3

(W) Are you still working in New York?

(M) Yeah, but I'm trying to apply for a job near my hometown so that I can spend more time with my family.

Question: Which statement is true about the conversation?

(A) The man is currently working in his hometown.

(B) The man is applying for a job in New York.

(C) The woman would like to spend more time with her family.

(D) The man is currently looking for a new job.

No. 4

(M) Excuse me, I'm James Clinton in Room 201. I'm afraid the air-conditioner isn't working properly.

(W) Oh, I'm sorry, Mr. Clinton. The regular rooms are fully booked, so I'll upgrade your room for free. Our staff will be there soon with a key.

Question: Who most likely is the woman?

(A) A hotel employee.

(B) A repair person.

(C) A bookstore clerk.

(D) A traveler.

No. 5

(M) Hello, it's me again. I've just remembered that I have a meeting in the evening. Could we possibly make it lunch instead of dinner?

(W) Erm..., no problem. I can have lunch, too. Let's meet at 12:30 in the usual restaurant.

Question: What is implied in the conversation between the man and the woman?

(A) The woman is busy all day.

(B) The man is going to make dinner for the woman.

(C) The man and woman have a meeting in the evening.

(D) The man and woman have agreed to have lunch together.

【PART 2】

In this part, you will hear a conversation between a man and a woman. After that, you will be asked four questions. Read the four choices on your test paper, choose the best one to the question, and write it on your answer sheet. You will hear the conversation and the questions two times.

(W) OK, let's start creating a video channel.

(M) Yep. Well, I've come up with this idea.

(W) Go on.

(M) It would be really cool to do a series of videos about Kagawa prefecture, but with a special angle.

(W) Oh, that sounds good. What's the angle?

(M) An hour to kill. So, say you're somewhere in Kagawa, and you have an hour to kill. We have a video of someone describing something to do in that place in an hour or less.

(W) I see. So, the target audience is tourists.

(M) It could be tourists and local people. Say you find yourself in a city that you don't know very well.

(W) OK.

(M) And you have a bit of spare time. By going onto our video channel, you get all kinds of suggestions of what to do or where to visit in under an hour. The clips are filmed on location, so you get to see the places, too.

(W) I like it. Who will be the presenters? Will you have any star names?

(M) No, we don't have any money! We can get local people to host each video clip, with just one camera, but really cool content.

(W) How often will we upload videos?

(M) Well, how about once a month?

(W) That's good. What about a name?

(M) How about One Hour Wonders?

(W) One Hour Wonders. I like it!

Question No. 1: What is the purpose of this conversation?

(A) To make decisions about their video channel.

(B) To know each other's favorite videos.

(C) To determine their vacation plans.

(D) To discuss where they should eat local food.

Question No. 2: What are they planning to make videos about?

(A) About how to upload videos.

(B) About the countries to visit during the vacation.

(C) About how to take pictures with a special angle.

(D) About what people can do in a limited time in Kagawa.

Question No. 3: Who could be their target audience?

(A) Presenters and travel agents.

(B) Travel agents and film makers.

(C) Local people and tourists.

(D) Film makers and local people.

Question No. 4: Which is true about this conversation?

(A) They are going to spend one hour to make videos.

(B) They are planning to post a video every month.

(C) They are planning to present a camera to local people.

(D) They are going to use several cameras.

【PART 3】

In this part, you will hear one speech. Summarize the speech by writing the answers in Japanese on your answer sheet. You'll hear the speech two times.

Now, listen.

Archaeology suggests that humans have had dogs as pets for over 12,000 years. Even now dogs remain our most popular pet. A survey taken in 2018 reported that 11.5% of Japanese people have a dog and 10.1% have a cat. While in the U.K., 25% of people have a dog and 17% have a cat. Pets are often kept for companionship and are considered a member of the family. In fact, another survey in the U.K. reported that 12% of people said that they loved their pet more than their partner. Another 9% admitted loving their pet more than their children!

Pets provide owners with emotional support. Studies have shown that stroking pets lowers heart rates and stress levels. Some scientists suggest that the bacteria pets bring into the house could reduce allergies in later life. Also, dogs keep their owners active and social, as many people say they often chat to other dog walkers. Other studies have shown that people with pets sleep better and visit the doctor less. However, this could be due to the fact that people who own pets are often wealthier.

The downside of keeping pets is that it can cost a lot of money if the animal gets sick. They can also bring fleas and diseases into the house.

述べられている内容について，次の(　①　)～(　⑤　)にあてはまる日本語や数字を，それぞれ書け。

| | |
|---|---|
| ペットと人類との関わり | 考古学上，人類は(　①　)年以上前から犬をペットとして飼っていた。 |
| ペットを飼うことのメリット | 【1】ペットを(　②　)ことで，心拍数やストレスレベルが下がった。<br>【2】ペットが家に持ち込むバクテリアによって，その後の(　③　)を抑える可能性がある。<br>【3】犬の飼い主は活動的かつ(　④　)的になる。<br>【4】ペットを飼っている人はよく眠れ，医者にかかる回数が減る。 |
| ペットを飼うことのデメリット | 【1】ペットが(　⑤　)ときに多くのお金がかかる。<br>【2】ノミや病気を家の中に持ち込む可能性がある。 |

This is the end of the Listening Comprehension Section.

(☆☆☆◎◎◎◎)

【２】英語の授業で，次の(1)～(4)のとき，授業者は生徒に英語でどのように言うかを書け。

(1)　ペア活動で，相手と向き合うように指示を出すとき。

(2)　授業後にワークシートを提出するように指示を出すとき。

(3)　答えが分かる人がいるかどうかを確認するとき。

(4)　文に下線を引くように指示を出すとき。

(☆☆◎◎◎◎)

【３】次の(1)～(4)の各組において，a)とb)がほぼ同じ意味になるように，b)の(　　)内にあてはまる最も適切な一語をそれぞれ書け。

(1)　a)　The matter is not important.

　　b)　The matter is(　　)no(　　).

(2)　a)　You were careless to leave your camera in the train.

　　b)　(　　)was careless(　　)you to leave your camera in the train.

(3)　a)　Every time I see my nephew, I hug him.

　　b)　I(　　)see my nephew(　　)hugging him.

(4)　a)　Besides being a good athlete, he is a brilliant student.

　　b)　(　　) (　　)to being a good athlete, he is a brilliant student.

(☆☆◎◎◎◎)

【４】次の(1)～(4)のそれぞれについて，日本語の意味になるように，(　　)内にあてはまる最も適切な一語をそれぞれ書け。

(1)　私の知る限りでは，彼はまだ来ていない。

　　(　　) (　　)as I know, he has not come.

(2)　読書が大好きだ。

　　I'm(　　) (　　)reading.

(3)　私の仕事を手伝ってくれてありがとう。

　　Thank you for(　　)me(　　)my work.

(4)　ここだけの話だが，彼は少し内気だと思うんだ。

　　(　　) (　　) , I think he is rather shy.

(☆☆◎◎◎◎)

## 【中学校】

【1】中学校学習指導要領(平成29年告示)の「第2章　第9節　外国語」に関して，次の(1)，(2)の問いに答えよ。

(1)　次の文は，「第1　目標」の一部を示そうとしたものである。文中の(　①　)，(　②　)にあてはまる語句をそれぞれ書け。

| コミュニケーションを行う(　①　)や場面，状況などに応じて，日常的な話題や社会的な話題について，外国語で簡単な情報や考えなどを理解したり，これらを(　②　)して表現したり伝え合ったりすることができる力を養う。 |
|---|

(2)　次の文は，「第2　各言語の目標及び内容等　英語　1　目標　(5)書くこと」を示そうとしたものである。文中の(　①　)～(　③　)にあてはまる語句をそれぞれ書け。

| ア　関心のある事柄について，簡単な語句や文を用いて(　①　)に書くことができるようにする。<br>イ　日常的な話題について，事実や自分の考え，気持ちなどを(　②　)し，簡単な語句や文を用いてまとまりのある文章を書くことができるようにする。<br>ウ　社会的な話題に関して聞いたり読んだりしたことについて，考えたことや感じたこと，その(　③　)などを，簡単な語句や文を用いて書くことができるようにする。 |
|---|

(☆☆☆◎◎◎◎)

【2】次の(1)～(3)の日本語を英語で書け。

(1)　文化祭　　(2)　生徒会　　(3)　指導案

(☆☆◎◎◎◎)

【3】次の英文を読み，以下の(1)～(7)の問いに答えよ。

When you purchase fresh-cut flowers, do you think about where they came from? ①It might make sense to think they were grown somewhere nearby. The reality, though, is that the cut flower trade is increasingly international. Today, thanks to airplanes and high-tech cooling systems, even the most delicate flower can be exported, and sold in a florist thousands of kilometers away from where ②it was grown. [ A ]

The country that dominates the world cut flower trade is the Netherlands. It handles about 60 percent of the world's cut flowers. And its auction houses are very large. Aalsmeer, near Amsterdam, is an auction house in the sense that Tokyo is a city, or Everest a mountain. [ B ] Nineteen million flowers are sold here on an average day, including roses, lilies, and of course, tulips.

The Netherlands is also a world leader in developing new flower varieties. Dutch companies and the government ( ③ ) a considerable amount of money in flower research. Their scientists look for ways to lengthen a flower's vase life, to strengthen flowers to prevent them from being damaged while traveling, and also to strengthen the natural fragrance of the flowers. [ C ]

Despite the Netherlands' dominance of the flower market, there are many places with a better climate for growing flowers, and the climate of Ecuador is almost perfect. Mauricio Dáavalos is the man responsible for starting Ecuador's flower industry. "④Our biggest edge is nature," he claims. "Our roses are the best in the world." With predictable rainy periods and 12 hours of sunlight each day, Ecuador's roses are renowned for their large heads and long, straight stems. Every year, Ecuador sells about 500 million flowers to the U.S. alone. [ D ] "My family has TV now. There are radios," says Yolanda Quishpe, 20, who picked roses for four years.

To others, the increasingly international nature of the flower trade is very bad news. In recent years, local growers in the U.S. faced huge ( ⑤ ) from international flower companies, and many lost their businesses. Lina Hale, an independent rose grower in California, said her father had predicted the situation in the 1980s. "I see a freight train coming down the track," he warned her, "and it's coming straight towards us." [ E ]

(1)　下線部①の英語を日本語に直して書け。

(2)　下線部②のitが示す具体的な内容を，次のア～エから一つ選んで，その記号を書け。

ア　a florist　　イ　the cut flower trade　　ウ　the country

エ　the most delicate flower

(3)　本文中の③の(　　)内にあてはまる最も適切な語を，次のア～エから一つ選んで，その記号を書け。

ア　purchase　　イ　invest　　ウ　refund　　エ　reproduce

(4)　下線部④について，その内容について最も適しているものを，次のア～エから一つ選んで，その記号を書け。

ア　良い花を育てるために自然を守っていく責任がある

イ　エクアドルで花を育てることは自然なことである

ウ　良い花を育てるのに適した自然があることが強みである

エ　切り花産業と自然はこれからも支え合っていく必要がある

(5)　本文中の⑤の(　　)内にあてはまる最も適切な語を，次のア～エから一つ選んで，その記号を書け。

ア　competition　　イ　surplus　　ウ　prospect　　エ　reward

(6)　次のア，イの文は，本文中の［A］～［E］のいずれかに入る。最も適切な箇所を一つ選んで，その記号をそれぞれ書け。

ア　The industry has brought employment opportunities and a stronger economy to regions of the country.

イ　About 120 soccer fields would fill its main building.

(7)　本文の内容と一致するものを，次のア～オから二つ選んで，その記号を書け。

ア　Nineteen million flowers are grown in Aalsmeer's auction house.

イ　The flower trade with the U.S. helps the locals in Ecuador live better lives.

ウ　Lina Hale's father could actually see a freight train carrying roses.

エ　It is possible that flowers people buy come from distant places.

オ　The researchers on flowers work on improving the durability of flower vases.

(☆☆☆◎◎◎◎)

【4】次の(1)～(3)の日本語を英語に直して書け。

(1)　間違いは，言語学習において自然なことである。

(2)　日本では，オリーブの約90％が香川で生産されている。

(3)　香川は日本で最もせまい県だが，たくさんの観光地がある。

(☆☆◎◎◎◎)

【5】中学3年生の授業で「中学校の昼食は，給食ではなく弁当にするべきだ」というテーマのディベートをするために，聞き手に伝わりやすい文を書く指導を行う。賛成，反対の立場を明確にし，生徒の参考例となるよう，40語以上の英語で書け。ただし，ピリオドやクエスチョンマークなどは下線の間に記入し，語数には含めない。

| | | | | | |
|---|---|---|---|---|---|
| ＿＿＿ | ＿＿＿ | ＿＿＿ | ＿＿＿ | ＿＿＿ | ＿＿＿ |
| ＿＿＿ | ＿＿＿ | ＿＿＿ | ＿＿＿ | ＿＿＿ | ＿＿＿ |
| ＿＿＿ | ＿＿＿ | ＿＿＿ | ＿＿＿ | ＿＿＿ | ＿＿＿ |
| ＿＿＿ | ＿＿＿ | ＿＿＿ | ＿＿＿ | ＿＿＿ | ＿＿＿ |
| ＿＿＿ | ＿＿＿ | ＿＿＿ | ＿＿＿ | ＿＿＿ | ＿＿＿ |
| ＿＿＿ | ＿＿＿ | ＿＿＿ | ＿＿＿ | ＿＿＿ | ＿＿＿ |
| ＿＿＿ | ＿＿＿ | ＿＿＿ | ＿＿＿ (40語) | ＿＿＿ | ＿＿＿ |
| ＿＿＿ | ＿＿＿ | ＿＿＿ | ＿＿＿ | ＿＿＿ | ＿＿＿ |
| ＿＿＿ | ＿＿＿ | ＿＿＿ | ＿＿＿ | ＿＿＿ | ＿＿＿ |
| ＿＿＿ | ＿＿＿ | ＿＿＿ | ＿＿＿ | ＿＿＿ | ＿＿＿ |

(☆☆☆◎◎◎◎)

## 【高等学校】

【1】次の文は，高等学校学習指導要領(平成30年告示)「第2章　第8節　外国語　第2款　各科目　第1　英語コミュニケーションⅠ　1　目標」

の一部を示そうとしたものである。次の①～④の(　　)内にあてはまる語句を書け。

| (3) 話すこと[やり取り]<br>ア (　①　)的な話題について，使用する語句や文，対話の(　②　)などにおいて，多くの(　③　)を活用すれば，基本的な語句や文を用いて，(　④　)や考え，気持ちなどを話して伝え合うやり取りを続けることができるようにする。 |
|---|

(☆☆☆◎◎◎◎)

【2】次の英文を読み，以下の(1)～(11)の問いに答えよ。

The research on〔　①　〕has just started, considering the length of human history. In 1966, a scientist who was studying the relationship between the environment and character formation visited a wealthy couple. They had just adopted a newborn girl and were going to rear her as their own daughter. The scientist who visited them was Professor Peter Nubauer from New York University Research Institute of Analytic Psychology. The baby, who was named Beth, was one of identical twins. The other twin named Amy, was adopted into a rough family where the parents were poor and always quarreling. ②<u>The professor's aim was to observe these twins who were adopted into different environments in order to prove his theory that "the environment makes personality."</u>

Ten years later, to his disappointment, his theory turned out to be wrong, as was proved by the results of ③<u>his own research</u>. Beth had a habit of wetting her bed and chewing her nails, even at the age of 11. Amy also had exactly the same problems as Beth — bed-wetting, chewing nails, and poor performance at school. The professor concluded that it was quite likely that the environment in which a child grows does not play a more important role than the genes in forming personality. However, could it be possible that ④<u>the result of this long-term research was merely a matter of coincidence</u>?

In the 1960s, around the time that the study on Beth and Amy had been carried out, there was indeed quite a lot of criticism towards this study, claiming that the result was coincidental. Then in the 1990s, thousands of studies that examined twins were carried out. The results of these studies showed that twins behave very similarly to their twin siblings, in the way they fold arms, have a favorite dance, etc.

〔 ⑤ 〕, having the same actions or postures is also common among friends. For example, when you look at two women friends having a chat, you may notice that they have similar postures. If the two are close friends and have the same opinion towards the topic they are talking about, they have almost identical postures — their chins resting upon their hands, their legs crossed, etc. Even more surprising is that they change postures concurrently. If one takes her head off her hand, the other one does the same. This is not done〔 ⑥ 〕. Without knowing, they enter into a state called posture echo. In other words, they are echoing their partner's action as a natural display that shows intimacy. When they take the same posture as their friends, they are enjoying the situation by exchanging messages such as "You and I are exactly the same."

This posture echo is also used deliberately by psychiatrists in counseling, when they want to establish a good rapport with their patients. It is thought to be impossible for a patient to feel friendly towards the doctor if he examines the patient while adopting a〔 ⑦ 〕posture — standing, looking down on him from behind. Instead, the doctor usually sits on a stool in a bent-forward posture and waits for the patient to speak.

Whether the concord or discord of actions is caused by the genes or the environment still remains ⑧<u>controversial</u>. There are many cases where brothers and sisters with the same genes have different characters and behave very differently. In other cases a couple who have been together for a long time behave similarly. The genetic factor cannot be denied, however, as twins who live far from each other and have never met each other〔 ⑨ 〕.

(1) 本文中の①の〔　　〕内にあてはまる最も適切なものを，次のア～エから一つ選んで，その記号を書け。

ア　the reasons why genes determine human characters

イ　the relationship between human habits and their environment

ウ　the effects of genes and the environment on humans

エ　the roles of the environment in human history

(2) 下線部②を日本語に直して書け。

(3) 下線部③について，その結果とそこから彼が導き出した結論を本文の内容に即して日本語で書け。

(4) 下線部④の内容として最も適切なものを，次のア～エから一つ選んで，その記号を書け。

ア　この長期にわたる研究の結果は，強固な根拠に基づいたものであること

イ　この長期にわたる研究の結果は，たまたま見られた結果にすぎないということ

ウ　この長期にわたる研究の結果は，大多数の人から支持されているものであること

エ　この長期にわたる研究の結果は，今後の研究にさらなる知見を与えるものであること

(5) 本文中の⑤の〔　　〕内にあてはまる最も適切な語を，次のア～エから一つ選んで，その記号を書け。

ア　Briefly　　イ　Therefore　　ウ　Namely　　エ　However

(6) 本文中の⑥の〔　　〕にあてはまる最も適切な語を，次のア～エから一つ選んで，その記号を書け。

ア　intentionally　　イ　reluctantly　　ウ　simultaneously

エ　awkwardly

(7) 友人間で posture echo が起きるのはなぜか。またカウンセリングの場で posture echo が使われるのはなぜか。本文の内容に即してそれぞれ日本語で説明せよ。

(8) 本文中の⑦の〔　　〕内にあてはまる最も適切な語を，次のア～

エから一つ選んで，その記号を書け。

ア　defensive　　イ　dominant　　ウ　gentle　　エ　timid

(9)　下線部⑧の語とほぼ同じ意味を表す語として最も適切なものを，次のア～エから一つ選んで，その記号を書け。

ア　valid　　イ　contentious　　ウ　irrational　　エ　profound

(10)　本文中の⑨の〔　　〕内にあてはまる最も適切なものを，次のア～エから一つ選んで，その記号を書け。

ア　lead long lives　　イ　have different habits

ウ　talk on good terms　　エ　share many things in common

(11)　この文章につけるタイトルとして最も適切なものを，次のア～エから一つ選んで，その記号を書け。

ア　The Environment Is the Most Important in Deciding Personality.

イ　Is Personality Decided by the Genes or the Environment?

ウ　The Effect of Posture Echo in Counseling

エ　Do Twins Look Alike Even If They Live Apart?

(☆☆☆◎◎◎◎)

【3】次の文の下線部①，②を英語に直して書け。

何世紀も前，世界中の人々は，お互いに限られた交流しか持ちませんでした。①そのため，世の中の変化が起こる速度はゆっくりでした。しかし最近では，状況は非常に異なっています。グローバル化によって，人々はお互いにつながったり，とても簡単に考えや商品，サービスを共有したりできるようになりました。②この現象は私たちの世界を急速に変え，今やその世界のことを，多くの人が「グローバル・ヴィレッジ」と呼んでいるほどです。

(☆☆☆◎◎◎◎)

【4】英語の学習においてICTをどのように活用するのが有効であるか。次の三つの条件を踏まえて英語で書け。

条件1　40語以上であること。ただしピリオドやクエスチョンマークなどは下線の間に記入し，語数には含めない。

条件2　自分の意見を述べること。

条件3　理由を述べること。

| ________ | ________ | ________ | ________ | ________ | ________ |
|---|---|---|---|---|---|
| ________ | ________ | ________ | ________ | ________ | ________ |
| ________ | ________ | ________ | ________ | ________ | ________ |
| ________ | ________ | ________ | ________ | ________ | ________ |
| ________ | ________ | ________ | ________ | ________ | ________ |
| ________ | ________ | ________ | ________ | ________ | ________ |
| ________ | ________ | ________ | ________ (40語) | ________ | ________ |
| ________ | ________ | ________ | ________ | ________ | ________ |
| ________ | ________ | ________ | ________ | ________ | ________ |
| ________ | ________ | ________ | ________ | ________ | ________ |
| ________ | ________ | ________ | ________ | ________ | ________ |

(☆☆☆◎◎◎◎)

# 解答・解説

## 【中高共通】

【1】PART 1　No.1　(C)　No.2　(B)　No.3　(D)　No.4　(A)　No.5　(D)　PART 2　No.1　(A)　No.2　(D)　No.3　(C)　No.4　(B)　PART 3　①　12,000　②　なでる　③　アレルギー　④　社交　⑤　病気になった

〈解説〉PART 1　No.1　Check-in time begins at 3:40 p.m.を聞き取る。No.2　be congested「渋滞している」を聞き取る。　No.3　apply for～「～に応募する」から男性が新しい仕事を探していることがわかる。No.4　The regular rooms are fully bookedやI'll upgrade your roomなどか

ら，ホテルの従業員だとわかる。　No.5　Could we possibly～「～していただくことは可能でしょうか」。make it「都合がつく」。男性が，夕食を昼食に変更することを願い出て，女性は承諾している。　PART 2　香川県をテーマにした動画シリーズを特別な切り口で作ろうとする2人の対話。ターゲットは観光客だけでなく現地の人も含む。そのビデオチャンネルにアクセスすると，1時間以内に何をすべきか，どこに行くべきか，などいろいろな提案が得られるというもの。また，お金をかけられないので，カメラ1台で，現地の人に司会をしてもらい，月に1回くらい動画をアップロードしようとしている。　PART 3　聞き取るべき英文は，①　Archaeology suggests that humans have had dogs as pets for over 12,000 years，②　stroking pets lowers heart rates and stress levels，③　the bacteria pets bring into the house could reduce allergies in later life，④　dogs keep their owners active and social，⑤　it can cost a lot of money if the animal gets sickである。

【2】(1)　Face your partner.　(2)　Give your worksheet to me after class.　(3)　Who knows the answer?　(4)　Underline the sentence.

〈解説〉教室英語については，例えば(2)ではhand in「提出する」，(3)ではDoes anyone know the answer?など，解答例以外にもいろいろな表現をストックしておきたい。

【3】(1)　of, importance　(2)　It, of　(3)　never, without　(4)　In, addition

〈解説〉(1)〈前置詞＋抽象名詞〉で形容詞のように用いられる。of importance＝important。　(2)　人の性質を表す形容詞の場合，〈It is＋形容詞＋of＋人＋to不定詞〉で「～するとは〈人〉は～だ」という形になる。　(3)　never～without…ing「…せずに～することはない，～すれば必ず…する」。　(4)　besides～「～の他に，～に加えて」。In addition to～「～に加えて」。

【4】(1)　As, far　(2)　fond, of　(3)　helping, with　(4)　Between, ourselves

〈解説〉(1)　as far as～は範囲や程度を表し，as long as～は時や条件を表す。　(2)　be fond of～「～が好きだ」。　(3)　help O with～「Oの～を手伝う」。　(4)　between you and meも同意。

## 【中学校】

【1】(1)　①　目的　②　活用　(2)　①　正確　②　整理　③　理由

〈解説〉2022年度は，外国語科の「目標(3)」と，英語科の「目標(4)　話すこと[発表]」から出題されたことに注意する。過去問をさかのぼって，まだ出題されていないところのキーワードを中心に覚えておきたい。記述式での出題であるので，外国語科の目標と英語科の目標，及び「読むこと」などの5領域の目標については，正確な漢字表記も含め確実に覚えておくこと。

【2】(1)　cultural festival　(2)　student council　(3)　lesson plan

〈解説〉学校・指導関係の語彙は毎年出題されている。いくつかの教科書では生徒が英作文等で利用できるようにまとめてある。それらから出題されていると思われるので，目を通しておくとよい。

【3】(1)　それら(切り花)が，近くのどこかで栽培されたと考えると納得するかもしれない。　(2)　エ　(3)　イ　(4)　ウ　(5)　ア　(6)　ア　D　イ　B　(7)　イ，エ

〈解説〉(1)　make sense「意味をなす，うなずける，筋が通っている」。　(2)　下線部を含む文意は「今日では，飛行機や高度な冷却装置のおかげで，最もデリケートな花でも輸出され，それが栽培された場所から何千キロも離れた花屋で売られている」となる。　(3)「また，オランダは花の新品種開発で世界をリードしている」に続く文。「オランダの企業や政府は，花の研究にかなりの資金を投入している」となる。

invest「投資する，出資する」。　(4)　下線部は「私たちの最大の強みは自然だ」。エクアドルの雨季がはっきりしていることや，日照時間が12時間あることなど，よいバラの花を育てるのに自然が適していることを述べている。　(5)　空所を含む文意は「ここ数年，アメリカの地元生産者は国際的な花の会社との大きな競争にさらされ，その多くがビジネスを失っている」。face competition from～「～とせめぎ合う，～との競争に直面する」。　(6)　アは「この産業は，この国の地方に雇用の機会と経済の強化をもたらした」。この国とは，エクアドルのことを指し，4年間バラ摘みをした20歳のYolanda Quishpeさんの発言「今では，うちにテレビがある。ラジオもある」の前のDに入るのが適切。イは「本館はサッカー場120面ほどになる」。花市場の大きさを述べているので，Bに入るのが適切。　(7)　ア　第2段落参照。アールスメール花市場では花が売買されているのであって，栽培されているのではない。　イ　「アメリカとの花の取引はエクアドルの現地の人のより良い生活に役立っている」。第4段落最終文より，正しい。
ウ　最終段落参照。Lina Haleさんの父親は，1980年代にこの状況を予見して「私はバラを運ぶ貨物列車が線路を走ってくるのが見える」と言っていたのであって，実際にそのような列車を見たわけではない。
エ　「人々が買う花は遠くから届くこともある」。第1段落4文目より，正しい。　オ　第3段落参照。研究者が研究しているのは切り花の花もちをよくする方法であって，花瓶の耐久性を強める方法ではない。

【4】(1)　Errors are a natural part of language learning.　(2)　In Japan, around 90 percent of olives are produced in Kagawa.　(3)　Kagawa is the smallest prefecture in Japan, but it has a lot of sightseeing spots.
〈解説〉(1)ではmaking mistakes「間違いをすること」，(3)では tourist attractions「観光地」などを使用しても可。

【5】(解答例)　I don't agree with this opinion. I have two reasons for this. First, it's hard for my parent to make boxed lunch every day. Second, school lunch has a variety of food. We can eat healthy and balanced meals. So, I believe that school lunch is better than our own boxed lunch. (52 words)

〈解説〉解答例では，「給食でなく弁当にするべきだ」というテーマに反対の立場の意見を述べている。中学生の立場で，中学校レベルの語彙で解答をまとめる。指示された語数は「40語以上」であるが，解答用紙を見ると解答欄には最大60語まで書くことができる。日頃から50語程度で自分の意見を簡潔にまとめる練習をしておくとよいだろう。

## 【高等学校】

【1】① 日常　② 展開　③ 支援　④ 情報

〈解説〉外国語科・英語科の「目標」は頻出であるが，本自治体ではさらに細分化された各領域別の目標が出題されている。文言を正確に覚えていないと解答できない問題である。高等学校学習指導要領解説　外国語編・英語編(平成30年7月)の巻末資料には，「英語コミュニケーションⅠ・Ⅱ・Ⅲ」および「論理・表現Ⅰ・Ⅱ・Ⅲ」について，5領域別の目標が一覧表にまとめられている。それぞれどのような違いがあるか理解しやすいので，対照しながら読み込んでおいてほしい。

【2】(1)　ウ　(2)　教授の目的は，「環境が人格を形成する」という自身の理論を証明するために，異なる家庭環境に養子として引き取られた双子を観察することであった。　(3)　結果…育った環境が違うにも関わらず，ベスとエイミーは，全く同じ癖を持っていた。　結論…人格の形成には，子どもが成長する環境が遺伝子よりも重要な役割を果たしているとは言えない可能性がある。　(4)　イ　(5)　エ　(6)　ア　(7)　友人間…親密さを示すため。　カウンセリングの場…患者と良い関係を築くため。　(8)　イ　(9)　イ　(10)　エ　(11)　イ

〈解説〉(1)　本文は，一卵性双生児の観察から，環境と人格形成の関係について論じている英文である。よって「遺伝子や環境が人間に与える影響」に関する研究，とするのが適切。　(2)　observe～「～を観察

する」。be adopted「養子になる」。prove～「～を証明する」。　(3)　下線部直後の英文参照。2人の育った環境が違うにも関わらず，ベスはおねしょと爪を噛む癖があり，エイミーもベスと全く同じ問題を抱えていた。そこで教授は，人格形成において，遺伝子よりも生育環境が重要な役割を果たすことはないと結論付けた。　(4)　下線部は「この長期的な研究結果が単なる偶然であった」の意。　(5)　空所直前の文意は「双子の兄弟姉妹の行動が非常に似ている」。空所後の文意は「同じ行動や姿勢をとることは，友達同士でもよくあることだ」。よって「しかしながら」が適切。　(6)　空所前後は，「友達同士がおしゃべりしているとき，同じ姿勢になったり，彼らが同時に姿勢を変えたりするが，このことは『意図的に』行われているのではない。知らず知らずのうちに，姿勢の反響とよばれる状態になっている」という流れになる。　(7)　「友人間」の場合については第4段落8文目参照。as a natural display that shows intimacyを訳出する。「カウンセリングの場」については第5段落1文目参照。when they want to establish a good rapport with their patientsを訳出する。　(8)　空所には，患者が医師に対して親しみを感じることができない姿勢を表す語が入る。立って，後ろから見下ろすような「支配的な」姿勢とするのが適切。　(9)　controversial「物議を醸している」。contentious「議論を引き起こす」。　(10)　空所前の文意は「同じ遺伝子を持つ兄弟姉妹でも，性格が異なり行動も全く違うというケースは多い。また，長く連れ添った夫婦が同じような行動をとる場合もある」。その後に「しかし遺伝的な要素を否定することはできない」と続くことから，「遠く離れて暮らし，一度も会ったことのない双子にも『多くの共通点があるように』」とするのが適切。　(11)　人格形成が遺伝子か環境のどちらかによるものかは本文で結論付けられていない。最終段落1文目にも「行動の一致，不一致が遺伝子によるものか，環境によるものかはいまだ議論の余地がある」とある。よって，タイトルとして「人格は遺伝子または環境によって形成されるのか」が適切。

【3】① Therefore, changes happened to our world slowly. However, the situation is quite different nowadays. ② This phenomenon has rapidly changed our world, which many now refer to as a “global village”.

〈解説〉「世の中の変化が起こる速度はゆっくりだった」という表現は「世の中はゆっくりとした速度で変化した」などできるだけシンプルな表現にすることが解答のコツで，①はThe world was changing at a slow pace.などとも表せる。②はso rapidly that many now refer to it as～などを用いて簡潔に書くこともできる。

【4】(解答例) I think ICT tools are effective, when they are used, for example, to exchange with schools overseas through the internet because students can engage in authentic communication, experience diverse cultures and broaden their perspective. Also, introducing digital materials such as textbooks and worksheets will motivate each individual student to learn at his own pace according to his English skills. (59 words)

〈解説〉40語以上と指定されているが，公式の解答用紙では最大66語まで書くことができる解答欄になっている。おおよそ50～60語程度で自分の意見を簡潔に述べる練習をしておくとよいだろう。ICT活用については，文部科学省から出された文書等に目を通しておくこと。解答例では，インターネットによる海外の学校との交流で多様な文化に触れ視野を広げられることや，デジタル教材を導入し，個々の生徒が自分の能力に応じて学べることで学習意欲の向上に役立つことを，有効なICT活用の例として挙げている。そのほか，電子黒板の利用により板書時間を削減してその分言語活動の時間を多く確保したり，生徒のパフォーマンスを録音・録画したりすることで，生徒の振り返りや教師の評価にも有効活用できることを挙げてもよいだろう。

# 2022年度　実施問題

## 【中高共通】

【1】Listening Comprehension Section

Listening Comprehension Section is composed of three parts: PART 1, PART 2 and PART 3. In each part, you may take notes while listening.

【PART 1】

In this part, you will hear five conversations between two people. After listening to a conversation, you will hear a question about it. Read the four choices on your test paper, choose the best one to the question, and write it on your answer sheet. You will hear each conversation and question just one time.

No. 1

(M) How's your new apartment?

(W) It's great! It's near here, so instead of taking an hour to get to work, it only takes 20 minutes now.

Question: How long did it take the woman to get to work before?

(A) Twelve minutes.

(B) Twenty minutes.

(C) An hour.

(D) An hour and a half.

No. 2

(W) We're interested in taking one of your tours tomorrow. Can you tell me about the boat tour?

(M) Sure. The boat tour lasts a full day and includes two stops for swimming and lunch on an island.

Question: Where does this conversation most likely take place?

(A) On a ship.

(B) On a bus.

(C) At a travel agency.

(D) At a consulting firm.

No. 3

(M) I really like these food carts. And I really like eating!

(W) Yeah, me too. Speaking of eating, we've decided to have a potluck party at our office this Friday night. Do you want to come?

Question: Which is true about this conversation?

(A) The woman doesn't like food carts.

(B) The man has been to a potluck party.

(C) The woman likes speaking in a party.

(D) The man is being invited to a potluck party.

No. 4

(W) Now, then, I want to look at the new autumn dresses.

(M) If you are going to do that, I'll go to the men's clothing section and see if I can find a nice long-sleeved shirt.

Question: What does the man want to do?

(A) He wants to look for long-sleeved shirts.

(B) He wants to go to the men's restroom.

(C) He wants to buy a new dress for the woman.

(D) He wants to see if the new autumn dresses are good.

No. 5

(M) Excuse me. I'd like to take a train to ABC Station. Could you tell me which platform I should go to?

(W) The train departs from platform 15, but the trains are behind schedule due to some mechanical trouble.

Question: Why are the trains delayed?

(A) Because a big storm is approaching.

(B) Because the machine is not working properly.

(C) Because a big obstacle is on the railway.

(D) Because there are some problems at the platform.

【PART 2】

In this part, you will hear a conversation. After that, you will be asked four questions. Read the four choices on your test paper, choose the best one to the question, and write it on your answer sheet. You will hear the conversation and the questions two times.

(Bob) Hi, Sarah, You look sleepy. Didn't you sleep well last night?

(Sarah) Hi, Bob. I slept only six hours.

(Bob) How many hours do you sleep every night?

(Sarah) Usually, at least eight hours.

(Bob) Oh, eight hours. Do you need an alarm clock to wake you up?

(Sarah) I definitely have to have two alarm clocks and that will usually get me up.

(Bob) Oh, wow. I don't use an alarm clock at all. I can wake up exactly at the minute I want, any time.

(Sarah) That's amazing. I wish it was that way for me, but it's not.

(Bob) To me, an alarm clock is like somebody throwing cold water on me. I can't have a deep sleep if I know that it's going to ring and wake me up.

(Sarah) As for me, I'm always paranoid about being late so that's why I set two just in case one doesn't go off. Without alarms, I could sleep 12 hours and not wake up.

(Bob) Wow. You do like sleeping. I hope you can have a good sleep tonight.

Question No. 1: What are they mainly talking about?

(A) How to wake up.

(B) How to stay healthy.

(C) How to take a nap.

(D) How to have a long sleep.

Question No. 2: How many hours does Sarah usually sleep a night?

(A) Six hours.

(B) Eight hours.

(C) Ten hours.

(D) Twelve hours.

Question No. 3: Who needs an alarm clock?

(A) Bob.

(B) Sarah.

(C) Both of them.

(D) Neither of them.

Question No. 4: Which is true about this conversation?

(A) Bob has been splashed with water.

(B) Bob cannot wake up at the time he wants.

(C) Sarah is not afraid of being late for work.

(D) Sarah wishes she could wake up whenever she wants.

【PART 3】

In this part, you will hear one speech. Summarize the speech by writing the answers in Japanese on your answer sheet. You'll hear the speech two times.

Now, listen.

Coral is a partnership between two living things: the coral and algae. The coral builds the hard shell on the ocean floor, which is the pair's home. These two living things work together. The algae live inside the coral and help keep their home clean. The algae make oxygen and food from sunlight, carbon dioxide and water.

Coral reefs are known for their bright colors. But these colors are going away because of warming ocean waters. Warming oceans can cause coral stress, which turns coral white. This is called "bleaching." But some coral is turning bright colors instead. A coral scientist, and his teammates tried a test on this phenomenon.

The scientists put corals in warm water in the test. The algae started to leave their home. This causes bleaching. In their work, the scientists found not all the corals turn white and some corals make bright colors even in warmer water. The colors keep the coral safe from the sun and bring the algae back home. The algae came back to the bright corals faster. Those algae were better at making food, meaning they were healthier. The coral scientist says the bright colors only come from a low amount of stress. If it's too hot, the corals can't live. But bright colors on a reef are a good sign. Those corals are fighting back.

述べられている内容について，次の(　①　)～(　⑤　)にあてはまる日本語を，それぞれ書け。

| | |
|---|---|
| サンゴと藻類の関係 | サンゴは藻類と共生している。サンゴは藻類にすみかを提供し，藻類はすみかを(　①　)にしている。藻類はサンゴに(　②　)と栄養素を与える。 |
| 研究者たちによる実験とその結果 | 【1】 温かい海水にサンゴを入れた。<br>【2】 藻類がサンゴから離れた。それが原因となり，(　③　)色に変わるサンゴと，(　④　)色に変わるサンゴがあることが分かった。後者はその色により(　⑤　)から身を守っていることが分かった。<br>【3】 (　④　)色に変わったサンゴには藻類が早く戻ることが分かった。 |

This is the end of the Listening Comprehension Section.

(☆☆☆◎◎◎◎)

【2】次の(1)～(4)の場面で，授業者が生徒に英語でどのように言うかを書け。

(1) ペア活動で，役割を交代するよう指示するとき。

(2) 発表の場面で，発表を待っている生徒に順番がきたことを伝えるとき。

(3) 物語を読み終えたかを尋ねるとき。

(4) これから授業者が言うことを書きとめるよう指示するとき。

(☆☆◎◎◎◎)

【3】次の(1)～(4)の各組において，a)とb)がほぼ同じ意味になるように，b)の(　　)内にあてはまる最も適切な一語をそれぞれ書け。

(1) a) Whoever finds it can keep it.

b) (　　) (　　) finds it can keep it.

(2) a) This table is as large as that one.

b) This table is the (　　) (　　) as that one.

(3) a) Though he had a bad cold, he went to work as usual.

b) (　　) (　　) of his bad cold, he went to work as usual.

(4) a) Who owns this house?

b) (　　) is the (　　) of this house?

(☆☆◎◎◎◎)

【4】次の(1)～(4)のそれぞれについて，日本語の意味になるように，(　　)内にあてはまる最も適切な一語を書け。

(1) サービス料は請求書に含まれている。

Service is (　　) in the (　　).

(2) その事故はエンジンと何の関係もなかった。

The accident had (　　) to do (　　) the engine.

(3) 地面がぬれているので，昨夜雨が降ったにちがいない。

It must (　　) (　　) last night because the ground is wet.

(4) 彼が来ようが来まいが，私にとっては同じことだ。

It makes (　　) (　　) to me whether he will come or not.

(☆☆◎◎◎◎)

## 【中学校】

【1】中学校学習指導要領(平成29年告示)の「第2章　第9節　外国語」に

関して，次の(1)，(2)の問いに答えよ。

(1)　次の文は，「第1　目標」の一部を示そうとしたものである。文中の(　①　)，(　②　)にあてはまる語句をそれぞれ書け。

| 外国語の背景にある(　①　)に対する理解を深め，聞き手，読み手，話し手，書き手に配慮しながら，(　②　)に外国語を用いてコミュニケーションを図ろうとする態度を養う。 |
|---|

(2)　次の文は，「第2　各言語の目標及び内容等　英語　1　目標　(4)　話すこと[発表]」を示そうとしたものである。次の(　①　)～(　③　)にあてはまる語句をそれぞれ書け。

| ア　関心のある事柄について，簡単な語句や文を用いて(　①　)で話すことができるようにする。<br>イ　日常的な話題について，事実や自分の考え，気持ちなどを整理し，簡単な語句や文を用いて(　②　)のある内容を話すことができるようにする。<br>ウ　社会的な話題に関して聞いたり読んだりしたことについて，考えたことや感じたこと，その(　③　)などを，簡単な語句や文を用いて話すことができるようにする。 |
|---|

(☆☆☆◎◎◎◎)

【2】次の(1)～(3)の日本語を2語以内の英語で書け。

(1)　運動会　　(2)　暗記　　(3)　職員室

(☆☆◎◎◎◎)

【3】次の英文を読み，以下の(1)～(7)の問いに答えよ。

It may be hard to believe, but barely thirty years have passed since e-mail became available to the average person. E-mail messages were exchanged over private networks as early as the mid-1960s, but ①<u>it was not until the early 1990s that this type of communication became widespread</u>. [ A ]

E-mail was made widely available to ordinary people when U.S. Internet service companies, America Online and Delphi, connected their private systems to the World Wide Web in 1993. The improvement in ( ② ) compared to "snail mail" (postal delivery service) greatly decreased transfer time, and the ability to address a message to several individuals enabled us to easily reach more people than ever before. [ B ]

After the initial marriage of e-mail and the Internet, the next popular stage of electronic communication came around 1999 when blogging started becoming popular. Websites like Open Diary, Live Journal, and blogger.com allowed people to post ideas and opinions that others could read and even comment on. Famous stars and politicians began using blogs to keep in touch with their fans and supporters, but much of the communication was about minor events in people's daily lives. [ C ] However, blogging was still an important development in electronic communication.

The next big event in the evolution of electronic communication was the creation of SNSs (social network services). In 2003, students from Harvard University introduced the now famous Facebook which allowed students to create a network of "friends." With Facebook, members can communicate either one to one or within a large group. [ D ] However, an amazing number of people have access to SNS communications by simply accessing a webpage.

In more recent years, PDAs (personal digital assistants) have made electronic communication even more efficient. With PDAs, we can access electronic communications wherever a wireless network is available. This amazing ( ③ ) means that we can instantly communicate with many people almost anywhere in the world—④<u>a far cry from "snail mail."</u>

[ E ]

Before e-mail was invented, it seemed impossible that we would ever communicate on such a grand scale as we do today. We have come from sending paper mail to contacting numerous people instantly, from almost anywhere, at any time. Ray Tomlinson was not kidding when he said he invented e-mail because "⑤it was a neat idea."

(1) 下線部①の英語を日本語に直して書け。

(2) 本文中の②の(　　)内にあてはまる最も適切な語を，次のア～エから一つ選んで，その記号を書け。

ア automaticity　イ efficiency　ウ dependency
エ accuracy

(3) 本文中の③の(　　)内にあてはまる最も適切な語を，次のア～エから一つ選んで，その記号を書け。

ア publicity　イ disability　ウ complexity
エ portability

(4) 下線部④について，その内容について最も適しているものを，次のア～エから一つ選んで，その記号を書け。

ア 「スネイル・メール」も便利ではあるが
イ 「スネイル・メール」とは比べものにならない
ウ 「スネイル・メール」は使われなくなった
エ 「スネイル・メール」から派生して

(5) 下線部⑤のitが示す具体的な内容を，次のア～エから一つ選んで，その記号を書け。

ア blogging　イ SNS　ウ e-mail　エ PDA

(6) 次のア，イの文は，本文中の[ A ]～[ E ]のいずれかに入る。最も適切な箇所を一つ選んで，その記号をそれぞれ書け。

ア It is even more remarkable that within just three decades we are now able to reach thousands of people instantly.

イ E-mail requires adding a number of addresses to a message to contact multiple people, which can take a lot of time.

(7) 本文の内容と一致するものを，次のア～オから2つ選んで，その記号を書け。

ア In the mid-1960s, blogs began gaining in popularity.

イ The event that led to the widespread use of e-mail occurred in 1993.

ウ　Ray Tomlinson invented the system called Facebook.

エ　People were not willing to blog about minor events in their daily life.

オ　It was considered impossible to exchange information on a large scale before e-mail was invented.

(☆☆☆◎◎◎◎)

【4】次の(1)～(3)の日本語を英語に直して書け。

(1)　教員は従来の指導方法に固執すべきではない。

(2)　讃岐うどんの「讃岐」は香川県の昔の名前を使っている。

(3)　香川は美しい海や山に囲まれた，自然が豊かな県である。

(☆☆☆◎◎◎◎)

【5】中学3年生の授業で「中学生は自分たちで学校を掃除すべきか。」というテーマのディベートを通して，聞き手に伝わりやすい文を書くよう指導することになった。賛成，反対の立場を明確にし，生徒の参考例となるよう，40語以上の英語で書け。ただし，ピリオドやクエスチョンマークなどは下線の間に記入し，語数には含めない。

| ______ | ______ | ______ | ______ | ______ | ______ |
|---|---|---|---|---|---|
| ______ | ______ | ______ | ______ | ______ | ______ |
| ______ | ______ | ______ | ______ | ______ | ______ |
| ______ | ______ | ______ | ______ | ______ | ______ |
| ______ | ______ | ______ | ______ | ______ | ______ |
| ______ | ______ | ______ | ______ | ______ | ______ |
| ______ | ______ | ______ | ______ (40語) | ______ | ______ |
| ______ | ______ | ______ | ______ | ______ | ______ |
| ______ | ______ | ______ | ______ | ______ | ______ |
| ______ | ______ | ______ | ______ | ______ | ______ |

(☆☆☆◎◎◎◎)

## 【高等学校】

【1】高等学校学習指導要領(平成30年告示)に関して，次の問題に答えよ。
　次の文は，「第2章　第8節　外国語　第1款　目標」を示そうとしたものである。次の①～④の(　　)内にあてはまる語句を書け。

> 　外国語によるコミュニケーションにおける見方・考え方を働かせ，外国語による聞くこと，読むこと，話すこと，書くことの言語活動及びこれらを結び付けた(　①　)な言語活動を通して，情報や考えなどを(　②　)に理解したり適切に表現したり伝え合ったりするコミュニケーションを図る資質・能力を次のとおり育成することを目指す。
> (1)　外国語の音声や語彙，表現，文法，言語の働きなどの理解を深めるとともに，これらの知識を，聞くこと，読むこと，話すこと，書くことによる実際のコミュニケーションにおいて，(　③　)や場面，状況などに応じて適切に活用できる技能を身に付けるようにする。
> (2)　コミュニケーションを行う(　③　)や場面，状況などに応じて，日常的な話題や社会的な話題について，外国語で情報や考えなどの概要や要点，詳細，話し手や書き手の意図などを(　②　)に理解したり，これらを活用して適切に表現したり伝え合ったりすることができる力を養う。
> (3)　外国語の背景にある文化に対する理解を深め，聞き手，読み手，話し手，書き手に配慮しながら，(　④　)，自律的に外国語を用いてコミュニケーションを図ろうとする態度を養う。

(☆☆☆◎◎◎◎)

【2】次の英文を読み，以下の(1)～(11)の問いに答えよ。

1 Communication between people often comes in coded form. “DYK” this?  Sometimes we use [　①　] codes or make signals through body language while other times we use written codes.  Sometimes we use none of

these and rely on simple or complex tools to convey information. Among all of these methods, information can be shared and understood by everyone, or it can be secretive and known only by some. Whether secretive or not, such forms of communication have existed throughout human history and will no doubt continue to evolve in the future.

2 Long before the widespread use of telephones and the Internet, American Indians used to communicate by way of smoke signals. They made fires and manipulated the rising smoke to convey messages to their fellow Indians in the distance. [ A ] Signals like these relayed warnings of danger, summoned people to gather for meetings and transmitted news. [ B ] Even though most of the smoke signals were used to send secretive and unique messages between individuals, some were commonly understood. For instance, one ring of smoke meant "Attention!" and two meant, "All is well." Three rings indicated that there was some kind of danger or trouble, or that help was needed. [ C ] Although no longer used, this form of coded communication is often referred to as "Indian telegraphy." [ D ]

3 However, telegraphy as we know it was invented in the U.S. in the 1800s. Around this time, inventors developed the telegraph, a machine that could receive electronic messages known as telegrams. The system was simple and it involved two operators. One operator sent a communication for a customer, and the other [ ② ] and wrote it out for the recipient. To send messages, most telegraph operators used Morse code, a coded alphabet consisting of dots and dashes. The whole system was not very refined, but it was at the cutting edge of communication technology in those days.

4 [ ③ ], coded communication used by Native American Indians was not completely displaced by technology. While Morse code did play an important role during the First and Second World Wars, the Native Americans also played a vital role in transmitting coded messages by telephone and radio. This time, however, their messages did not involve smoke. During World War I, the U.S. military used Native American Indian languages,

especially Choctaw, to encode messages. Then, during World War Ⅱ members from the Navajo tribe were recruited as code talkers. The Navajo language is unwritten and intelligible only to those within the tribe. Because of this, the Japanese military, which was very skilled at breaking codes, could not break the codes of the bilingual Navajo speakers.

5 Nowadays, computers and hand-held devices are ④cutting-edge technology and are providing a popular means of communication—whether in code or not. In particular, ⑤sending short text messages has become a common pastime for billions of people, and this trend has led to a rapid [ ⑥ ] and use of coded words and expressions. For the novice, this coded language can be confusing. For instance, it is much more likely that the code "B4" in a text message means "before" rather than referring to a standardized paper size. Here is another example. What does "LOL" stand for? Is it "Laughing out loud," "Lots of love," or "Lots of luck"? Actually, the answer is all three, and this is no secret among today's users of this kind of code. They also know that "DYK" stands for "Do you know?" Now, did you know that?

注) Choctaw：チョクトー語　　Navajo：ナバホ族

(1) 本文中の①の[ 　]内にあてはまる最も適切な語を，次のア～エから一つ選んで，その記号を書け。

ア genetic　イ international　ウ telegraphic　エ verbal

(2) 次の文は，本文中の A ～ D のいずれかに入る。最も適当な箇所を一つ選んで，その記号を書け。

For example, they made the smoke twist like a spiral or ascend in circles and could even make letters resembling V or Y.

(3) 本文中の ② にあてはまる最も適切な語を，文脈から考えて一語で書け。

(4) 本文中の③の[ 　]内にあてはまる最も適切な語を，次のア～エから一つ選んで，その記号を書け。

ア Moreover　イ Nevertheless　ウ Briefly

エ　Consequently

(5)　アメリカ先住民の言語は戦時中にどのように使われたか。4段落の内容に即して，具体例を2つ挙げて，日本語で書け。

(6)　下線部④について，この文脈で置き換えられる最も適切なものを，次のア～エから一つ選んで，その記号を書け。

ア　state-of-the-art　　イ　out-of-date　　ウ　well-known

エ　in-depth

(7)　下線部⑤について，その内容について最も適しているものを，次のア～エから一つ選んで，その記号を書け。

ア　ショートメッセージでのやりとりの普及が様々な問題を引き起こしていること

イ　ショートメッセージでのやりとりに代わる新たなテクノロジーが生まれていること

ウ　ショートメッセージでのやりとりに省略形が使用されるようになってきていること

エ　ショートメッセージでのやりとりが人々の娯楽となっていること

(8)　本文中の⑥の[　　]内にあてはまる最も適切な語を，次のア～エから一つ選んで，その記号を書け。

ア　perception　　イ　application　　ウ　expansion

エ　modernization

(9)　5段落の内容に即して，次の表に示した2つのcodeが紛らわしい理由(ア)，(イ)を具体例を挙げながら日本語で説明せよ。

| code | 紛らわしい理由 |
|---|---|
| “B4” | (ア) |
| “LOL” | (イ) |

(10)　本文の内容と一致するものを，次のア～オから2つ選んで，その記号を書け。

ア　We make use of written codes to convey information at all times.

イ　Telegraphy was originally invented by American Indians in the 1800s.

ウ　Among American Indians, three rings of smoke meant that some kind of problem had occurred.

エ　The Japanese military broke the codes of the bilingual Navajo speakers during World War Ⅱ.

オ　Coded messages are likely to cause misunderstanding to some people receiving them.

(11)　本文のタイトルとして最も適しているものを，次のア～エから一つ選んで，その記号を書け。

ア　New Information Technology

イ　Coded Communication

ウ　The History of Native Americans

エ　Computer Development

(☆☆☆◎◎◎◎)

【3】次の文中の下線部①，②を英語に直して書け。

①自由とは社会にとってつねに重要な概念であるが，それは多種多様なものを意味し得る。実のところ，社会が変化するときはいつでも自由の概念も変化するように思われる。②自由は一部の人々の権利であったが，21世紀の初めにおいて，自由はあらゆる個人が自分自身を表現することを可能にした。この傾向には多くの文化的な意味合いが含まれている。

(☆☆☆◎◎◎◎)

【4】あなたは，自身の英語におけるスピーキング力を高めるために，何が大切だと考えるか。次の3つの条件を踏まえて英語で書け。

条件1　40語以上であること。ただし，ピリオドやクエスチョンマークなどは下線の間に記入し，語数には含めない。

条件2　自分の考えを述べること。

条件3　具体的な例を挙げること。

(40語)

(☆☆☆◎◎◎◎)

# 解答・解説

## 【中高共通】

【1】PART 1　No.1　(C)　No.2　(C)　No.3　(D)　No.4　(A)　No.5　(B)　PART 2　No.1　(A)　No.2　(B)　No.3　(B)　No.4　(D)　PART 3　①　清潔　②　酸素　③　白　④　鮮やかな　⑤　太陽

〈解説〉PART 1～PART 3の3つのパートに分かれており，説明はすべて英語でなされる。いずれも問題用紙に文字情報があるので，あらかじめ目を通して内容を予測したうえで臨むこと。　PART 1　男女2人による短い会話を聞いて，選択肢で解答するもの。質問は，この女性は，以前は通勤にどのくらい時間がかかったか」，「この会話はどこで行われている可能性が高いか」など，難度は高くないが1度しか放送されないため，集中して聞き取る必要がある。　PART 2　長めの対話文を聞いて選択肢で解答するもの。放送は2回ある。対話は女性の睡眠時間の話から始まり，それぞれいつもどうやって起きるかという内容になっている。 PART 3 スピーチの内容の要点を日本語で表を埋めながら解答するもの。放送は2回ある。サンゴと藻類の共生関係と，サンゴの色の変化に関する実験結果について述べられている。

【2】(1) Change roles. (2) It's your turn. (3) Have you finished reading the story? (4) Write down what I'm going to say.

〈解説〉解答例以外にも，switch「交代する」，take notes「メモを取る」など，複数の表現をストックしておきたい。新学習指導要領では，英語の授業は英語で実施することが推奨されている。授業の流れに沿って，挨拶から活動の説明，時間の指示から，活動の終わり，授業のまとめと振り返り，次回の予定の連絡と課題の指示，終わりの挨拶まで，すべて英語による授業を想定して練習しておくことが必要である。

【3】(1) Anyone, who (2) same, size (3) In, spite (4) Who, owner

〈解説〉(1) whoever～「～する人は誰でも」。 (2) be the same size as～「～と同じサイズである」。 (3) in spite of～「～にもかかわらず」。 (4) 動詞own「所有する」をowner「所有者」を使って書きかえる。

【4】(1) included, bill (2) nothing, with (3) have, rained (4) no, difference / matter

〈解説〉(1) be included in～「～に含まれている」。 (2) have nothing to do with～「～に無関係である」。 (3) must have＋過去分詞「～したに違いない」。 (4) matter「重大なこと」。make no matter「たいしたことではない」。make no difference「違いが生まれない，同じことである」。

## 【中学校】

【1】(1) ① 文化　② 主体的　(2) ① 即興　② まとまり
③ 理由

〈解説〉今回出題されている箇所は，他の自治体でも頻出である。
(1) 「外国語」の目標と併せて「英語」の目標も覚えておきたい。
(2) 「話すこと[発表]」は，平成29年度の改訂時に新設された領域である。同じく新設された「話すこと[やり取り]」とともに，学習指導要領解説外国語編を参照し，新設された背景，目標，具体的な内容，言語活動まで答えられるように整理しておきたい。

【2】(1) sports day　(2) memorization　(3) staff room

〈解説〉実際に教壇に立ってから必要となる学校・指導関係の語彙は，できるだけ多く身につけておこう。例えば，opening ceremony「始業式」，school picnic「遠足」，teachers' meeting「職員会議」などの学校行事や，student guidance「生徒指導」，classroom administration「学級経営」等の学校教育関係，affirmative sentences「肯定文」，using blackboard「板書」，grasping the context「内容の把握」等，英語学習関係の用語まで，幅広く押さえておきたい。

【3】(1) 1990年代初めになってようやく，この種のコミュニケーション手段が広く利用されるようになった。　(2) イ　(3) エ
(4) イ　(5) ウ　(6) ア A　イ D　(7) イ，オ

〈解説〉(1) It is not until～that…で「～になって初めて…する」。の意味。
(2) 電子メールと普通郵便を比較している。普通郵便と比べて，移送時間が大幅に減っているとあることから，イ「効率性」の改良が適切。
(3) PDAの特徴として「ワイヤレスネットワークが使えるところであればどこでも」という記述から，エ「可搬性」が適切。　(4) far cry from～「～から程遠い，非常な相違で」。　(5) 下線部を含む文意は「電子メールを発明したと言ったときレイ・トムリンソンはからかっていたのではない，なぜならそれ(電子メール)は素晴らしいアイデア

だったのだから」。　(6)　ア　挿入文は「たった30年のうちに，私たちが何千人もの人とすぐ連絡が取れるようになったということはさらに注目すべきことである」。電子メールの普及について述べている第1段落のAに挿入するのが適切。　イ　挿入文は電子メールの短所について述べられている。「電子メールは，多くの人とコンタクトを取るためメッセージに多くのアドレスを加える必要があり，それは多くの時間を要する」。挿入文は，ウェブページにアクセスするだけでコミュニケーションが取れるSNSの長所と対比されているので，Dが適切。
(7)　ア　第3段落参照。ブログが人気を得始めたのは1999年頃。
イ「電子メールが広く使用されるようになった出来事は1993年に起きた」。第2段落参照。　ウ　最終段落参照。レイ・トムリンソンは電子メールを発明した。　エ　第3段落参照。人々はブログで日常生活の些細な出来事を書いている。　オ「電子メールが発明されるまでは，大規模に情報を交換することは不可能だと考えられていた」。最終段落参照。

【4】(1)　Teachers shouldn’t stick to old-fashioned teaching methods.
(2)　The word “Sanuki” in Sanuki Udon is the old name of Kagawa Prefecture.　(3)　Kagawa prefecture is rich in nature with the beautiful sea and mountains.
〈解説〉解答例以外にも，次のような表現が使える。　(1)　cling to～「～にしがみつく，固執する」。traditional, conventional「従来の」。
(2)　previous～, former～「旧～」。　(3)　surrounded by～「～に囲まれた」。full of nature「自然豊かな」。

【5】(解答例) I think we should clean our school by ourselves. I have two reasons for this. First, we are less likely to litter up if we have to clean it by ourselves. Second, we can learn to collaborate with each other to get the cleaning done smoothly. (46 words)
〈解説〉解答例は，自分たちで掃除すべきだという立場である。自分たち

で掃除しなければならないなら散らかさなくなることと，スムーズに掃除するために互いに協力することを学べることを理由に挙げている。聞き手に伝わりやすいことを意識し，自分の意見と理由を明示する。使用語数は40語以上と指示されているので，40～60語程度を目安に，簡潔に自分の意見を述べる練習をしておくとよいだろう。

## 【高等学校】

【1】① 統合的　② 的確　③ 目的　④ 主体的

〈解説〉他の自治体などにおいても，最も頻出である目標の空所補充である。今年度は「外国語科」の目標からの出題であるが，次年度以降は，各科目の目標や指導計画の作成と内容の取扱いなどからの出題が予想される。記述式であるため正確に文言を覚えておくことが求められるが，やみくもに暗記しようとするのではなく，学習指導要領と併せて同解説外国語編・英語編を読み込み，内容を理解した上でキーワードを押さえることが必要である。

【2】(1) エ　(2) A　(3) received　(4) イ　(5) 第一次世界大戦中，アメリカ軍はアメリカ先住民の言語であるチョクトー語を使って，メッセージを暗号化し，第二次世界大戦では，書き言葉がなく，民族内の人にしかわからない言語を使用するナバホ族がメッセージを暗号化したり，暗号化されたメッセージを解読したりする役割を果たした。　(6) ア　(7) エ　(8) ウ　(9) (ア)「前に」という意味のbeforeと，用紙サイズのB4の2つの意味にとれるから。(イ)「大声で笑うこと」,「たくさんの愛」,「たくさんの運」などの意味にとることができるから。　(10) ウ，オ　(11) イ

〈解説〉(1) 第1段落では，人と人とのコミュニケーションの種類を挙げている。「ボディランゲージ」,「written code(書き言葉)」以外のコミュニケーションの種類としては,「verbal code(話し言葉)」が適切。

(2) 挿入文は「彼らは煙をらせんのようにねじったり，円を描くようにして上げたり，VやYに似た文字を作ったりすることさえできた」。

第2段落では，ネイティブアメリカンがのろしを使っていたことに言及している。空所Aの前の文で，「遠くの仲間にメッセージを伝えるために，彼らは火を起こし，立ち上る煙を操った」と述べていることから，挿入文はこの文について詳述したものと考えられる。また，空所Aの後で「これらののろしは危険を警告したり，人々を招集したり，ニュースを伝達したりした」と述べているのは，挿入文に説明を加えたものと判断できる。　(3)　電報について触れている箇所である。文頭のOne operator sent…と呼応しているので，the otherの後の動詞は「受け取る」となる。　(4)　空所前の第3段落は，当時合衆国で電報は伝達技術の最先端であったと締めくくられている。空所後は「ネイティブアメリカンによる符号化されたコミュニケーションは，テクノロジーに完璧にとって代わられたわけではない」とあるので，Nevertheless「それにもかかわらず」が適切。　(5)　第4段落の後半の，During World War Ⅰ…と，Then, during World War Ⅱ…の部分に書かれていることをまとめる。　(6)　cutting-edge「最先端の」と同意の表現を選ぶ。state-of-the-art「最新式の」，out- of-date「時代遅れの」，well-known「周知の」，in-depth「詳細な」。　(7)　下線部⑤のpastime「娯楽」が解答のカギである。　(8)　this trendは「ショートメッセージでのやりとりが人々の娯楽になっていること」を指し，続いて「それが符号化された言葉や表現の急速な使用と『拡大』につながっている」と述べている。　(9)　第5段落4～8文目参照。紛らわしいショートメッセージの例として，B4とLOLの例が挙げられているので，簡潔な日本語でまとめる。　(10)　ア　第1段落3文目参照。情報を伝える手段は書き言葉だけではない。　イ　第2段落の最終文参照。ネイティブアメリカンののろしは「インディアン　テレグラフ」と呼ばれている。電報をネイティブアメリカンが発明したということではない。　ウ「ネイティブアメリカンの間では，三つの煙の輪は何かしらの問題が起きていることを意味した」。第2段落の6文目参照。　エ　第4段落の最終文参照。日本軍は解読できなかった。　オ「符号化されたメッセージは受け手に誤解を引き起こす可能性がある」。第5段落3文目参照。

(11) 本文には，符号化されたコミュニケーションの変遷が書かれている。よって，ア「新しい情報テクノロジー」，ウ「ネイティブアメリカンの歴史」，エ「コンピューターの発達」などは不適。

【3】① Freedom is always an important concept to society, but it can mean many different things. ② Freedom used to be a right for some people. At the beginning of the 21st century, it allowed all individuals to express themselves.

〈解説〉日本語の文章の表現がやや硬いので，まず日本語を簡単な言い回しに置き換えてから英訳を考える。英語特有の無生物主語の表現をうまく使いこなすことが解答のポイントである。

【4】(解答例) I think I should maintain the motivation to improve my English speaking skills. I'll make the most of each class, which is conducted completely in English, and chances to talk with native speakers outside of class. Also, I'll take English proficiency tests regularly to evaluate my own English speaking level.(50 words)

〈解説〉解答例では，スピーキング力を高めるためにはモチベーションを保つことが大切で，オールイングリッシュの授業や授業外でネイティブ話者と話す機会を最大限利用することと，自身のレベル確認のために定期的に英語試験を受験することを具体例として挙げている。指定語数は40語である。40～60語を目安に簡潔にまとめられるよう練習しておくとよいだろう。

# 2021年度　実施問題

## 【中高共通】

【1】Listening Comprehension Section

Listening Comprehension Section is composed of three parts: PART 1, PART 2 and PART 3. In each part, you may take notes while listening.

【PART 1】

In this part, you will hear five conversations between two people. After listening to a conversation, you will hear a question about it. Read the four choices on your test paper, choose the best one to the question, and write it on your answer sheet. You will hear each conversation and question just one time.

No. 1

(M) When you travel, do you like to try the local food?

(W) Yes, of course. I usually ask a taxi driver the name of a good restaurant.

Question: What does the woman usually ask a taxi driver when she travels?

(A) The name of a local food.

(B) The name of a taxi driver.

(C) The name of a beautiful place to visit.

(D) The name of a good place to eat.

No. 2

(M) I think a sense of humor is the most important. I like people who are funny!

(W) I like to laugh, but what I care about the most is how smart people are.

Question: What does the woman care about the most when she meets people?

(A) The wealth.

(B) The appearance.

(C) The intelligence.

(D) The sense of humor.

No. 3

(M) When I was a child, my family had dinner together every night.

(W) It's great! Our family did so just on weekends, but we had breakfast together every day.

Question: What did the man say about his childhood?

(A) His family had dinner together on weekends.

(B) His family had dinner together every night.

(C) His family had breakfast together every day.

(D) His family had breakfast together on weekdays.

No. 4

(M) How often do you take public transportation?

(W) Every day. I don't drive, so I have to take the subway to work.

Question: How does the woman go to her workplace?

(A) By bus.

(B) By taxi.

(C) By subway.

(D) On foot.

No. 5

(W) I think the best way to keep fit is to ride a bicycle regularly.

(M) Really? I think walking up five flights of stairs every day is the most effective.

Question: What does the man think is the best way to keep fit?

(A) Going up the stairs.

(B) Walking in a park.

(C) Riding a bicycle.

(D) Having a nice flight.

【PART 2】

In this part, you will hear an interview. After that, you will be asked four questions. Read the four choices on your test paper, choose the best one to the question, and write it on your answer sheet. You will hear the interview and the questions two times.

(M) Thank you for joining this interview.

(W) My pleasure.

(M) Let me ask some questions. First, would you tell me about your job?

(W) Sure. I write market reports about the chemical industry.

(M) How do you do that?

(W) I talk to people in the industry. I read related articles to follow the markets.

(M) What kind of equipment do you use?

(W) Well, I use the phone a lot, but my computer is the most important piece of equipment. There are some good websites that give a lot of information. In fact, sometimes there is too much information. My doctor says I spend too much time in front of a screen, but I have no choice.

(M) Where do you work?

(W) I work at home in New York. When I lived in Canada, I worked in an office in Toronto, but I moved to the States two years ago, and found I could do the job from home. I have a very small room with my fax, my phone, and my computer. In fact, it's not really big enough for me and all my equipment, but I manage somehow.

(M) And do you work normal office hours?

(W) Yes. I start at about nine and work until three thirty. This gives me enough time to go and pick up my kids.

(M) So no business lunches?

(W) No, unfortunately. I usually have a quick sandwich by myself, then go back upstairs. It was nice before to have lunch with my colleagues.

Now. I only speak to them on the phone. Sometimes it's too quiet in my house.

(M) So which do you prefer, the traditional way or the way you work now?

(W) It depends. I feel I work more efficiently at home, but I do want to see my colleagues.

(M) Thank you.

(W) Thank you.

Question No. 1: What does the woman do?

(A) Working in a computer company.

(B) Making websites.

(C) Working in the chemical industry.

(D) Researching and making reports.

Question No. 2: How and where does the woman work now?

(A) In her house by herself.

(B) In her house without a phone.

(C) In an office with her colleagues.

(D) In an office with a computer.

Question No. 3: Who did the woman have lunch with before?

(A) Alone.

(B) With her colleagues.

(C) With her kids.

(D) With her husband.

Question No. 4: Which is true about the content of the interview?

(A) The woman does not talk with her colleagues on the phone.

(B) The woman works efficiently at home.

(C) The woman goes out for business lunches very often.

(D) The woman has found only bad points about her present way of working.

【PART 3】

In this part, you will hear one speech. Summarize the speech by writing the answers in Japanese on your answer sheet. You'll hear the speech two times.

Now, listen

Michelangelo painted his fresco on the ceiling of the Sistine Chapel in 1512. The painting shows scenes from the Bible and is widely thought of as a masterpiece of the Renaissance era. It has been restored just once, but it still has very clear and strong colors. Though time is one problem for the painting, there are other factors which cause damage to it, and so new systems have been introduced to keep the painting in a good condition for the future.

There are a purification system which cleans the air and a lighting system which now uses LED lights. Thanks to the LED lights, there is no heat damage to the monument. As well as helping to preserve the colors, this new lighting allows the detail of the painting to be seen very clearly, which makes the people who care for the masterpiece very happy. There are sensors and cameras on the walls which count the number of people in the chapel, so that the air quality and temperature can be controlled. The Vatican is so worried about the large number of visitors that in the future they may need to limit how many people can enter the chapel.

述べられている内容について，次の(　①　)～(　⑤　)にあてはまる日本語や数字を，それぞれ書け。

ミケランジェロの「システィーナ礼拝堂天井画」は(　①　)年に描かれ，ルネサンス時代の傑作とされている。良い状態で保存するために，新しい2つの装置が導入された。その一つが，(　②　)による影響のない照明装置である。もう一つは，壁に設置されたセンサーとカメラが(　③　)を数えて，空気の状態や(　④　)を制御する装置である。将来的には，この礼拝堂への(　③　)を(　⑤　)することも検討されている。

This is the end of the Listening Comprehension Section.

(☆☆☆◎◎◎◎)

【2】英語の授業で，次の(1)～(4)のとき，授業者が生徒に英語でどのように話すかを書け。

(1) 自分の席に戻るように指示を出すとき。

(2) 4人グループを作るように指示を出すとき。

(3) 相手を変えてもう一度質問をするように指示を出すとき。

(4) これは誰についての話かと尋ねるとき。

(☆☆◎◎◎◎)

【3】次の(1)～(4)の各組において，a)とb)がほぼ同じ意味になるように，b)の(　　)内にあてはまる最も適切な一語をそれぞれ書け。

(1) a) What a good singer she is!

b) How (　　) she (　　)!

(2) a) Without his shyness, he would be a good actor.

b) (　　) it were (　　) for his shyness, he would be a good actor.

(3) a) I said to Mary, "Don't cry."

b) I (　　) Mary not (　　) cry.

(4) a) Because I felt tired, I went to bed early.

b) (　　) (　　), I went to bed early.

(☆☆◎◎◎◎)

【4】次の(1)～(4)のそれぞれについて，日本語の意味になるように，(　　)内にあてはまる最も適切な一語を書け。

(1) いくらか安くしてもらえませんか。

Could you (　　) me a (　　), please?

(2) 昨日，事務所を掃除してもらった。

We (　　) our office (　　) yesterday.

(3)　今のところ，順調です。

(　　) (　　), it's going well.

(4)　2時間雨が降り続いている。

It (　　) (　　) raining for two hours.

(☆☆☆◎◎◎)

## 【中学校】

【1】中学校学習指導要領(平成29年告示)の「第2章　第9節　外国語」に関して，次の(1)，(2)の問いに答えよ。

(1)　次の文は，「第1　目標」の一部を示そうとしたものである。文中の(　①　)，(　②　)にあてはまる語句をそれぞれ書け。

> 外国語の音声や語彙，表現，文法，(　①　)の働きなどを理解するとともに，これらの知識を，聞くこと，読むこと，話すこと，書くことによる実際のコミュニケーションにおいて活用できる(　②　)を身に付けるようにする。

(2)　次の文は，「第2　各言語の目標及び内容等　英語　1　目標　(1)聞くこと」を示そうとしたものである。次の(　①　)～(　③　)にあてはまる語句をそれぞれ書け。

> ア　はっきりと話されれば，日常的な話題について，必要な(　①　)を聞き取ることができるようにする。
> イ　はっきりと話されれば，日常的な話題について，話の(　②　)を捉えることができるようにする。
> ウ　はっきりと話されれば，社会的な話題について，短い説明の(　③　)を捉えることができるようにする。

(☆☆☆☆◎◎◎◎)

【2】次の(1)～(3)の日本語を英語で書け。

(1) 体育館　(2) 復習　(3) 校長

(☆☆◎◎◎◎)

【3】次の英文を読み，あとの(1) ～(7)の問いに答えよ。

Sometimes a building can come to symbolize a country: the Pyramids in Egypt, the Kremlin in Russia and the Taj Mahal in India. Arguably, one of the world's most famous constructions, and one that is inescapably linked to the city and country it stands in, is Eiffel Tower. It is the most visited paid monument in the world, having welcomed over 200 million people since it was built in 1889. ①Standing at 324 meters tall at its highest point, it is the tallest structure in Paris. When it was constructed, it was the tallest man-made structure in the world.

The Eiffel Tower was named after the man who constructed it, Gustave Eiffel, sometimes referred to as 'The Magician of Iron'. This civil engineer was born in the French city of Dijon to a well-to-do family in 1832. The young Eiffel developed an ( ② ) in science partly due to the influence of an uncle, who owned a chemical works in Dijon. This led him to enroll in the famous higher education and research institute, École Centrale Paris, which specializes in engineering and science. [ A ]

After graduation, Eiffel found himself working in the railway industry. He became involved with bridge design, and in particular, bridges made of iron. His first big solo project was the construction of Bordeaux Bridge in south-west France. Spanning a larger river, this bridge would be 500 meters long, and Eiffel was only 27 years old when he completed ③it. He would go on to have a highly successful career in the railway industry, building bridges, locomotives and stations. However, it is for the iconic tower in Paris that he is best ( ④ ). [ B ]

To celebrate the centennial of the French revolution, the 1889 World's Fair was to be held in Paris. A tower, initially designed by two employees in

Eiffel's company, Emile Nouguir and Maurice Koechlin, was selected to be ⑤<u>the exposition's centrepiece</u>. The proposed structure would be over 300 meters tall, making it the largest man-made structure in the world at that time, and was therefore a massive engineering undertaking. [ C ]

The levels of detail and precision involved in putting together the Eiffel Tower were simply staggering. In total 1,700 general drawings were made, and a further 3,629 detailed drawings of the 18,038 different parts were produced. All these drawings needed to be incredibly precise, often to the nearest 0.1 mm. The various sections of the tower were constructed at a nearby factory and then transported to the site to be joined together with over 2.5 million rivets. [ D ]

The tower was completed in two years, in time for the opening of the World's Fair, and was an immediate success with the public. On the various levels, visitors could buy a souvenir newspaper, actually printed in the tower, eat cake at a patisserie, or send a postcard from the post office at the top. [ E ]

Over 100 years later. Eiffel's wonder of engineering is still standing and still delighting visitors from across the globe.

P.Z.Graham, G.A.Reid; Eurekal — *Great Discoveries and Achivements in Science, Engineering, and Technology* —

(1)　下線部①の英語を日本語に直して書け。

(2)　本文中の②の(　　)内にあてはまる最も適切な語を，次のア～エから一つ選んで，その記号を書け。

ア　economy　　イ　interest　　ウ　objective　　エ　opinion

(3)　下線部③のitが示す具体的な内容を次のア～エから一つ選んで，その記号を書け。

ア　the long railway

イ　his first big solo project

ウ　the construction of the Eiffel Tower

エ　the world's Fair in Paris

(4) 本文中の④の(　　)内にあてはまる最も適切なものを，次のア～エから一つ選んで，その記号を書け。

ア understood　　イ resented　　ウ organized

エ remembered

(5) 下線部⑤について，その内容について最も適しているものを，次のア～エから一つ選んで，その記号を沓け。

ア 博覧会で最も精密な作品

イ 博覧会場の中心に位置する作品

ウ 博覧会の最大の目玉作品

エ 博覧会で最も多くの寄付が集まった作品

(6) 次の文は，本文中の[　A　]～[　E　]のいずれかに入る。最も適切な箇所を一つ選んで，その記号を書け。

ア Eiffel graduated near the top of his class in 1855 with a degree in chemistry.

イ At night, the tower was illuminated by hundreds of gas lamps.

(7) 本文の内容と一致するものを，次のア～オから2つ選んで，その記号を書け。

ア エッフェル塔は完成以来，200億人以上が訪れるパリの象徴である。

イ エッフェルは大学卒業後すぐに化学工場で働いた。

ウ エッフェル塔はエッフェルが20代の時に建てられた。

エ エッフェル塔はフランス革命の100周年を祝う博覧会に合わせて建てられた。

オ エッフェル塔は近くの工場で作られた部品を組み合わせて建てられた。

(☆☆☆☆◎◎◎◎)

【4】次の(1)～(3)の日本語を英語に直して書け。

(1) 英語を学ぶうえで最も重要な要因は，年齢ではなく，動機付けである。

(2)　瀬戸内の気候は年間を通じておだやかである。

(3)　香川県は17の市や町から成り立っている。

(☆☆☆◎◎◎◎)

【5】「中学校の修学旅行先を海外にすべきだ」という意見に対してあなたは賛成か反対か。理由を添えて自分の意見を30語以上の英語で書け。ただし，ピリオドやクエスチョンマークなどは下線の間に記入し，語数には含めない。

| ______ | ______ | ______ | ______ | ______ | ______ |
|---|---|---|---|---|---|
| ______ | ______ | ______ | ______ | ______ | ______ |
| ______ | ______ | ______ | ______ | ______ | ______ |
| ______ | ______ | ______ | ______ | ______ | ______ |
| ______ | ______ | ______ | ______ | ______ | ______ (30語) |
| ______ | ______ | ______ | ______ | ______ | ______ |
| ______ | ______ | ______ | ______ | ______ | ______ |
| ______ | ______ | ______ | ______ | ______ | ______ |

(☆☆☆◎◎◎◎◎)

## 【高等学校】

【1】次の文は，高等学校学習指導要領(平成30年告示)「第2章　第8節　外国語　第1款　目標」の一部を示そうとしたものである。次の①～⑥の(　　)内にあてはまる語句を書け。

> 外国語によるコミュニケーションにおける見方・考え方を働かせ，外国語による聞くこと，読むこと，話すこと，書くことの言語活動及びこれらを結び付けた統合的な言語活動を通して，情報や考えなどを的確に理解したり適切に表現したり伝え合ったりするコミュニケーションを図る資質・能力を次のとおり育成することを目指す。
>
> (1)　外国語の音声や語彙，表現，文法，言語の働きなどの理解

を深めるとともに，これらの(　①　)を，聞くこと，読むこと，話すこと，書くことによる実際のコミュニケーションにおいて，目的や場面，状況などに応じて適切に活用できる(　②　)を身に付けるようにする。

(2)　コミュニケーションを行う目的や場面，状況などに応じて，(　③　)的な話題や(　④　)的な話題について，外国語で情報や考えなどの概要や要点，詳細，話し手や書き手の意図などを的確に理解したり，これらを活用して適切に表現したり伝え合ったりすることができる力を養う。

(3)　外国語の背景にある(　⑤　)に対する理解を深め，聞き手，読み手，話し手，書き手に配慮しながら，主体的，自律的に外国語を用いてコミュニケーションを図ろうとする(　⑥　)を養う。

(☆☆☆☆◎◎◎◎)

【2】次の英文を読み，あとの(1)～(7)の問いに答えよ。

[1] Scientists speculate that human beings evolved as runners about two million years ago. Our tall, lean bodies, muscle structure and strong arches gave us the spring we needed for speed and stamina. Our species survived in part by successfully running down wild animals for food.

[2] East Africa, where our human species began, now seems to produce faster runners than any other part of the world. East African racers dominate sprints and long distance competitions alike. Kenyan Geoffrey Mutai, for example, recently set a new record in the famous NYC Marathon. ①Ethiopian Haile Gebrselassie won several Olympic races after years of practice running six miles daily, barefoot, from his farm to his school.

[3] The Tarahumara Indians of northwest Mexico are runners famous for their endurance. ②They have developed stamina by running barefoot between their isolated mountain villages for centuries. For instance, in seven hours,

one barefoot Tarahumara man ran a distance that took a horseback rider three days to complete. In their own language, Tarahumara males are called Raramori, "foot runners."

4 But no human athlete can match Earth's fastest animals. Speed and endurance depend on how quickly oxygen flows through the body. Each breath pushes oxygen into the lungs. The oxygen travels through the bloodstream into the heart. The heart pumps the oxygen-filled blood into the muscles, where it turns into energy, But the human heart is small, so our ③<u>aerobic system</u> can't produce super energy. Superb runners such as the cheetah, greyhound and pronghorn antelope* convert oxygen to energy much faster than we do.

5 The heart of a greyhound—the fastest species of dog—pumps twice as much blood to its aerobic system as the human heart does. Greyhounds, like racing camels—another speedy species—sometimes become airborne, with all four feet off the ground! The cheetah, the world's swiftest land animal, much smaller than a horse, can race 70 mph*, but only for a few seconds.

6 For combined speed and endurance, the American pronghorn antelope takes the prize. Pronghorns can run 60 mph for an hour at a time. "They've evolved over millennia," explains one physiologist. "In ancient times pronghorns probably developed their [　④　] to evade cheetahs. They developed [　⑤　] to escape wolf packs, which hunt over long distances." The pronghorn's aerobic system is twice as efficient as ours.

7 Even the two-inch Etruscan shrew*, thin as a dime, can race at superb speeds, If it were the size of a human being, it could sprint a mile in 40 seconds. No human being could match this feat even over shorter distance.

8 Human beings survived by developing big brains and toolmaking abilities. But many animals survive only thanks to their speed and endurance. They truly must run for their lives!

注)　pronghorn antelope: プロングホーン(草食動物の一種)
　　mph: miles per hour　※1マイル＝約1.6km

Etruscan shrew: コビトジャコウネズミ

(1) 下線部①のエチオピアのHaile Gebrselassie選手は，オリンピックのマラソンで勝つためにどのような練習をしていたか。本文の内容に即して日本語で具体的に書け。

(2) 下線部②について，(ア) その方法と，(イ) そのことが分かる実例を，本文の内容に即して日本語で具体的に書け。

(3) 下線部③の仕組みについて，本文の内容に即して日本語で具体的に書け。

(4) Which of the following statements best describes paragraph 4 ?

ア Stamina is very important for animals to run fast.

イ Some animals can convert oxygen to energy much faster than human beings do.

ウ The heart of a human being is the central part of its aerobic system.

エ Oxygen travels through the bloodstream into the heart.

(5) 6 段落の④，⑤の[ ]内にあてはまる適切な一語を，文中からそれぞれ抜き出して書け。

(6) 次の表は，本文の内容に即して，あとのA～Eを走りの特徴ごとに分類しようとしたものである。表中の( ア )～( ウ )に，A～Eを全て分類し，記号で書け。

| 走りの特徴 | A～Eを分類 |
|---|---|
| 持久力に優れている | ( ア ) |
| 速さに優れている | ( イ ) |
| 持久力・速さの両方を備えている | ( ウ ) |

A the Tarahumara Indians B the cheetah

C the greyhound D the American.pronghorn antelope

E the Etruscan shrew

(7) 次の文の( )内にあてはまる最も適切なものを，あとのア～エから一つ選んで，その記号を書け。

From this story, we can conclude that ( ).

ア intelligence may be the most important in order for human beings to survive

イ　if human beings practice much harder, they can run faster than Etruscan shrew

ウ　very tiny animal species have little hope of surviving

エ　some animals are more intelligent than human beings

(☆☆☆☆◎◎◎◎)

【3】次の文中の下線部①，②を英語に直して書け。

①最近の考え方や出来事あるいは問題が，ニュースであるかどうかを，私たちはどのように決めるのだろうか。それらの中からニュースになるものとならないものをどうやって素早く見極め，選り分けたらよいのだろうか。このニュースは，読者やリスナーや視聴者に本当に関心をもたせることができるのだろうか。②これらの問いに答えるため，全てのニュースに共通する複数の要素を検討してみよう。

(☆☆☆☆◎◎◎◎)

【4】英語を学ぶ上で大切なことは何だと考えるか。あなたの考えを理由も含めて，40語以上の英語で書け。ただし，ピリオドやクエスチョンマークなどは下線の間に記入し，語数には含めない。

| | | | | | |
|---|---|---|---|---|---|
| ＿＿＿＿ | ＿＿＿＿ | ＿＿＿＿ | ＿＿＿＿ | ＿＿＿＿ | ＿＿＿＿ |
| ＿＿＿＿ | ＿＿＿＿ | ＿＿＿＿ | ＿＿＿＿ | ＿＿＿＿ | ＿＿＿＿ |
| ＿＿＿＿ | ＿＿＿＿ | ＿＿＿＿ | ＿＿＿＿ | ＿＿＿＿ | ＿＿＿＿ |
| ＿＿＿＿ | ＿＿＿＿ | ＿＿＿＿ | ＿＿＿＿ | ＿＿＿＿ | ＿＿＿＿ |
| ＿＿＿＿ | ＿＿＿＿ | ＿＿＿＿ | ＿＿＿＿ | ＿＿＿＿ | ＿＿＿＿ |
| ＿＿＿＿ | ＿＿＿＿ | ＿＿＿＿ | ＿＿＿＿ | ＿＿＿＿ | ＿＿＿＿ |
| ＿＿＿＿ | ＿＿＿＿ | ＿＿＿＿ | ＿＿＿＿ (40語) | ＿＿＿＿ | ＿＿＿＿ |
| ＿＿＿＿ | ＿＿＿＿ | ＿＿＿＿ | ＿＿＿＿ | ＿＿＿＿ | ＿＿＿＿ |
| ＿＿＿＿ | ＿＿＿＿ | ＿＿＿＿ | ＿＿＿＿ | ＿＿＿＿ | ＿＿＿＿ |
| ＿＿＿＿ | ＿＿＿＿ | ＿＿＿＿ | ＿＿＿＿ | ＿＿＿＿ | ＿＿＿＿ |

(☆☆☆◎◎◎◎◎)

# 解答・解説

## 【中高共通】

【1】Part1　No.1　(D)　No.2　(C)　No.3　(B)　No.4　(C)　No.5　(A)　Part2　No.1　(D)　No.2　(A)　No.3　(B)　No.4　(B)　Part3　①　1512　②　熱　③　入場者数　④　気温　⑤　制限

〈解説〉男女の短い会話とその内容に関する質問を聞いて，問題用紙に印刷された4つの選択肢から正答を選ぶ。会話と質問の放送は1回のみ。PART1　No.1　the name of a good restaurant→(D) The name of a good place to eatに言い換えている。　No.2　how smart people are→(C) The intelligenceに言い換えている。　No.3　男性は子どものころ毎晩夕食を家族で食べていて，女性は毎朝と週末は家族で食事したとある。No.4　take the subway → (C) by subwayに言い換えている。
No.5　walking up five flights of stairs → going up the stairsに言い換えている。flightは「(階段の)一続き」という意味。　PART 2　短めのインタビューとその内容に関する4つの質問を聞いて，問題用紙の選択肢から正答を選ぶ。インタビューと質問は2回放送される。　No.1　男性のwould you tell me about your job?に対し，I write market reportsと答えている。また，How do you do that?に対し，I talk to people in the industryとI read related articlesと，調査していることを述べていることから判断する。　No.2　Where do you workという質問にI work at homeと答え，さらにI usually have a quick sandwich by myselfやSometimes it's too quiet in my houseなどから，自宅で1人で働いていることがわかる。No.3　女性の7番目の発言で，It was nice before to have lunch with my colleaguesと述べている。　No.4　女性の8番目の発言で，I feel I work more efficiently at homeと述べていることから判断する。　PART 3　スピーチを聞いて要約文(和文)の空所を補充する記述式問題。問題用紙にスピーチの要約文が印刷されており，空所に入る適語を日本語で書く。スピーチは2回放送される。　① 第1段落1文目のin 1512から判断する。　② 第2段落2文目のThanks to the LED lights, there is no heat damage to the monumentから判断する。　③・④ 第2段落4文目のThere are sensors and cameras on the walls which count the number of people … so that the air quality and temperature can be controlledから判断する。　⑤ 第2段落5文目の they may need to limit how many people can enter the chapelから判断する。

【2】(1) Go back to your seat.　(2) Make groups of four.　(3) Change partners and ask your questions again.　(4) Who is this story about?

〈解説〉授業を行う際の指示の表現はまとめて覚えておこう。Open your books to page 25.「25ページを開きなさい」など教室活動の準備に必要な指示や，Point at the picture that I said.「私が言った絵を指さしなさい」など活動時の具体的な指示，Put your cards face up「カードの表を上にして置きなさい」など特定のゲームで出す指示，Please sit down, when you are done.「終わったら座ってください」など終了の指示，そのほか注意を促す表現やほめる表現，活動のまとめ，次回までの宿題の指定や，授業終了時の挨拶まで，授業を一通り英語で行うには，実に多くの指示が必要となる。活動に応じて様々な状況をシミュレーションしておくことが大切である。

【3】(1) well, sings　(2) If, not　(3) told, to　(4) Feeling, tired

〈解説〉(1) 〈What＋a(an)＋形容詞＋名詞＋主語＋動詞～〉＝〈How＋形容詞＋主語＋動詞～〉。singerを派生語である動詞singに言い換えている。　(2) If it were not for～=Without～= But for～で表される。
(3) tell＋(人)＋to doで「(人)に～するよう命じる」という意味になり，命令文に近いニュアンスが出る。　(4) 分詞構文。接続詞を含む節の接続詞と主語を取り，feltを現在分詞のfeelingにする。

【4】(1) give, discount (2) had / got, cleaned (3) So, far
(4) has, been

〈解説〉(1) give＋(人)＋a discount「(人)に割引をする＝安くする」。
(2) 主語自らがするのではなく，他の人にさせるのは使役動詞を使い，have [get]～＋過去分詞「～を…してもらう」。our officeは「掃除される」と考え，cleanedと過去分詞にする。 (3)「今のところ」はso farで表す。 (4) 2時間前から今に至る2時間ずっと雨が降っていると考え，現在完了の進行形have＋been＋doingを用いる。

## 【中学校】

【1】(1) ① 言語 ② 技能 (2) ① 情報 ② 概要
③ 要点

〈解説〉学習指導要領における「外国語の目標」及び「英語の目標」，さらに「5領域の各目標」を確実に覚えておくこと。 (1) ② 実際のコミュニケーションにおいて活用できるのは知識だけでなく技能と考える。 (2) 英語を聞くことの目標として，「日常的な話題」では「必要な情報を聞き取り」，「話の概要を捉える」こと，「社会的な話題」では「短い説明の要点を捉える」ことと覚えておく。

【2】(1) gym(gymnasium) (2) review (3) principal/headmaster

〈解説〉学校関連の単語はまとめて覚えておこう。teachers' room「職員室」，infirmary「保健室」，homeroom(class)teacher「学級担任」，school events「学校行事」，student on day duty「日直」，basic scholastic ability「基礎学力」，teaching objectives「教育目標」などのように，施設や校務分掌から学習一般関連まで，英語教諭が知っておかなければならない語は数多くある。

【3】(1) それ(エッフェル塔)は最も高い地点では324メートル高さがあり，パリで最も高い建築物である。 (2) イ (3) イ
(4) エ (5) ウ (6) ア A イ E (7) エ，オ

〈解説〉(1)　stand at～は「(数字が)～である，～に達する」という意味。付帯状況を表す分詞構文で，同時を表す。　(2)　空所の直後にinがあるので，interest in～「～の興味」。科学に興味があり，それが有名な高等教育研究機関であるエコール・サントラル・パリ入学へ導いたとなる。　(3)　直前の文に「彼の最初の単独プロジェクトはBordeaux Bridgeの建設」とあり，続いて「この橋は500メートルの長さで，それを完成させたときEiffelはわずか27歳だった」とあることから判断できる。　(4)　空所を含む文は「彼がもっともよく～なのはパリにある象徴的な塔のためである」という意味。第1段落の3文目に「エッフェル塔が建てられて以来，世界で最も訪れられた有料の記念建築物で，2億人以上の人々を迎え入れてきた」とあるので，「もっともよく覚えられている」と考える。　(5)　centrepieceは「中央に位置したもの」ではなく「最重要なもの」という意味。　(6)　ア「エッフェルは化学の学位を取って，1855年に彼のクラスのトップ近い成績で卒業した」という意味。Aの後の第3段落の最初に「卒業後」と始まっているので，Aは卒業に関連する話だと見当をつける。　イ「夜に，エッフェル塔は何百ものガス灯で照らされた」という意味。第6段落で，エッフェル塔は世界博覧会の開幕に間に合うように完成したとある。Eの直前で，塔の中で新聞が印刷されたり，塔の頂上の郵便局ではがきが送られたりしていたとあり，それと同列で，塔で行われていたことと考える。　(7)　エは第4段落の1文目と一致する。オは第5段落の4文目と一致する。

【4】(1)　The most important factor in learning English is not age, but motivation.　(2)　The climate in Setouchi area is mild all through the year.　(3)　Kagawa prefecture consists of 17 cities and towns.

〈解説〉(1)　文の構造はThe factor is not age, but motivation.となる。「～の要因」はfactor in～で表す。　(2)　文の構造はThe climate is mild.となる。「～の気候」はclimate in～，「年間を通じて」はall through the yearやthroughout the yearなどで表す。　(3)「～から成り立つ」はconsist of

～や，be made up of～で表す。

【5】(解答例)　I think that the junior high school students should go abroad for school trip. Because students can realize cultural differences and diverse values by interacting with people in foreign countries. This experience can help students to broaden their horizons. Moreover, students will be motivated to study English harder to communicate with people in foreign countries. (55 words)

〈解説〉まず賛成か反対かを述べ，そのあとでその理由を2つか3つ述べる。moreoverなどのつなぎ言葉で情報をつなぐとよい。語数は30語以上という指定であるが，逆にあまり長くなりすぎないよう簡潔にまとめること。解答例は賛成の場合である。海外へ行き現地の人々と交流することで，異なる考え方や価値観に触れ，生徒の視野が広まること，さらに，生徒の英語学習の動機付けにもなることを挙げている。

## 【高等学校】

【1】①　知識　②　技能　③　日常　④　社会　⑤　文化　⑥　態度

〈解説〉外国語の語彙や文法などの知識を身につけるだけでなく，それを活かす5つの技能が必要である。日常的，社会的な話題を，話し相手の文化背景を考慮しながら，コミュニケーションを積極的にとろうという態度で表現し伝え合うことが大切と考える。

【2】(1)　自分の農場から学校まで毎日6マイル(約10km)を裸足で走った。　(2)　ア　何世紀にもわたり山中の離れた村々を走って移動してきた。　イ　馬で3日間かかる距離を7時間で走った男性がいた。　(3)　呼吸によって，酸素は肺に送られ，血流を通して心臓に入る。その後，(酸素は)心臓から筋肉へ送られて，エネルギーに変わる。　(4)　イ　(5)　④　speed　⑤　endurance / stamina　(6)　ア　A　イ　B，C，E　ウ　D　(7)　ア

〈解説〉(1)　第2段落の4文目のafter years of practiceのあとに，具体的にどういう練習をしたかが述べられている。　(2)　下線部②のあとに，by doing～「～することによって」と方法が述べられている。また，その次の文のFor instance以降に，実例が述べられている。　(3)　下線部③のある文から，「私たちのaerobic systemはスーパーエネルギーを作り出せないが，チータや猟犬やプロングホーンのような最高のランナーは私たちよりもはるかに早く酸素をエネルギーに変える」とある。
(4)「走る速さを決めるspeedとendurance(持久力)は，肺に入った酸素が血液とともにいかに早く心臓→筋肉に行き渡りエネルギーに変わるか」と述べられていることから判断する。　(5)　第6段落は，「(チータのようにスピードが速ければ普通は持久力はないのだが)スピードと持久力を兼ね備えたアメリカンプロングホーンは別格である」から始まり，プロングホーンの特徴が述べられている。その2つを兼ね備えた理由として，チータから逃れるためにはスピードで，オオカミの群れから逃げるためには持久力が必要だと考える。　(6)　A　the Tarahumara Indiansは第3段落1文目を参照。　B　the cheetahは第4段落最後の文，第5段落の最後の文を参照。　C　the greyhoundは第4段落の最後の文，第5段落1文目を参照。　D　the American pronghorn antelopeは第6段落参照。　E　the Etruscan shrewは第7段落参照。
(7)　第8段落1文目に「人間は大きな脳と道具を作る能力を発達させて生き残ってきた」を言い換えた，ア「知性は人類が生き残るために最も重要であるかもしれない」が適切。

【3】①　How do we determine whether a current idea, an event or a problem is a piece of news?　②　To answer these questions, examine the elements common to all news.
〈解説〉①「～かどうかを決める」はdetermine whether 主語＋動詞～で表す。　②「～に共通の」はcommon to ～で表し，common to all newsが後ろからelementsを修飾する。

【4】(解答例)　English is the most important language as an international communication tool in a global society we live in. Therefore, we need to learn not only English language itself but also practical communication skills such as giving presentations, participating in debates, leading discussions and so on. By acquiring practical skills, we will come to feel confident with exchanging our opinions freely with English speaking people. (64 words)

〈解説〉指定は40語以上。解答例では，英語はグローバル社会におけるコミュニケーションツールとして重要であること，よって言語そのものを学ぶだけでなく，プレゼンテーションやディベートなど実際のコミュニケーションスキルを身につけることが大切であり，スキルが身につくことで英語話者と自信をもって意見交換できるようになることを挙げている。

# 2020年度　実施問題

## 【中高共通】

【 1 】Listening Comprehension Section

There are three parts to this section, with special directions for each part. You may take notes while you are listening.

【PART1】

Now, let's begin PART 1. In this part, you will hear five conversations between two people. After each conversation, a third person will ask a question about what was said. Read the four possible answers on your test paper, choose the best answer to each question, and write it on your answer sheet. You will hear each conversation and question just one time.

No.1

(M) What did you think of the lecture?

(W) It had some interesting points at first, but the latter half got very difficult to understand.

Question : How was the lecture for the woman?

(A) Too easy.

(B) Very boring.

(C) Interesting at the beginning.

(D) Difficult as a whole.

No.2

(W) I think bungee jumping is much more dangerous than sky diving.

(M) Really? I think they're both very frightening. I don't think one is safer than the other.

Question : What does the man think about sky diving?

(A) As dangerous as bungee jumping.

(B) Not as dangerous as bungee jumping.

(C) Much more dangerous than bungee jumping.

(D) As safe as bungee jumping.

No.3

(M) What would you do if you won the lottery?

(W) In my dreams! But what would I do? Well, I might just give it all away to a dogs' home. No, actually, I would travel the world.

Question : What would the woman actually do if she won the lottery?

(A) Buy a world-famous dog.

(B) Build a dogs' home.

(C) Go on a trip around the world.

(D) Donate all to a dogs' home.

No.4

(W) Did you have a good time in London?

(M) We had a great time. There's so much to do. It's a really exciting city. And there are so many people from all over the world. I think it's nearly as cosmopolitan as New York.

Question : What does the man think about London?

(A) It has so many beautiful historical buildings and castles.

(B) It is composed of people from many parts of the world.

(C) It is an exciting city because of the Cosmopolitan Museum.

(D) It is so large that we can't visit the whole city.

No.5

(M) Thanks for returning the book. How did you like it?

(W) I couldn't put it down. He writes so well and the story was very exciting.

Question : Which statement is true about the conversation?

(A) The woman returned the book without reading it through.

(B) The woman wrote an exciting story.

(C) The woman couldn't put things away.

(D) The woman was so amused that she couldn't stop reading.

【PART2】

Now, let's go on to PART 2. In this part, you will hear a conversation. After that, you will be asked four questions. Read the four possible answers on your test paper, decide which one is the best answer to the question you heard, and write it on your answer sheet. You will hear the conversation and questions two times.

(M) Hi, Wanda. Did you have a good holiday?

(W) Oh, yeah, we had a great time. But I have to tell you — the most amazing thing happened.

(M) Really? What was that?

(W) Well, Roy and I were at the beach near the hotel and we were swimming in the sea — it was our first day — and a huge wave came along and knocked my sunglasses in to the water. I ...

(M) Why were you swimming in your sunglasses?

(W) I'd just left them on the top of my head. I'd forgotten they were there. Anyway, they were gone. I couldn't find them anywhere. I was really upset. You know Roy had given me those sunglasses for my birthday and they were really expensive.

(M) I remember — exactly ￡150.

(W) Yeah. Anyway, I had to have sunglasses, so I bought a new pair — just a cheap pair for just ￡15 this time. The next day I was lying on the beach, sunbathing. Then, suddenly another huge wave ...

(M) You didn't lose another pair of sunglasses?

(W) No, no. You'll never believe this — there was another huge wave. It completely covered me. I was so wet and ...

(M) Are you sure this was a good holiday?

(W) Yeah — but listen! When I looked down, there on the sand, right next to me, were my expensive sunglasses. The one I had lost the day before! I couldn't believe my eyes!

(M) You're joking! That is amazing!

Question No. 1 : Where were the sunglasses just before the woman lost them?

(A) In her bag.

(B) In her hand.

(C) On her head.

(D) On the sand.

Question No. 2 : How much were the sunglasses the woman lost?

(A) £15.

(B) £50.

(C) £115.

(D) £150.

Question No. 3 : What was the woman doing when another huge wave covered her?

(A) She was enjoying talking on the beach.

(B) She was lying on the beach.

(C) She was making a sand castle on the beach.

(D) She was swimming in the sea.

Question No. 4 : Why did the man think this was an amazing story?

(A) Because a big wave returned her expensive sunglasses to her.

(B) Because a big wave returned her cheap sunglasses to her.

(C) Because she found her lost sunglasses under the sea.

(D) Because she lost two pairs of sunglasses.

【PART3】

In this part, you will hear one speech. Summarize the speech by writing the answers in Japanese on your answer sheet.

You'll hear the speech two times.

Now, listen

Right-hand traffic means that cars must use the right side of the road and left-hand traffic means the opposite. In general, the former British colonies now use left-hand traffic. Japan is also a left-hand traffic country, because they introduced the traffic rules from Britain. Now many people are driving outside their country, so such a basic traffic rule should be united to reduce accidents. So right-hand traffic or left-hand traffic? I support right-hand traffic for the following reasons.

The first reason is that more countries use right-hand traffic in the world. Right-hand traffic is used in 163 countries, left-hand traffic in 76 countries. Originally, left-hand traffic was more common than right-hand traffic probably because many people are right-handed, but Napoleon of France chose right-hand traffic for his military strategy. He imposed this system all over Europe, but Britain didn't follow him. When America became independent from Britain, they chose right-hand traffic. As America became powerful, many countries followed America. Right-hand traffic is now more common in the world, so all countries should accept right-hand traffic for traffic safety.

The second reason is that water traffic and air traffic both use right-hand traffic, because the USA supports it. Now that right-hand traffic is the common rule on the sea and in the air, why not on the land?

Nothing is more important than international traffic safety. I believe the world should consider this issue more seriously.

述べられている内容について，次の(　①　)～(　⑥　)にあてはまる日本語や数字を，それぞれ書け。ただし，(　①　)～(　③　)には国名を書け。

| 日本が左側通行の理由 | (　①　)の交通規則を導入したため。 |
|---|---|
| 右側通行を支持する第一の理由 | (　②　)や(　③　)の影響で，現在は<br>(　④　)か国が右側通行を採用しているから。 |
| 右側通行を支持する第二の理由 | (　⑤　)交通と航空交通も右側通行であるから。 |
| 最も大切なことは何か | 国際的な(　⑥　)。 |

This is the end of the Listening Comprehension Section.

(☆☆☆◎◎◎◎)

【2】英語の授業で，次の(1)～(4)のとき，授業者が生徒に英語でどのように話すかを書け。

(1) 空欄を埋めるように指示を出すとき。

(2) 教科書の70ページを開くように指示を出すとき。

(3) 用紙を後ろから前に手渡しするように指示を出すとき。

(4) このページの上から3行目を見るように指示を出すとき。

(☆☆◎◎◎◎)

【3】次の(1)～(4)の各組において，a)とb)がほぼ同じ意味になるように，b)の(　　)内にあてはまる最も適切な一語をそれぞれ書け。

(1) a) She advised me to attend the party.

b) She advised me that (　　) (　　)attend the party.

(2) a) Why do you think it was a lie?

b) (　　) (　　)you think it was a lie?

(3) a) I was so shocked that I couldn't move.

b) I was (　　)shocked (　　)move.

(4) a) As soon as she saw her mother, she smiled brightly.

b) (　　) (　　)her mother, she smiled brightly.

(☆☆◎◎◎◎)

【4】次の(1)～(4)のそれぞれについて，下線部の①～④のいずれかに一箇所誤りがある。その箇所の番号と正しい表現に直したものを書け。

(1) ①In this area, ②a lot of car ③accidents ④are happened every day.

(2) Please ①click ②on the name of the country ③where you ④live in.

(3) I ①am looking forward ②to ③meet your ④parents.

(4) The doctor ①insisted ②to ③changing ④the dosage.

(☆☆◎◎◎◎)

【5】次の(1)～(4)のそれぞれについて，日本語の意味になるように，(　　)内にあてはまる最も適切な一語を書け。

(1) 援助に感謝いたします。

I (　　) your (　　).

(2) あなたは医者に診てもらう方がよい。

You (　　) better (　　) a doctor.

(3) お困りですか。

(　　) you in (　　)?

(4) ここに座っても構いませんか。

Would you (　　) (　　) I sit here?

(☆☆☆◎◎◎)

## 【中学校】

【1】次の文は，中学校学習指導要領(平成29年3月告示)「第2章　第9節　外国語　第2　各言語の目標及び内容等　英語」から「1　目標　(3) 話すこと[やり取り]」を示したものである。次の①～③の(　　)内にあてはまる語句を書け。

ア　関心のある事柄について，簡単な語句や文を用いて(　①　)で伝え合うことができるようにする。

イ　(　②　)な話題について，事実や自分の考え，気持ちなどを整理し，簡単な語句や文を用いて伝えたり，相手からの質問に答えたりすることができるようにする。

ウ　(　③　)な話題に関して聞いたり読んだりしたことについて，考えたことや感じたこと，その理由などを，簡単な語句や文を用いて述べ合うことができるようにする。

(☆☆☆☆◎◎◎◎)

【2】次の(1)～(3)の日本語を英語で書け。

(1) 時間割　　(2) 卒業式　　(3) 給食

(☆☆◎◎◎◎)

【3】次の英文を読み，あとの(1)～(7)の問いに答えよ。

If our era is the next Industrial Revolution, as many claim, A.I. is surely one of its driving forces.

It is an especially exciting time for a researcher like me. When I was a graduate student in computer science in the early 2000s, computers were barely able to detect sharp edges in photographs, let alone recognize something as loosely defined as a human face. But ①thanks to the growth of big data, advances in algorithms like neural networks and an abundance of powerful computer hardware, something momentous has occurred: A.I. has gone from an academic niche to the leading differentiator in a wide range of industries, including manufacturing, health care, transportation and retail.

I worry, however, that enthusiasm for A.I. is preventing us from reckoning with its potential effects on society. Despite its name, there is nothing "artificial" about this technology — it is made by humans, it is intended to behave like humans and it affects humans. So if we want it to play a positive role in tomorrow's world, it must be guided by human ( ② ).

I call this approach "human-centered A.I." It consists of three goals to guide the development of intelligent machines.

First, A.I. needs to reflect more of the depth that characterizes our own intelligence. Consider the richness of ③human visual perception. It's complex and deeply contextual, and naturally balances our awareness of the obvious with a sensitivity to nuance. By comparison, machine perception remains strikingly narrow.

Sometimes this difference is trivial. For instance, in my lab, an image-captioning algorithm once fairly summarized a photo as "a man riding a horse" but failed to note that both were bronze sculptures. Other time, the difference is more profound, as when the same algorithm described an image of zebras grazing on a savanna beneath a rainbow. While the summary was technically correct, it was entirely devoid of aesthetic awareness, failing to detect any of the vibrancy or depth a human would naturally appreciate.

[ A ]

Reconnecting A.I. with fields like cognitive science, psychology and even sociology will give us a far richer foundation on which to base the development of machine intelligence. And we can expect the resulting technology to collaborate and communicate more naturally, which will help us approach the second goal of human-centered A.I.: enhancing us, not ( ④ ) us. [ B ]

Imaging ⑤the role that A.I. might play during surgery. The goal need not be to automate the process entirely. Instead, a combination of smart software and specialized hardware could help surgeons focus on their strengths — traits like dexterity and adaptability — while keeping tabs on more mundane tasks and protecting against human error, fatigue and distraction. [ C ]

No amount of ingenuity, however, will fully eliminate the threat of job displacement. Thus the third goal of human-centered A.I.: ensuring that the development of this technology is guided, at each step, by concern for its effect on humans. [ D ]

(The New York Times, March 8, 2018)

(1) 下線部①を解答欄の日本語に合うように，英語を日本語に直して書け。

(2) 本文中の②の(　　)内にあてはまる最も適切な語を，次のア～エから一つ選んで，その記号を書け。

ア relations　イ concerns　ウ indifferences　エ thoughts

(3) 下線部③のhuman visual perceptionに対して，機械の視野はどのようであるか。日本語で書け。

(4) 本文中の④の(　　)内にあてはまる最も適切なものを，次のア～エから一つ選んで，その記号を書け。

ア changing　イ replacing　ウ revolving　エ enhancing

(5) 下線部⑤について，その内容について最も適しているものを，次のア～エから一つ選んで，その記号を書け。

ア 手術の工程を完全に自動化してしまうこと。

イ　器用さと適応力のような特性のバランスを取ること。

ウ　機械的な作業を省略すること。

エ　人間のミス，疲労や注意の散漫を常にチェックすること。

(6)　次の文は，本文中のA～Dの[　　　]のいずれかに入る。最も適切な箇所を一つ選んで，その記号を書け。

However autonomous our technology becomes, its impact on the world — for better or worse — will always be our responsibility.

(7)　本文の内容と一致するものを，次のア～エから2つ選んで，その記号を書け。

ア　第2次産業革命が起こったとしても，人工知能はその原動力となることは決してない。

イ　人工知能の発達により，手術などの手順も自動化されることが期待できる。

ウ　筆者が言う人間中心の人工知能は，知能の高い機械を開発するうえで，3つの目標を有している。

エ　認知科学や心理学，社会学に関するAIは，知能の高い機械の開発の基盤となる。

(☆☆☆☆◎◎◎◎)

【4】次の(1)，(2)の日本語を英語に直して書け。

(1)　私は，英語を効果的に勉強する方法を教えてほしいと頼まれた。

(2)　香川県の課題の一つは人口が減少していることである。

(☆☆☆◎◎◎◎)

【5】「中学生は必ず何らかのボランティア活動に参加しなければならない」という意見に対して，あなたは賛成か反対か。理由を添えて，自分の意見を30語以上の英語で書け。ただし，ピリオドやクエスチョンマークなどは，語数には含めない。

(☆☆☆◎◎◎◎◎)

## 【高等学校】

【1】高等学校学習指導要領(平成30年告示)に関する次の(1)，(2)の問いに答えよ。

(1) 次の文は，「第2章　第8節　外国語　第1款　目標」の一部を示そうとしたものである。ア～エの(　　)内にあてはまる語句を書け。

> 外国語によるコミュニケーションにおける見方・(　ア　)を働かせ，外国語による聞くこと，読むこと，話すこと，書くことの言語活動及びこれらを結び付けた(　イ　)な言語活動を通して，(　ウ　)や考えなどを的確に理解したり適切に表現したり伝え合ったりするコミュニケーションを図る(　エ　)・能力を次のとおり育成することを目指す。

(2) 「第2章　第8節　外国語　第2款　各科目　第1　英語コミュニケーションⅠ」の「1　目標」で示されている「五つの領域」は何か。省略せずにすべて書け。

(☆☆☆☆◎◎◎◎)

【2】次の英文を読み，あとの(1)～(8)の問いに答えよ。

Did you know that the average person throws away the equivalent of 1,212 PET bottles every year? Moreover, we use too much plastic and cardboard wrapping for sending packages by post, as simple items such as food is often over packaged. If we want clean oceans, ①<u>this</u> has got to stop. Our oceans now have five very large plastic pollution areas, called “garbage patches.” These are huge swirling areas of wastes that are ruining the ecosystem, killing fish and other forms of sea life. The largest one is the “Great Pacific Garbage Patch,” and it is several times the size of Hokkaido. Where is the garbage coming from? An article in *Nature* magazine reported that 86% comes from rivers in Asia. (　②　), as time goes by, the plastic breaks into smaller fragments that are eaten by many marine life forms, which die. Further up the food chain, the fragments of toxic plastic enter the human body when we consume sea products.

However, there is hope of finding a solution to this dangerous problem. One day, a 16-year-old schoolboy from the Netherlands was scuba diving in the ocean. His name is Boyan Slat. He said, "I could see more plastic bags than fish," and was very shocked at seeing such pollution. This included plastic bags, PET bottles, bottle caps, wrappers, plastic spoons, forks and straws. That year, he had to do a science project for one of his high school classes, so ③he chose the topic of cleaning the oceans of plastic. Then, a spark of genius came to him. It was the idea of letting the sea naturally do the work. ( ④ ) using machines, you use nature itself.

However, many people said, "Impossible. The garbage patches are too big." But Boyan didn't give up. He had a vision and believed it could ( ⑤ ). He dropped out of the Aerospace Engineering program at university to concentrate on his goal. He soon received support from many people, and the video of his presentation in the TED Talk presentation series became well known. The 23-year-old founder and CEO of Ocean Cleanup now has a mission to clean all of the world's oceans and seas.

How does Boyan's approach go? ⑥Ironically, he uses the aerospace engineering principle of fluid flow dynamics. Ocean current velocity is at its maximum at the ocean surface, about 16 to 17cm/s (cm per second), which decreases to 3 or 4 cm/s in deeper places and makes a big difference. A floater is put on the ocean surface, and it has a long U-shaped screen that goes deep into the ocean. The screen is not a net, so it doesn't ( ⑦ ) or entangle sea life, and it has weights at the bottom to prevent drifting. ⑧Moreover, since it is near the surface, ocean currents and winds push the floater and it moves faster than if it were in the deep ocean, thus enabling the screen to catch garbage in the water. Boyan's idea is relatively simple — let's hope his vision of garbage-free oceans and seas can be realized in the not-too-distant future.

(1) 下線部①が指すものは何か。本文の内容に即して具体的に日本語で書け。

(2)　文中の②の(　　)内にあてはまる最も適切な語を，次のア～エから一つ選んで，その記号を書け。

ア　Probably　　イ　Definitely　　ウ　Unfortunately

エ　Suddenly

(3)　下線部③について，Boyanはどのような経験をし，その後，何をする必要があったからこうしたのか。日本語で具体的に書け。

(4)　文中の④，⑤の(　　)内にあてはまる最も適切な語句を，次のア～エからそれぞれ一つずつ選んで，その記号を書け。

④　ア　By means of　　イ　Instead of　　ウ　For the sake of

エ　As a result of

⑤　ア　work　　イ　see　　ウ　stop　　エ　fail

(5)　下線部⑥は，なぜそのように言っているのか。その理由について最も適しているものを，次のア～エから一つ選んで，その記号を書け。

ア　TEDトークによって，彼の計画が世界中に知れ渡り，多額の寄付を得ることになったため。

イ　世界中の海の汚染をなくすミッションを果たすための会社の創立者になることになったため。

ウ　大学では宇宙工学の研究をあきらめたが，その知識を結果的に使うことになったため。

エ　高校生の時に取り組んだ科学プロジェクトの成果がやっと今になって認められたため。

(6)　文中の⑦の(　　)内にあてはまる最も適切な語を，次のア～エから一つ選んで，その記号を書け。

ア　protect　　イ　separate　　ウ　damage　　エ　save

(7)　下線部⑧を日本語に直して書け。

(8)　本文の内容と一致するものを，次のア～エから一つ選んで，その記号を書け。

ア　Plastic fragments kill many marine life forms, but they don't harm human health.

イ　Boyan came up with an idea to use an electric spark to remove plastics in the sea.

ウ　The ocean current velocity at the surface is about the same as that in deeper places.

エ　Boyan's idea to use some physical principle sheds a light on cleaning plastics pollution areas.

(☆☆☆☆◎◎◎◎)

【3】次の文中の下線部①，②を英語に直して書け。

人生は山登りのようだ，と人はよく言う。①頂上に辿り着くまでに様々な苦難があり，山を下るところが最も難しいこともある。だが，カナダの冒険家でコンサルタントのスティーヴ・ドナヒュー氏は，この考え方に反対である。彼は，人生は，実際はどちらかというと砂漠のようだと主張する。②山には明確なゴール，つまり頂上があるが，砂漠には道がなく，どこへ向かっているのかはっきりとわからない。ドナヒュー氏は，砂漠を賢く横断する方法をいくつか，自身の経験に基づいて提案している。

(☆☆☆☆◎◎◎◎)

【4】「外国語の学習を始める年齢は，低ければ低いほどよい」という意見に対して，あなたはどう考えるか。そう考える理由も含めて，30語以上の英語で書け。

(☆☆☆◎◎◎◎◎)

# 解答・解説

## 【中高共通】

【1】Part1　No.1　(C)　No.2　(A)　No.3　(C)　No.4　(B)　No.5　(D)　Part2　No.1　(C)　No.2　(D)　No.3　(B)　No.4　(A)　Part3　①　イギリス　②　アメリカ　③　フランス　④　163　⑤　海上／水上　⑥　交通安全

〈解説〉リスニング問題は3つのパートに分かれている。PART 1は，2人による短い会話を聞いて選択肢で解答するもの。難度は高くないが1度しか放送されないことに注意すること。2人目の発言が解答する際のヒントになることが多い。PART 2は長めの対話文を聞いて選択肢で解答するもので，対話文と質問が2度放送される。PART 3は右側通行を支持する理由についてのスピーチを聞き，表の空欄に日本語を補充して内容の要点をまとめるもの。スピーチは2 度放送される。first, secondなどの単語に注意をして聞くと要点をつかみ易い。また問題用紙に文字情報があるので，あらかじめ目を通して内容を予測したうえで臨むことが肝要である。

【2】(1)　Fill in the blanks.　(2)　Open your textbook to page 70.　(3)　Pass your sheet from the back to the front.　(4)　Look at the third line from the top of the page.

〈解説〉英語で授業を行う際に必要な生徒への指示文の出題である。実際の授業を行うことを想定し，様々な表現を覚えておきたい。　(1)　fill in「～を埋める」。　(2)　pageの前に置く前置詞toに気をつける。イギリス英語ではatになる。　(3)　pass「渡す」，from ～ to …「～から…まで」。　(4)「何行目」は序数を使って表す。

【3】(1)　I, should　(2)　What, makes　(3)　too, to　(4)　On, seeing

〈解説〉(1)　advise O to V「OにVするよう忠告する」をadvise O that S＋Vに書き換える。　(2)「なぜそれが嘘だったと思うのですか？」→「それが嘘だったと何が思わせるのですか？」。make O V「OにVさせる」。　(3)「私はとてもショックを受けたので動くことができなかった」。too ～to…「とても～なので…できない」。　(4)「彼女は自分の母親を見るとすぐに，明るくほほ笑んだ」。on ～ing「～するとすぐに」。

【4】(1)　番号…④　　正しい表現…happen　　(2)　番号…③　　正しい表現…which/that　　(3)　番号…③　　正しい表現…meeting
(4)　番号…②　　正しい表現…on

〈解説〉(1)「この地域では，毎日，多くの自動車事故が起きている」。happenは自動詞で受動態にはできない。　(2)「あなたが住んでいる国の名前をクリックしてください」。関係副詞whereは前置詞＋関係代名詞と同じ働きをするので，which に変える。　(3)「私はあなたの両親に会えるのを楽しみにしています」。look forward to～ing「～することを楽しみにしている」。　(4)「その医師は服用量を変えるように言い張った」。insist on ～「～を言い張る」。

【5】(1)　appreciate，help　　(2)　had，see　　(3)　Are，trouble
(4)　mind，if

〈解説〉(1)　appreciate「感謝する」。　(2)　had better ～「～した方がいい」。see a doctor「医者に診てもらう」。　(3)　be in trouble「やっかいな状況にいる」。　(4)　Would you mind if ～?「～してもいいですか？」。

## 【中学校】

【1】①　即興　　②　日常的　　③　社会的

〈解説〉「中学校学習指導要領」(平成29年3月告示)の「第2章　第9節　外国語　第2　各言語の目標及び内容等　英語　1　目標」には，出題されている「話すこと[やり取り]」の他に，「聞くこと」「読むこと」「話すこと[発表]」「書くこと」における各目標が示されているので，これらにも目を通しておきたい。さらに学習指導要領と併せて同解説を熟読しておくことが必要である。

【2】(1) schedule/class schedule/timetable (2) graduation ceremony/commencement (3) school lunch

〈解説〉学校の行事や施設に関連した語彙を身につけておきたい。英語で授業を行う際に必要となる場面があるので，普段から意識しておきたい。

【3】(1) 大容量データ(ビッグデータ)，神経回路のようなアルゴリズムの発達，および大量の強力なコンピューター機械装置(ハードウェア)のおかげで，〔重要な何かが起きている。〕 (2) イ (3) 機械の視覚は非常に狭い。 (4) イ (5) イ (6) D (7) ウ，エ

〈解説〉(1) thanks to ～「～のおかげ」，algorithms「アルゴリズム(計算や問題を解決するための手順)，neural network「神経回路」，abundance「大量」。thanksからhardwareまで副詞句。 (2) 空欄を含む文の意味は「もし人工知能に明日の世界でプラスの役割を果たして欲しいと思うのなら，それは人間の関心事に従って動かなければならない」。さらに直後の文でこれを「人間中心の人工知能」と言い換えている。
(3) 第5段落最終文のBy comparison以下を和訳する。strikingly「著しく」，narrow「狭い」。 (4) 空欄を含む文の意味は「私たちは様々な分野と協力し，より自然に意思疎通を図ることができる科学技術が生まれることを期待する。その科学技術は，人間中心の人工知能の2つ目の目標に近づくのに役立つであろう。すなわち，人工知能が私たちにとって代わるのではなく，私たちを高めるのである」。 (5) 第8段落3文目がthe roleの具体的内容。dexterity「器用さ」。 (6) 挿入文の意味は「どんなに科学技術が自動化しても，世界に対するその影響は，良くも悪くも，常に私たちの責任だろう」。第6段落では人間の視野と機械の視野の違いについて，第7段落では人間中心の人工知能の2つ目の目標について，第8段落では人工知能が手術中に果たす役割につい

て述べられている。よって空欄A，B，Cは不適。人工知能が人間に及ぼす影響について書かれているのは第9段落なのでDが適切。

(7) ア 第1段落1文目に，第2次産業革命が起これば，人工知能は原動力の一つになると書かれている。 イ 人工知能の目標が手術の自動化であるという記述はない。ウは第4段落の2文目に合致する。エは第7段落の1文目に合致する。

【4】(1) I was asked to tell how to learn/study English effectively.

(2) One of the problems in Kagawa Prefecture is decreasing the population.

〈解説〉(1) ask O to V「OにVするよう頼む」を受動態に変えて用いる。how to ～「～の仕方」。 (2) 「～のうちの一つ」はone of ～，「人口が減少している」はdecreaseを動詞で用いてdecreasing the population，または名詞として使うとthe decrease in the populationなどが考えられる。

【5】(解答例) I agree with this opinion. Junior high school students may experience a lot of difficult time in their period of youth because of drastic physical and mental changes. Some students could have problems being emotional, desperate, or violent. Through volunteer activities, students should realize how they are needed and cared by others and how important it is to be considerate of others. (59words)

〈解説〉解答例は賛成の立場の意見で，「意見→中学生が経験する思春期の急激な変化→問題を抱える中学生も現れる→ボランティア活動によって期待できる効果」で構成されている。「中学生」が必ずボランティア活動に参加すべきか否かを問われていることに留意する。語数は30語以上という指定であるが，逆にあまり長くなりすぎないよう簡潔にまとめること。

## 【高等学校】

【1】(1)　ア　考え方　　イ　統合的　　ウ　情報　　エ　資質

(2)　聞くこと，読むこと，話すこと[やり取り]，話すこと[発表]，書くこと

〈解説〉空所補充と記述問題からなる。高等学校学習指導要領は平成30年3月告示の改訂版からの出題である。今後は新学習指導要領からの出題が増える可能性が考えられる。文部科学省のホームページで「高等学校学習指導要領比較対照表」を参照し，現行版と改訂版との差異を確認したうえで，新旧の学習指導要領及び同解説を熟読されたい。教科及び各科目の「目標」は頻出である。全文暗記をしておくことが望ましい。

【2】(1)　毎年大量のペットボトルなどが捨てられたり，食料や郵便物などを包むのに大量のプラスチックや紙が使われていること。

(2)　ウ　　(3)　海でスキューバダイビングをしていた時，魚よりもプラスチックの袋やペットボトルなどを見ることの方が多く，このような海の汚れにショックを受けたから。そして，高校の理科の授業の課題をする必要があったから。　　(4)　④　イ　　⑤　ア　　(5)　ウ

(6)　ウ　　(7)　その上，U字スクリーンは海面近くにあるので，海流や風が浮きを押し，海中深くにある場合より速く移動する。そうすることでスクリーンは水中のゴミをとることができる。　　(8)　エ

〈解説〉(1)　下線部①を含む文の意味は「もし私たちが海をきれいにしたいなら，これを止めなければならない」。thisが指す内容は直前の文が表す内容。　(2)　海にはきれいな場所とごみが溜まる場所があり，そこに溜まるゴミの大半はアジアの川から来るという文脈である。空欄②を含む文の意味は「残念なことだが，時が経つにつれて，そのプラスチックが砕けて小さくなり，それらを海洋生物が食べて死ぬ」。

(3)　下線部③を含む文の意味は「彼は海からプラスチックを取り除くテーマを選んだ」。第2段落2文目から5文目にそのテーマを選ぶきっかけとなったBoyanの経験，そして6文目にその後，彼がする必要があっ

たことについて書かれている。 (4) ④ ④を含む文の意味は「機械を使うのではなく，自然そのものを使う」。直前で海に自然にその作業(海からプラスチックをなくす)をさせるというアイデアを思いついたとあることから考える。 ⑤ 空欄の直前でBoyanはあきらめなかったとあるので，機械の手を借りずに，自然を使うという考えが「うまくいく」と彼は思っていたのである。 (5) 下線部⑥を含む文の意味は「皮肉なことだが，彼は流体力学という航空宇宙工学の原理を使うことになる」。なぜ皮肉なのかが書かれているのは第3段落5文目である。 (6) ⑦を含む文の意味は「そのスクリーンはネットではないので，海洋生物を傷つけたり，からまったりしない」。 (7) sinceは理由を表す接続詞。if it were ～は仮定法過去の形になっている。enablingは分詞構文で付帯状況を表す。 (8) ア 第1段落最終文に海産物を食べると，有毒なプラスチックの小さな破片が体内に入るとある。 イ Boyanが電気火花を使って海のプラスチックを取り除くアイデアが浮かんだという記述はない。 ウ 最終段落3文目に，海面を流れる海流の速度とより深い海中での速度は異なると書かれている。 エ 最終段落最終文に合致する。

【3】① Until you reach the top, there are all kinds of difficulties, and the hardest thing can be coming down from the mountain. ② Mountains offer a clear goal, the summit, but deserts are trackless, and people don't know for sure where to go.

〈解説〉① On the way to the top of the mountain, we have all kinds of trouble も可。 ② 「明確なゴール，頂上がある」は「明確なゴール，頂上を提供する」と読み換える。Deserts do not have any tracks (paths), people do not clearly know where they are goingも可。

【4】I agree with this statement. This is because the earlier we begin to study foreign languages, the easier it is to acquire the pronunciation and accent. As we get older, we find it difficult to acquire these skills because we are more affected by our mother tongue.　(47 words)

〈解説〉解答例は賛成の立場の意見で，「意見→理由→まとめ」で構成されている。語数は30語以上という指定であるが，逆にあまり長くなりすぎないよう簡潔にまとめること。本問のような英語教育，言語習得などに関するトピックについては，自分の意見を英語で述べられるように日頃から練習をしておくことが必要である。

# 2019年度　実施問題

## 【中高共通】

【1】Listening Comprehension Section

There are three parts to this section, with special directions for each part. You may take notes while you are listening.

【PART1】

Now, let's begin PART 1. In this part, you will hear five conversations between two people. After each conversation, a third person will ask a question about what was said. Read the four possible answers on your test paper, choose the best answer to each question, and write it on your answer sheet. You will hear each conversation and question just one time.

No.1

(M) My 10-year-old daughter has a cold and a sore throat. Do you have any good medicine for children?

(W) This is our most popular brand. Children under 12 should take one tablet three times a day.

Question: How many times a day should children under 12 take the medicine?

(A) Once.

(B) Twice.

(C) Three times.

(D) Twelve times.

No.2

(W) I need to go see the dentist tomorrow. My tooth really hurts! They're open till 5, right?

(M) No, it's Saturday, so they close at noon.

Question: What is the man doing?

(A) He is asking the woman when to go.

(B) He is correcting the woman's misunderstanding.

(C) He is introducing a dentist to the woman.

(D) He is treating the woman's tooth.

No.3

(M) I'd like two tickets for the 3 p.m. bus to Johnsonville tomorrow, please.

(W) Sorry, there's only one seat left, but I could get you on the 5 p.m. bus.

Question: What was the man's original plan for the next day?

(A) To buy one ticket for the 5 p.m. bus.

(B) To sell two tickets for the 3 p.m. bus.

(C) To leave Johnsonville at 5 p.m.

(D) To take the bus at 3 p.m.

No.4

(W) Excuse me, Professor Jones, do you have a minute? I wanted to ask about this week's assignment.

(M) I'm afraid I have to attend a departmental meeting, but I'm free from 10 to 12 tomorrow morning. Please drop by my office then.

Question: What will the woman most likely do the next day?

(A) She will go to the professor's office in the morning.

(B) She will finish the week's assignment by 10 a.m.

(C) She will work on the week's assignment alone until noon.

(D) She will take part in a departmental meeting with the professor.

No.5

(W) Welcome back! How was your trip to Toronto?

(M) Well, my return flight was delayed two hours due to snow. But the conference itself went well and I met some interesting people.

Question: What does the man think of his trip to Toronto?

(A) It was perfect because everything was fine.

(B) It was rather good because the purpose of the trip was accomplished.

(C) It was disappointing because he had some problems on the way to and from Toronto.

(D) It was terrible because the conference was boring.

【PART2】

Now, let's go on to PART 2. In this part, you will hear a conversation. After that, you will be asked four questions. Read the four possible answers on your test paper, decide which one is the best answer to the question you heard, and write it on your answer sheet. You will hear the conversation and questions two times.

(W) Hello, Andy. I'm Elena Briggs, the manager here at the Bluebird Bakery.

(M) Nice to meet you, Ms. Briggs. Here's my résumé.

(W) Let's see... So you're a student at Carter College?

(M) Yes, I'm in my second year.

(W) Well, one of our other part-time workers, Kelly, is leaving soon. We're looking for someone to take her place. What days are you available?

(M) I can work any days after 3, except on Sundays and Mondays.

(W) Hmm... We'll need someone on Wednesday afternoons from 4 to 8. Do you have any problem with working the same hours on Saturday, too?

(M) No, that's fine.

(W) Wonderful. Your main task will be to serve the customers at the counter, plus cleaning up after we close at 7:30. We'll pay you $9.00 an hour and you'll also get a 20% staff discount off all our bread.

(M) Is there a uniform?

(W) No. You're free to wear whatever you like as long as it's suitable for work. You do need to wear proper shoes — sneakers would be fine. We'll give you an apron.

(M) Sounds good. When should I start?

(W) How's next Wednesday? That's Kelly's last day, so she can show you around.

(M) OK, thank you.

(W) Welcome to the Bluebird Bakery team!

Question No.1: When will the man work at the bakery?

(A) Both on Sundays and on Mondays.

(B) Only on Wednesdays.

(C) Either on Wednesdays or on Saturdays.

(D) Both on Wednesdays and on Saturdays.

Question No.2: How many hours a day will the man work at the bakery?

(A) Two hours.

(B) Three hours.

(C) Four hours.

(D) Eight hours.

Question No.3: What will the woman prepare for the man?

(A) A counter.

(B) A uniform.

(C) Shoes.

(D) An apron.

Question No.4: Which is true about the Bluebird Bakery?

(A) It has only one part-time worker.

(B) It closes at 7:30.

(C) It doesn't hire college students.

(D) It is looking for a new manager.

【PART3】

In this part, you will hear one lecture about a device. Summarize the lecture by filling in the blanks from one to six and write the answers on your answer sheet. You'll hear the lecture two times.

Now, listen.

Hi, class! Today, I'd like to show you a picture. Look at this matchbox-sized, printer-like device on this person's arm. What do you think this is? — No one? Okay.

This is a prototype of a skin-cancer detection device invented by four Canadian engineering students as part of a class project. The idea behind this handheld scanner is pretty simple. When the skin is cooled, cancerous cells warm up again faster than normal cells because they have a higher metabolic rate, and this scanner can detect the higher temperature.

According to the WHO, one in every three cancers in the world is skin cancer. Right now, diagnosing skin cancer largely depends on a doctor's visual inspection, so you have to wait for annual check-ups. If a device like this became widely available for everyone in the future, we could frequently check our skin on our own. The idea is so promising it won the International James Dyson Award last year — Dyson is a large British technology company by the way — and the students received about 50 thousand Canadian dollars.

This device is, however, made of cheap and standard electronic components. You see, there are always chances to generate new ideas from our everyday life if you stay open-minded. You could be the next big inventor, who knows?

述べられている内容について，次の(　①　)～(　⑥　)にあてはまる日本語を，それぞれ書け。

| 装置の用途 | (　①　) の発見 |
|---|---|
| 装置の考案者 | 工学を専攻している４人の（　②　）人の学生 |
| 考案者の着眼点 | 冷やされると、(　③　) は (　④　) よりも早く再び温まる。 |
| 装置の優れている点 | (　⑤　) に頼らず調べられるようになる。<br>(　⑥　) ありふれた電子部品でできている。 |

This is the end of the Listening Comprehension Section.

(☆☆☆◎◎◎◎)

【２】次の(1)～(4)の各組において，a)とb)がほぼ同じ意味になるように，b)の(　　)内にあてはまる最も適切な一語をそれぞれ書け。

(1)　a)　It is three years since Taro went to Australia.

　　b)　Three years (　　) (　　) since Taro went to Australia.

(2)　a)　I very much appreciate your kindness.

　　b)　I can't (　　) you (　　) much for your kindness.

(3)　a)　Mike said to me, "Are you busy?"

　　b)　Mike (　　) me (　　) I was busy.

(4)　a)　We changed our plans because he was absent.

　　b)　We changed our plans because (　　) (　　) absence.

(☆☆☆◎◎◎◎)

【3】次の(1)～(4)のそれぞれについて，下線部の①～④のいずれかに一箇所誤りがある。その箇所の番号と正しい表現に直したものを書け。

(1)　Mr. Brown is ①in ②his sixties, but he is very active and ③look ④much younger.

(2)　Alex ①awoke ②to find ③himself ④surrounding by his friends.

(3)　①When it ②goes to ③cooking, no one ④is better than my grandmother.

(4)　①Strict speaking, the ②rainy season has ③begun ④by mid-June.

(☆☆◎◎◎◎)

【4】次の(1)～(4)のそれぞれについて，日本語の意味になるように，(　　)内にあてはまる最も適切な一語を書け。

(1)　今日は何曜日ですか。

(　　) (　　) is it today?

(2)　鳥のように飛べたらいいのになあ。

I (　　) I (　　) fly like a bird.

(3)　ごゆっくり。

(　　) your (　　).

(4)　遠慮なく質問をしてください。

Please (　　) free (　　) ask questions.

(☆☆☆◎◎◎◎)

## 【中学校】

【1】次の文は，中学校学習指導要領(平成29年3月告示)「第2章　第9節　外国語　第1　目標」の一部を示そうとしたものである。次のア～ウの(　　)内にあてはまる語句を書け。

> (2)　コミュニケーションを行う目的や場面，(　ア　)などに応じて，日常的な話題や(　イ　)な話題について，外国語で簡単な情報や考えなどを理解したり，これらを活用して表現したり(　ウ　)することができる力を養う。

(☆☆☆☆◎◎◎◎)

【2】次の(1)～(3)の日本語を英語で書け。

(1)　始業式　　(2)　休み時間　　(3)　予習

(☆☆◎◎◎◎)

【3】英語の授業で，次の(1)～(4)のとき，授業者が生徒に英語でどのように話すかを書け。

(1)　カードを机の上に広げるよう指示するとき。

(2)　活動中に，もう1分延長することを言うとき。

(3)　何問正解したか尋ねるとき。

(4)　次回の授業を図書室ですることを言うとき。

(☆☆◎◎◎◎)

【4】次の英文を読み，あとの(1)～(9)の問いに答えよ。

Every year, humans produce about 300 million tons of plastic all over the world. Of which, 8 million tons is said to flow into the ocean as plastic waste. ①Plastic waste has been not only destroying the landscape but also endangering the marine ecological system and other environments.

②Nearly half of plastic is used for packaging, especially for food packages such as bottles, bags, or trays. In the United Kingdom, the leading supermarkets and the food retail industry ( ③ ) nearly 1 million tons of plastic packaging waste annually. In early 2018, British Prime Minister Theresa May called for the installation of display shelves that collect products with no plastic packaging at all. A group started a campaign to ( ④ ) the idea; however, most stores in the United Kingdom were reluctant to commit to setting up ⑤such shelves. [ A ]

The campaign group has a partner in the Netherlands, which is a nationwide organic retail chain. To raise ⑥awareness, they have decided to introduce the world's first plastic-free aisle to its Amsterdam store. On the shelves of a single aisle are more than 700 products that do not use plastic packaging, such as meat, dairy products, confectionery, etc., as well as ⑦perishable foods such as vegetables and fruits. Instead of plastic packaging, the products come in, for example, biodegradable substances, glass bottles and jars, and cardboard containers. The organic supermarket chain plans to introduce similar shelves to its 74 branches by the end of this year. Their decision has inspired many other European supermarkets, and now they are considering about setting up such plastic-free aisles as well. [ B ]

Changes are happening in the United Kingdom too. Despite the reluctance at the beginning, some stores are considering to offer fresh fruits and vegetables without any plastic packaging. Some other stores have started to encourage customers to bring their own containers or boxes ( ⑧ ) they can buy meat and fish from the counter without packaging, and they expect that the movement rolls out nationwide soon. [ C ]

It is true that food packed in plastic ⑨( keep fresh / could / longer / wrapped / goods / than ) in paper or other materials, but only a few days longer. On the other hand, the plastic waste remains almost permanently. To pass on the healthy environment to our next generation, ⑩consumers have to consider what is the most important thing for the planet and re-evaluate their priorities.

(1)　下線部①が地球に与える影響について，述べられていることを2

つ日本語で書け。

(2) 下線部②が表すものに最も近いものを，次のア～エから一つ選んで，その記号を書け。

ア about 300 million tons　イ about 150 million tons

ウ about 8 million tons　エ about 4 million tons

(3) 文中の③，④の(　)内にあてはまる最も適切な語を，次のア～オからそれぞれ一つずつ選んで，その記号を書け。

ア invent　イ create　ウ refuse　エ discover

オ support

(4) 下線部⑤が指すものを本文の内容に即して，具体的に日本語で書け。

(5) 下線部⑥，⑦について，この文脈で置き換えられる最も適切な語を，次のア～エからそれぞれ一つずつ選んで，その記号を書け。

⑥ ア hands　イ profit　ウ kindness

エ consciousness

⑦ ア processed　イ preserved　ウ uncooked

エ delicious

(6) 文中の⑧の(　)内にあてはまる最も適切な語を，次のア～エから一つ選んで，その記号を書け。

ア so　イ though　ウ how　エ which

(7) 下線部⑨の(　)内の語句を本文の内容に即して並べかえ，英語で書け。

(8) 下線部⑩を日本語に直して書け。

(9) 次の文は，本文中のA～Cの[　]のいずれかに入る。最も適切な箇所を一つ選んで，その記号を書け。

Also, the British government is discussing a possibility of banning single-use plastic products such as drinking straws or cotton buds within the year.

(☆☆☆◎◎◎◎)

【5】次の(1)，(2)の日本語を英語に直して書け。

(1)　日本人が英語を勉強するのにはいくつかの理由がある。

(2)　私は小さな子どもの世話をするのが得意である。

(☆☆☆◎◎◎◎)

【6】「中学生には制服が必要である」という意見に対して，あなたは賛成か反対か。理由を添えて，自分の意見を30語以上の英語で書け。

(☆☆☆◎◎◎◎)

## 【高等学校】

【1】高等学校学習指導要領(平成21年3月告示)に関する次の(1)，(2)の問いに答えよ。

(1)　次の文は，「第2章　第8節　外国語　第1款　目標」を示そうとしたものである。ア～エの(　　)内にあてはまる語句を書け。

| 外国語を通じて，言語や(　ア　)に対する理解を深め，積極的にコミュニケーションを図ろうとする(　イ　)の育成を図り，(　ウ　)や考えなどを的確に理解したり適切に伝えたりする(　エ　)を養う。 |
|---|

(2)　次のア～オの各文は，「第1章　総則　第3款　各教科・科目の履修等」及び「第2章　第8節　外国語」に基づいて述べたものである。内容の正しいものをア～オから2つ選んで，その記号を書け。

ア　「コミュニケーション英語Ⅰ」の標準単位数は3単位である。

イ　「コミュニケーション英語Ⅰ」及び「英語表現Ⅰ」をすべての生徒に履修させなければならない。

ウ　「コミュニケーション英語Ⅱ」は，「コミュニケーション英語Ⅰ」を履修した後に履修させることを原則とする。

エ　「英語表現Ⅰ」は，「コミュニケーション英語Ⅰ」を履修した後に履修させなければならない。

オ　「コミュニケーション英語Ⅰ」において，言語活動と効果的に関連付けて取り扱う文法事項の中に，仮定法は含まれていない。

(☆☆☆◎◎◎◎)

【2】英語の授業で，次の(1)～(4)のとき，授業者が生徒に英語でどのように話すかを書け。

(1) カードを机の上に広げるよう指示するとき。

(2) 活動中に，もう1分延長することを言うとき。

(3) 何問正解したか尋ねるとき。

(4) ノートを明後日までに提出するよう指示するとき。

(☆☆☆☆◎◎◎◎)

【3】次の英文を読み，あとの(1)～(8)の問いに答えよ。

A long time ago, many people believed that learning two or more languages would harm children's linguistic abilities. Therefore, immigrant children or children whose parents spoke different languages were strongly encouraged to concentrate on only one language, which usually was the locally spoken one where they lived.

However, this has been changing. Scientists have ①gleaned sufficient evidence that there are a lot of benefits to knowing more than one language. Bilingual or multilingual children usually develop better cognitive abilities; for example, they tend to be more creative, better at filtering out distractions or have better memories. Moreover, it is said that multilingual individuals have less likelihood of developing dementia. In multilingual people's brain, varying parts are active simultaneously, and they are used to switching between language systems according to the language they are operating in. Acquiring languages other than one's mother tongue is a powerful ( ② ) to the brain.

Not only the cognitive benefits mentioned above, but social and emotional benefits are also significant: Scientists have found evidence that learning multiple languages improves one's tolerance in many ways. Learning a new language is, at the same time, learning a new culture, ③( different / familiarizing / includes / oneself / ways / which / with ) of thinking and doing things. ④By realizing that not everyone in the world thinks or acts in the same ways as they would, they can deepen their understanding of cultural diversity and grow open-minded, and foster greater tolerance toward differences.

Another aspect of social or emotional benefits is that bilingual or multilingual individuals are better at dealing with unfamiliar or unexpected situations than monolingual people. This is because, upon speaking foreign languages, they constantly encounter foreign situations, and so they are used to swiftly adapting to the new setting by, for example, guessing the meaning of unknown words, reading signs and analyzing the situation. ⑤Many of them even feel ( X ) when facing unfamiliar milieus rather than being ( Y ). This way, they also have better tolerance of ambiguity.

Such quality is certainly an asset for young people to ably act in the modern, globalized society. However, despite many advantages that language education could offer, most universities in the United States are not ( ⑥ ) to give their students opportunities to learn languages. Although, over 350 languages are spoken in the United States, and more than 20 % of American households speak a language besides English at home, according to the 2010 Census. Today, universities tend to be judged by the high salaries their graduates earn, and so are less focused on fostering their students' ( ⑦ ). Thus, most American universities encourage them to acquire more practical skills and have a minimal language requirement.

( ⑧ ) the trend, nevertheless, ⑨Princeton, one of the Ivy League universities, announced in 2016 that all students would be required to study an additional language other than English. Princeton is a highly prestigious school. If more universities follow Princeton's lead, it could dramatically improve tolerance of cultural diversity on campus and in society.

(1)　下線部①について，この文脈で置き換えられる最も適切なものを，次のア～エから一つ選んで，その記号を書け。

ア　failed to discover　　イ　patiently collected　　ウ　suddenly lost
エ　managed to create

(2)　本文中の②の(　　)内にあてはまる最も適切な語を，次のア～エから一つ選んで，その記号を書け。

ア　threat　　イ　imagination　　ウ　impression　　エ　stimulus

(3)　下線部③の(　　)内の語を，本文の内容に即して並べかえ，英語で書け。

(4)　下線部④を日本語に直して書け。

(5)　下線部⑤のX，Yの(　　)内に入る組み合わせとして最も適切なものを，次のア～エから一つ選んで，その記号を書け。

ア　X　excited or amused　　Y　proud or confident
イ　X　embarrassed or confused　　Y　afraid or nervous
ウ　X　excited or amused　　Y　afraid or nervous
エ　X　embarrassed or confused　　Y　proud or confident

(6)　本文中の⑥～⑧の(　　)内にあてはまる最も適切なものを，次のア～エからそれぞれ一つずつ選んで，その記号を書け。

⑥　ア　keen　　イ　surprised
　　ウ　reluctant　　エ　hesitant
⑦　ア　sense of economy　　イ　proficiency in business
　　ウ　media literacy　　エ　emotional intelligence
⑧　ア　In addition to　　イ　Compared to
　　ウ　Contrary to　　エ　Thanks to

(7)　下線部⑨が発表したことは何か。本文の内容に即して，具体的に日本語で書け。

(8)　本文の内容と一致するものを次のア～オから2つ選んで，その記号を書け。

ア　移民の子どもたちや両親が異なる言語を話す子どもたちは，多くの場合，彼らの暮らす土地で話されている言語だけを使うよう奨励されていた。

イ　複数の言語を使う子どもは，そうでない子どもよりも，創造性や記憶力に優れているが，将来，認知症になる可能性が高い。

ウ　複数の言語を学ぶ人は，認知的負荷がかかるため，色々な面で忍耐力が失われることが分かっている。

エ　複数の言語を使う人は，そうでない人よりも，慣れない状況や予想外のことに対処するのが得意である。

オ　アメリカ合衆国では，350を超える言語が話され，英語以外の言葉を話す家庭も20パーセントを上回るため，多くの大学で言語教育に力を入れている。

(☆☆☆◎◎◎◎)

【4】次の文中の下線部①，②を英語に直して書け。

読書は知識を与えてくれる。①私たちは，様々な種類の本を読むことで，知らなかった多くの事柄を学ぶことができる。また，読書は私たちの人生を豊かにもしてくれる。本は私たちに楽しみを与え，悩んだ時には答えのヒントも与えてくれるのだ。②本は人生において最も重要な師であり，最も身近な助言者であると言っても過言ではない。

(☆☆☆◎◎◎◎)

【5】「インターネット上で意見を述べるときには本名を名乗るべきである」という意見に対して，あなたはどう考えるか。そう考える理由も含めて，30語以上の英語で書け。

(☆☆☆◎◎◎◎)

# 解答・解説

## 【中高共通】

【1】PART 1　No.1　(C)　No.2　(B)　No.3　(D)　No.4　(A)　No.5　(B)　PART 2　No.1　(D)　No.2　(C)　No.3　(D)

No.4 (B)　PART 3 ①　皮膚がん　②　カナダ　③　がん細胞　④　正常な細胞　⑤　医者　⑥　安価で

〈解説〉リスニング問題は3つのパートに分かれている。PART1は，2人による短い会話を聞いて，選択肢で解答するもの。難度は高くないが1度しか放送されないので，聞き逃さないように。PART2は，長めの対話文を聞いて選択肢で解答するもので，対話文と質問が2度放送される。PART3は，ある装置についての説明を聞き，表の空欄に日本語を補充して内容の要点をまとめる。説明は2度放送される。医療関係のトピックであるが，難解な専門用語は出てこない。いずれも問題用紙に文字情報があるので，あらかじめ目を通して内容を予測したうえで臨むこと。

【2】(1)　have，passed　(2)　thank，too　(3)　asked，if/whether　(4)　of，his

〈解説〉(1)　現在完了の文に書き換える。Three years have passed since ～「～以来3年が経過した」。　(2)「あなたの親切には感謝してもしきれない」。can't ～ too …「どんなに～してもし過ぎることはない」。

(3)　Yes-No疑問文を間接話法に書き換える。ask ～ whether［if］S＋V。

(4)　because節を，because of ～を使って句に書き換える。

【3】(1)　番号…③　正しい表現…looks　(2)　番号…④　正しい表現…surrounded　(3)　番号…②　正しい表現…comes

(4)　番号…①　正しい表現…Strictly

〈解説〉(1)「Mr. Brownは60代だが，とても活動的でずいぶん若く見える」。lookの主語はMr. Brownなので，3単元のsが必要。　(2)「Alexは目覚めると自分が友達に囲まれていることに気付いた」。himself (Alex) is surroundedという受動の文が成立する。　(3)「料理のことになると，私の祖母より上手な人はいない」。when it comes to ～「～のことになると，～に関して言えば」。　(4)「厳密に言えば，梅雨の季節は6月中旬に始まっている」。strictly speaking「厳密に言えば」。慣用的な分詞構文である。

【4】(1)　What, day　(2)　wish, could　(3)　Take, time　(4)　feel, to

〈解説〉(1)　what day (of the week)「何曜日」。　(2)　仮定法過去なので，過去形のcouldを使う。　(3)　Take your time「時間をかけなさい，ごゆっくり」。　(4)　feel free to ～「自由に～する，遠慮なく～する」。

## 【中学校】

【1】ア　状況　イ　社会的　ウ　伝え合ったり

〈解説〉「中学校学習指導要領(平成29年告示)解説　外国語編」(平成29年7月)の「第2章　外国語科の目標及び内容　第2節　英語　1　目標」には，出題の(2)項は「外国語科における『理解していること・できることをどう使うか』という『思考力，判断力，表現力等』の育成に関わる目標として掲げたものである」と示されている。今回の改訂により，目標は旧版に比べかなり詳しく記されている。改訂の趣旨と要点をおさえた上で，キーワードを中心に覚えておこう。学習指導要領と併せて同解説を熟読しておくことが必要である。

【2】(1)　opening ceremony　(2)　recess　(3)　preparation

〈解説〉関連して学校の行事や施設などの語彙を身につけておきたい。実際教壇に立ってから必要となる場面も多々予想される。

【3】(1)　Spread the cards out on the desks.　(2)　I'll give you one more minute.　(3)　How many questions did you answer correctly?　(4)　We will have our next class in the library.

〈解説〉授業中の生徒への指示文の出題である。いろいろな表現をストックしておきたい。　(1)　spread (out)「広げる」。　(2)　one more minute「もう1分」。　(3)　answer correctly「正解する」。なお，correct answerは「正解」である。　(4)　next class「次回の授業」。

【4】(1)　・景観を破壊する　　・海洋生態系やその他の環境を危機にさらす　(2)　イ　(3)　③　イ　④　オ　(4)　プラスチック包装を全く使わない商品を並べている陳列棚　(5)　⑥　エ　⑦　ウ　(6)　ア　(7)　could keep fresh longer than goods wrapped　(8)　消費者は地球のために何が最も重要なのかを考え，優先事項を再考しなければならない。　(9)　C

〈解説〉(1)　下線部①を含む文のdestroying the landscapeとendangering the marine ecological system and other environmentsが解答にあたる部分。(2)　nearly half「約半数」。第1段落の1文目のabout 300 million tonsの半分を指す。　(3)　③　空欄を含む文の意味は「英国では，主要なスーパーや食品小売業が年間約100万トンのプラスチック包装廃棄物を出している」。　④　空欄を含む文の意味は「あるグループはこの考えを支持するキャンペーンを始めた。しかし英国のほとんどの店はそのような棚を準備する約束に乗り気でなかった」。　(4)　第2段落3文目の，Theresa May (テリーザ・メイ)英国首相が設置を呼びかけた棚を指す。　(5)　⑥　awareness「意識，認識」なので，consciousness「意識，自覚」が適切。　⑦　perishable「腐りやすい」なので，uncooked「調理されていない，生の」が適切。　(6)　so (that) they can buy meat and fish from the counter without packaging「包装なしでカウンターから肉や魚を買えるように」。so that S can ～「Sが～できるように」。本文ではthatが省略されている。　(7)　下線部を含む文の意味は「プラスチックで包装されている食べ物は，紙や他の素材で包装されている商品より鮮度を長く保つことができるのは事実であるが，ほんの数日長いだけである」。keep fresh「新鮮な状態を保つ」。　(8)　consumer「消費者」，re-evaluate「再評価する」，priority「優先，優先事項」である。
(9)　第2段落では，プラスチックの使用を減らすことに英国の店は消極的であったこと，第3段落ではオランダを中心にヨーロッパの店にプラスチックの使用を控える動きが広がったことが記されている。よって挿入文「また英国政府は年内に，飲み物のストローや綿棒のような使い捨てのプラスチック製品を禁止する可能性について検討している」は空欄AやBには不適。第4段落で初めて，英国にもプラスチックの使用に関して変化が起きている，と述べているのでCが適切。

【5】(1)　There are some reasons why Japanese people study English.
(2)　I am good at taking care of small children.
〈解説〉(1)　関係副詞のwhyを使い，「SがVする理由」をa reason why S＋Vで表す。　(2)「～することが得意である」はbe good at～ing，「～の世話をする」はtake care of～で表せばよい。

【6】I agree with this opinion. These are my reasons. First, students don't have to worry about what to wear every morning and they can save time. Second, having school uniforms can save their parents' money. I think school uniforms are good for both students and their parents. (47 words)
〈解説〉解答例は賛成の立場の意見で，「意見→理由→まとめ」で構成されている。語数は30語以上という指定であるが，逆にあまり長くなりすぎないよう簡潔にまとめること。

## 【高等学校】

【1】(1)　ア　文化　　イ　態度　　ウ　情報　　エ　コミュニケーション能力　　(2)　ア，ウ
〈解説〉空所補充と正誤判断形式の問いからなる。本問は現行の学習指導要領からの出題であるが，高等学校学習指導要領は平成30年3月告示の改訂版がすでに公表されており，今後は新学習指導要領からの出題の可能性も考えられる。文部科学省のホームページで「高等学校学習指導要領比較対照表」を参照し，現行版と改訂版との差異を確認したうえで，新旧の学習指導要領及び同解説を熟読されたい。　(1)「目標」は頻出である。全文暗記をしておくこと。　(2)　イ「コミュニケーション英語Ⅰ」は必履修科目であるが，「英語表現Ⅰ」は選択科目である。　エ　この記述はない。　オ　文法事項に関しては全ての項目を扱うこととされている。

【2】(1) Spread the cards out on the desks. (2) I'll give you one more minute. (3) How many questions did you answer correctly? (4) Hand in your notebook by the day after tomorrow.

〈解説〉授業中の生徒への指示文の出題である。いろいろな表現をストックしておきたい。 (1) spread (out)「広げる」。 (2) one more minute「もう1分」。 (3) answer correctly「正解する」。なお，correct answerは「正解」である。 (4) hand in，turn in「提出する」。

【3】(1) イ (2) エ (3) which includes familiarizing oneself with different ways (4) 世界の誰もが自分たちと同じように考えたり行動したりするわけではないと気づくことにより，文化的多様性への理解を深め，心を開き，違いに対する寛容性を高めることができる。 (5) ウ (6) ⑥ ア ⑦ エ ⑧ ウ (7) 全ての学生が英語以外のもう一つの言語を学ぶことを要求されること。 (8) ア，エ

〈解説〉(1) 昔は2か国語より多くの言語を学ぶことは子どもの言語能力に差しつかえると考えられていたが，近年その考えが変化してきているという文脈である。下線部①を含む文は「1か国語より多く知っていることにたくさんの恩恵があるという十分な証拠を科学者たちは根気よく集めた」。glean「こつこつ収集する」。 (2)「多数の言語を話す人の脳では様々な部分がいっせいに活発になり，使用している言語により言語システムを切り替えることに慣れている」に続く文なので，「母国語以外の言語を獲得することは脳に大きな刺激となる」が適切。 (3) 下線部③を含む文の意味は「新しい言語を学ぶことは，同時に新しい文化を学ぶことである。それには物事の異なる考え方ややり方に慣れ親しむことも含まれる」。familiarize oneself with ～「～に慣れ親しむ」。 (4) not everyone in the world thinks and acts in the same way「世界の誰もが同じように考えたり行動したりするわけではない」。not everyoneは部分否定。grow open-minded「寛容になる，広い心になる」。 (5) 第4段落は，バイリンガルやマルチリンガルの人は，モノリンガ

ルの人より，慣れない状況や予想外のことに対処するのが得意であるという内容。よって「バイリンガルやマルチリンガルの人は，慣れない状況に直面すると，恐れたり緊張したりするよりむしろ，わくわくしたり楽しく感じたりすることさえある」とする。 (6) ⑥を含む文はHoweverで始まることに着目すると，「合衆国のたいていの大学は，言語を学ぶ機会を学生たちに提供することに乗り気ではない」。be keen to ～「～することに乗り気になっている，しきりに～したがっている」。⑦を含む文の意味は「今日，大学は卒業生が稼ぐ高給により評価されがちなので，学生の心の知能(感情知性)を育むことに焦点を当てていない」。言語を学ぶことは感情的な側面から有益だとする第4段落の内容からエを選択する。⑧を含む文にnevertheless「それにもかかわらず」があることから，第6段落は前言に反する内容がくると考えられる。よってcontrary to the trend「この傾向に反して」。 (7) プリンストン大学が発表した内容はthat以下にある。additional「追加の」。 (8) ア　第1段落の2文目の内容と合致する。 イ　将来認知症になる可能性があるという記述はない。 ウ　第3段落の2文目に忍耐力が発達するとある。 エ　第4段落の1文目の内容と合致する。 オ　第5段落の5文目より，「多くの大学が言語教育に力を入れている」という部分が誤り。

【4】① By reading various kinds of books, we can learn a lot of things that we haven't known. ② It is not too much to say that books are the most important teacher and the closest adviser in life.

〈解説〉① Reading various kinds of books enables us to learn a lot of things …も可。 ② It is not too much to say that ～, It is no exaggeration to say that ～「～と言っても過言ではない」。

【5】I agree with this opinion. The reason is that anonymous online comments can be sometimes inconsiderate because we don't have to face the consequences. We should not write what we would never say in person. So, I think we need our true identities to comment online. (46 words)

〈解説〉解答例は賛成の立場の意見で,「意見→理由→まとめ」で構成されている。語数は30語以上という指定であるが,逆にあまり長くなりすぎないよう簡潔にまとめること。本問のような現代の風潮に関するトピックについては,自分の意見を英語で述べられるように日頃から練習をしておくことが必要である。

# 2018年度　実施問題

## 【中高共通】

【1】Listening Comprehension Section

There are three parts to this section, with special directions for each part. You may take notes while you are listening.

【PART1】

Now, let's begin PART 1. In this part, you will hear five conversations between two people. After each conversation, a third person will ask a question about what was said. Read the four possible answers on your test paper, choose the best answer to each question, and write it on your answer sheet. You will hear each conversation and question just one time.

No.1

(M) I have to pick up my dry cleaning on the way home tonight. The shop closes at 6, right?

(W) No, today is Friday, so they're open till 8.

Question: When will the man go to the shop?

(A) At 6 in the morinig.

(B) After 8 p.m.

(C) Before he gets home.

(D) As soon as the shop opens.

No.2

(M) Excuse me, I'm looking for the imported cheese. Didn't it used to be in aisle five?

(W) All the cheese was moved to aisle seven. We have more varieties now for you to choose from.

Question: Where does this conversation most likely take place?

(A) At a supermarket.

(B) In an airplane.

(C) At a pizza stand.

(D) At a TV station.

No.3

(W) Oh, hi, Paul, I'm glad I caught you! I wanted to ask you if the sales report is ready.

(M) Nearly. I just need to check a few more things with the finance department first.

Question: What is the woman asking the man about?

(A) About a good coat.

(B) About the Ministry of Finance.

(C) About a department store.

(D) About the sales report.

No.4

(W) I'd like to try a mild coffee. What do you recommend?

(M) How about today's special blend? It's milder than our regular coffee, and it's good hot or iced.

Question: What suggestion is the man making to the woman?

(A) To make the regular coffe milder.

(B) To drink a mild coffee with ice cream.

(C) To try today's special blend.

(D) To buy the cafe's hot regular coffee.

No.5

(M) Professor Brown, I have a doctor's appointment tomorrow, so I'll miss your class. May I have the handouts?

(W) They're not ready yet, but send me an email this evening and I'll be happy to send them to you.

Question: What will the man do this evening?

(A) He will attend the woman's class.

(B) He will send the woman a message by email.

(C) He will hand in his handouts to the woman.

(D) He will make an appointment with the woman.

【PART2】

Now, let's go on to PART 2. In this part, you will hear a conversation. After that, you will be asked four questions. Read the four possible answers on your test paper, decide which one is the best answer to the question you heard, and write it on your answer sheet. You will hear the conversation and questions two times.

(W) Hello, Tsuyoshi. Thanks for coming in. I'm Liane Richardson from Global Voyage.

(M) Nice to meet you, Ms. Richardson.

(W) Call me Liane. So, we are looking for college interns to help as volunteers on our next trip. We have 100 high school students participating, including 20 Japanese. I understand you are bilingual?

(M) Yes. I was brought up in Japan and then I attended high school in New Zealand. I'm currently a science major at the University of Auckland.

(W) That's great. Do you speak any other languages?

(M) I studied Spanish in high school, but I'm not fluent.

(W) Well, you would probably be working mainly with the Japanese students on this trip. Our ship will visit seven different countries in six weeks.

(M) What will we be doing there?

(W) The students will participate in various environmental and charity projects in each place.

(M) That sounds great! Would I be helping with those, too?

(W) Yes, but you wouldn't have to lead the activities. Local people will lead everyone. Our ship departs on December 15 from Kobe and returns at the end of January. Will that be a problem?

(M) No, it's actually perfect for me, as it's during my summer vacation.

(W) Wonderful! I'm happy to offer you an intern position.

Question No. 1: Who most likely is the woman?

(A) A science professor.

(B) The president of the University of Auckland.

(C) A college intern applying for the trip.

(D) A staff member working for the voyage.

Question No.2: How many Japanese high school students will join the voyage?

(A) Twelve.

(B) Fifteen.

(C) Twenty.

(D) One hundred.

Question No. 3: Which is true about Tsuyoshi?

(A) He majors in science at university.

(B) He is a fluent speaker of Spanish.

(C) He is asked to lead all the activities during the trip.

(D) He is worried about skipping his classes during the trip.

Question No.4: What has the woman decided to do?

(A) To interview the man one more time.

(B) To employ the man as a regular employee.

(C) To welcome the man as a volunteer.

(D) To give the man a call of refusal.

【PART3】

PART 3. In this part, you will hear an explanation followed by a conversation two times. Before listening, you should read the instructions carefully so that you can write the answers on the answer sheet. You have 10 seconds to read the instructions.

Now, listen.

(M) Let me explain punctuation today. Many of you may have learned that in a list of three or more items, like "apples, oranges, and bananas," you are supposed to put "and" before you name the last item, and also, put a comma before this "and," that is "apples comma oranges comma and bananas."

This comma is called the "Oxford comma," or the "serial comma." It was traditionally used by editors at Oxford University Press, and long considered as the standard punctuation. However, a lot of people today think it's an optional comma. Some people would put it in, and some would leave it out. Like, "apples comma oranges and bananas."

The Oxford comma is still common in books and academic papers. On the other hand, most news organizations tend to omit the comma, unless it is confusing without. The important thing is that either one style or the other should be used consistently.

This is the end of my explanation.

(W) Excuse me, professor. I have a question for you. So, are you saying we can choose whichever style we like?

(M) Basically yes, but be careful. This year in the United States, truck drivers won in a dispute over their missing overtime payment. The judge ruled in favor of the drivers, because the lack of the Oxford comma made part of the overtime law too ambiguous.

I generally suggest that my students stick with the traditional use. It's never wrong to stay on the safer side, is it?

(1)　述べられている内容について，次の①～④の(　　)内に入る日本語を書け。

| | |
|---|---|
| 教授の説明 | オックスフォードコンマを書くのは、長らく標準的なスタイルとされていたが、今日では、多くの人が任意だと考えている。（ ① ）や（ ② ）では今でも一般的に使われているが、混乱を招く場合以外は、ほとんどの報道機関はこのコンマを省く傾向にある。大切なのは、（ ③ ）を使うことである。 |
| 学生からの質問に対する教授の応答 | オックスフォードコンマを（ ④ ）ほうが良い。 |

(2)　述べられている説明に従って，次の英語にオックスフォードコン

マを使ったスタイルでコンマを書き入れよ。

“Spring summer autumn and winter.”

This is the end of the Listening Comprehension Section.

(☆☆☆☆◎◎◎◎)

## 【中学校】

【1】次の文は，中学校学習指導要領(平成20年3月告示，平成27年3月一部改正)「第2章　第9節　外国語　第2　各言語の目標及び内容等」の「2　内容　(2)言語活動の取扱い」の一部を示そうとしたものである。次の1～3の(　　)内にあてはまる語句を書け。

> 第2学年までの学習を基礎として，言語の使用場面や言語の働きを一層広げた言語活動を行わせること。その際，第1学年及び第2学年における学習内容を(　1　)指導し定着を図るとともに，様々な(　2　)や意見などの中から(　3　)が図れるような話題を取り上げること。

(☆☆☆☆◎◎◎◎)

【2】次の(1)～(3)の日本語を英語で書け。

(1)　あいさつ　　(2)　学期　　(3)　修学旅行

(☆☆☆◎◎◎)

【3】英語の授業で，次の(1)～(4)のとき，授業者が英語でどのように話すかを書け。

(1)　電気を消すようお願いするとき。

(2)　今日の授業は45分であることを言うとき。

(3)　他に質問があるか尋ねるとき。

(4)　机を後ろに下げるよう指示するとき。

(☆☆☆◎◎◎◎)

【４】次の(1)～(4)の各組において，a)とb)がほぼ同じ意味になるように，b)の(　　)内にあてはまる最も適切な一語をそれぞれ書け。

(1) a) She plays the piano well.

b) She (　　) a good (　　).

(2) a) Why did you come here?

b) (　　) brought (　　) here?

(3) a) With a little more patience, he would have accomplished the task.

b) If he (　　) (　　) a little more patient, he would have accomplished the task.

(4) a) I went to the museum, but I found it was closed.

b) I went to the museum, (　　) (　　) find it was closed.

(☆☆☆◎◎◎◎)

【５】次の(1)～(4)のそれぞれについて，下線部の①～④のいずれかに一箇所誤りがある。その箇所の番号と正しい表現に直したものを書け。

(1) I was ①<u>laughed</u> by my sister ②<u>because</u> I was wearing my T-shirt inside out. It was ③<u>such</u> an ④<u>embarrassing</u> moment.

(2) Ms. Yamada was here ①<u>a moment</u> ②<u>ago</u>, so this bag ③<u>must</u> be ④<u>her</u>.

(3) My mother gave me ①<u>these</u> shoes ②<u>for</u> my birthday ③<u>last</u> month. ④<u>How</u> do you think?

(4) It's a perfect day for ①<u>going</u> on a hike, ②<u>isn't</u> it? ③<u>Are</u> everyone ready ④<u>to start</u>?

(☆☆☆◎◎◎◎)

【６】次の(1)～(4)のそれぞれについて，日本文の意味になるように，(　　)内にあてはまる最も適切な一語を書け。

(1) 電話番号をお間違えのようです。

I think you have the (　　) (　　).

(2) お体に気をつけて。

Take (　　) of (　　).

(3) お願いがあるのですが。

May I ask a (　　) (　　) you?

(4) ご家族によろしくお伝えください。

Please say (　　) (　　) your family.

(☆☆☆◎◎◎◎)

【7】次の英文を読み，あとの(1)～(7)の問いに答えよ。

Viola Desmond was born on July 6, 1914, in Halifax, Nova Scotia, Canada. Her father was a barber from a middle-class black family, and her mother, who had moved there from the United States, was a white person. Although interracial marriages were (　a　) in the early 20th century, Viola's parents were accepted into the black community, becoming active and highly regarded in various organizations. Viola ①( in / with / family / ten / a large / raised / was ) siblings.

Motivated by her hard-working parents, Viola decided to become a businesswoman. She noticed the absence of beauty care products for black women and wanted to start a new business in this field; however, people of African descent were not allowed to take beautician training in Halifax. So she had to receive her training in Montreal and New York. When she came back to Halifax, she started her own beauty salon and later established an esthetician school. [ A ]

One day in 1946, she went to a movie theater in a small town. As she took a seat on the main floor, an usher told her that she could not take that seat with her ticket, and ②it was against the theater's policy to give main floor seats to black people. Yet she refused to sit in the balcony designated for them. She was, then, forcibly removed from the theater and arrested. She was charged with ③tax evasion for not paying the mere one-cent difference in tax between a main floor seat and a seat in the segregated section.

She decided to fight the charge in court. The government insisted that it was a case of tax evasion and never admitted that it was racial discrimination.

B

After the trial, she closed her business and moved to Montreal, and then eventually settled in New York, where she died in 1965 at the age of 50.

Viola's story, however, began to receive public attention again through the efforts of her younger sister, Wanda Robson. In 2003, Wanda enrolled in a college course at the age of 73. The professor who taught the course ④( to / a / on / her / book / publish / encouraged / based ) Viola's experience.

Finally, in 2010, the government of Nova Scotia (　b　) for prosecuting Viola. It acknowledged her efforts to resist discrimination, and granted her a posthumous pardon. [ C ] In 2016, ⑤the Bank of Canada announced that Viola would be featured on the new 10-dollar bill in 2018, making her the first woman in Canada except Queen Elizabeth Ⅱ to appear on a bank note.

(1)　文中のa，bの(　　)内にあてはまる最も適切な語を，次のア～エからそれぞれ一つずつ選んで，その記号を書け。

a　ア　popular　　イ　legal　　ウ　compulsory　　エ　rare

b　ア　asked　　イ　apologized　　ウ　prepared　　エ　fought

(2)　下線部①，④の(　　)内の語句を，本文の内容に即して並べ替え，英語で書け。

(3)　下線部②が指している内容は何か。日本語で書け。

(4)　下線部③の具体的な内容は何か。日本語で書け。

(5)　下線部⑤を日本語に直して書け。

(6)　次の文は，本文中のA～Cの[　　]のいずれかに入る。最も適切な箇所を一つ選んで，その記号を書け。

Viola and her lawyer were unsuccessful.

(7)　次のa～cのそれぞれについて，本文の内容と合っていれば○を，合っていなければ×を書け。

a　ヴィオラは，黒人の母親と白人の父親の間に生まれた。

b　ヴィオラは，ハリファックスで美容師の訓練を受けることができなかった。

c　人種差別に抵抗したのはヴィオラではなく，妹のワンダであった。

(☆☆☆◎◎◎◎)

【8】次の(1)，(2)の日本語を英語に直して書け。

(1)　先生は私に間違いを恐れずもっと英語を話しなさいと言った。

(2)　香川県への外国人観光客の数が増加しているのは良いことだ。

(☆☆☆◎◎◎◎)

【9】「中学生は必ず何かの部活動に参加しなければならない」という意見に対して，あなたは賛成か反対か。理由を添えて，自分の意見を30語以上の英語で書け。

(☆☆☆☆◎◎◎◎◎)

## 【高等学校】

【1】次の各文は，高等学校学習指導要領(平成21年3月告示)の「第2章　第8節　外国語　第4款　各科目にわたる指導計画の作成と内容の取扱い」の一部を示そうとしたものである。1～6の(　　)内にあてはまる語句を，それぞれ書け。

(1)　教材については，外国語を通じて(　1　)を総合的に育成するため，各科目の目標に応じ，実際の言語の(　2　)や言語の働きに十分配慮したものを取り上げるものとすること。

(2)　(　3　)の補助として，発音表記を用いて指導することができること。

(3)　(　4　)の活用の指導などを通じ，生涯にわたって，自ら外国語を学び，使おうとする積極的な態度を育てるようにすること。

(4)　各科目の指導に当たっては，指導方法や指導体制を工夫し，ペア・ワーク，(　5　)などを適宜取り入れたり，視聴覚教材やコンピュータ，情報通信ネットワークなどを適宜指導に生かしたりすること。また，(　6　)などの協力を得て行うティ

| ーム・ティーチングなどの授業を積極的に取り入れ，生徒のコミュニケーション能力を育成するとともに，国際理解を深めるようにすること。 |
|---|

(☆☆☆☆◎◎◎◎◎)

【2】英語の授業で，次の(1)～(4)のとき，授業者が英語でどのように話すかを書け。

(1)　電気を消すようお願いするとき。

(2)　今日の授業は45分であることを言うとき。

(3)　もっと大きな声でもう一度発表させたいとき。

(4)　ペアになり，机を合わせるよう指示するとき。

(☆☆☆◎◎◎◎◎)

【3】次の(1)～(4)の各組において，a)とb)がほぼ同じ意味になるように，b)の(　　)内にあてはまる最も適切な一語をそれぞれ書け。

(1)　a)　She plays the piano well.

b)　She (　　) a good (　　).

(2)　a)　Why did you come here?

b)　(　　) brought (　　) here?

(3)　a)　With a little more patience, he would have accomplished the task.

b)　If he (　　) (　　) a little more patient, he would have accomplished the task.

(4)　a)　I went to the museum, but I found it was closed.

b)　I went to the museum, (　　) (　　) find it was closed.

(☆☆☆◎◎◎◎)

【4】次の(1)～(4)のそれぞれについて，下線部の①～④のいずれかに一箇所誤りがある。その箇所の番号と正しい表現に直したものを書け。

(1)　I was ①laughed by my sister ②because I was wearing my T-shirt inside out. It was ③<u>such</u> an ④<u>embarrassing</u> moment.

(2) Ms. Yamada was here ①<u>a moment</u> ②<u>ago</u>, so this bag ③<u>must</u> be ④<u>her</u>.

(3) My mother gave me ①<u>these</u> shoes ②<u>for</u> my birthday ③<u>last</u> month. ④<u>How</u> do you think?

(4) It's a perfect day for ①<u>going</u> on a hike, ②<u>isn't</u> it? ③<u>Are</u> everyone ready ④<u>to start</u>?

(☆☆☆◎◎◎◎)

【5】次の(1)～(4)のそれぞれについて，日本文の意味になるように，(　　)内にあてはまる最も適切な一語を書け。

(1) 電話番号をお間違えのようです。

I think you have the (　　) (　　).

(2) お体に気をつけて。

Take (　　) of (　　).

(3) お願いがあるのですが。

May I ask a (　　) (　　) you?

(4) ご家族によろしくお伝えください。

Please say (　　) (　　) your family.

(☆☆☆◎◎◎◎)

【6】次の英文を読み，あとの(1)～(7)の問いに答えよ。

When Japan ended *sakoku* and opened up the country to trade with the West in the middle of the 19th century, Japanese art and culture began to find its way to Europe and America. The Dutch, the British, and the Americans collected Japanese artworks and took ①<u>them</u> out of ②<u>the country</u>.

Most popular among them were ukiyo-e woodblock prints. Unlike ukiyo-e paintings, prints were inexpensive and ideal for mass production to meet the boosting demand for souvenirs. At first, foreign merchants would purchase any print, but [　　　　　　], works of such masters as Kitagawa Utamaro and Katsushika Hokusai became studiously sought after by collectors.

Hokusai's-designs were particularly popular and were received with ( ③ ) in Europe, and soon they became a source of inspiration for many of his western counterparts of that era. The man who first championed Hokusai's works was a French painter and lithographer named Félix Bracquemond. In about 1856, he found Hokusai's Manga sketchbooks in Paris and started to copy motifs from them. He praised those Japanese designs in his art salon and drew his fellow artists' attention to their flat ( ④ ), clean lines, and unmodulated colors. Hokusai's influences stretched to artists such as Manet, Toulouse-Lautrec, Degas, Monet, van Gogh, Gauguin, and Klimt; Debussy is said to have composed *La Mer* inspired by Hokusai's *The Great Wave off Kanagawa*. Thus, a new style called Art Nouveau, and its variation, Japonism, emerged in Europe.

Those ukiyo-e prints that went abroad had *rakkan*, the artists' signature and seal, as the sign of their ( ⑤ ). A great number of Hokusai's prints that remain to this day are signed "Hokusai, eighty-eight years old." Why was he able to produce so many prints at such an old age, when he was suffering from palsy? They have actively been discussing the matter at international conferences and symposiums, and publishing papers about it.

Some progressive scholars in Europe have been considering the possibility that some of his designs were created by one of his daughters, Ei. ⑥<u>Hokusai himself once admitted his daughter's superb talent, saying that his hand skill in painting women could not compare with that of Ei</u>; however, today there are only about 10 paintings remaining worldwide that are signed with Ei's painting name, Oui.

This is because the production of Hokusai's prints and paintings was probably done as his studio's work, or his family business, rather than Hokusai's solo work, these scholars think. Hokusai's signature and seal was, so to speak, a trademark to protect their family's brand and secure the value of their products. Thus, a considerable amount of works done by ( ⑦ ) could have been marked and considered as ( ⑧ ).

Unfortunately, many of ⑨( are / by / existing works / such as / Oui's / owned / foreign organizations ) the Boston Museum of Fine Arts and the Cleveland Museum of Art, but some museums in Japan also have her pieces in their collections. In 2014, the Boston Museum of Fine Arts organized a traveling Hokusai exhibition and it toured through Japan. Oui's *Three Women Playing Musical Instruments* was also displayed to the public amongst her father's works.

(1) 下線部①が指すものと，下線部②の具体的な国名は何か。それぞれ日本語で書け。

(2) 次の文は，本文中のどこかに入る。最も適切な場所に戻したとき，直後に来る文の最初の3語を書け。

This question has long been intriguing many western scholars and researchers.

(3) 次のア～エのうち，本文中の[　　]に入る最も適切なものはどれか。一つ選んで，その記号を書け。

ア　because many ukiyo-e paintings were not expensive

イ　though they wanted to produce more works

ウ　as western appreciation for ukiyo-e increased

エ　if they had understood the essence of ukiyo-e

(4) 本文中の③～⑤の(　　)内にあてはまる最も適切な語を，次のア～オからそれぞれ一つずつ選んで，その記号を書け。

ア　authenticity　　イ　biography　　ウ　enthusiasm

エ　perspectives　　オ　quantity

(5) 下線部⑥を日本語に直して書け。人名はカタカナで表記すること。

(6) 本文中の⑦，⑧の(　　)内にあてはまる適切な一語を，それぞれ本文中から抜き出して書け。

(7) 下線部⑨の(　　)内の語句を，本文の内容に即して並べかえ，英語で書け。

(☆☆☆☆◎◎◎◎)

【7】次の文は，あることわざの使い方について説明したものである。文中の下線部①，②を英語に直して書け。

「①彼がどんなに落ち込んでいても，厳しく接した方がいいよ。情けは人のためならずって言うだろう。」……このような「情けは人のためならず」の使い方は，本来の意味と合っていません。本来は，「②他人に親切にしなさい，そうすればあなたが困ったとき誰かが助けてくれるでしょう。つまり，人に情けをかけていれば，めぐりめぐって自分に良い報いが来る。」といった意味になります。

(☆☆☆◎◎◎◎)

【8】「高校生が英語を学習するときには，電子辞書ではなく紙の辞書を使うほうがよい」という意見に対して，あなたはどう考えるか。そう考える理由も含めて，30語以上の英語で書け。

(☆☆☆☆◎◎◎◎)

# 解答・解説

## 【中高共通】

【1】PART1　No.1　(C)　No.2　(A)　No.3　(D)　No.4　(C)　No.5　(B)　PART2　No.1　(D)　No.2　(C)　No.3　(A)　No.4　(C)　PART 3　(1)　①　書籍　②　学術論文　③　どちらか一方のスタイル　④　使う　(2)　“Spring, summer, autumn, and winter.”

〈解説〉リスニング問題では，放送が始まる前に選択肢に一通り目を通しておくとよい。PART 1は短い会話で放送は1回のみ，PART 2は長めの会話，PART 3は説明文とそれに続く会話で，それぞれ放送は2回ずつある。　PART 1　No.1　男性の発言のon以下「家に帰る途中で」と言っている。　No.2　男性女性ともにaisleと言っているのは，いわゆる陳列棚の間の通路のこと。 No.3 女性のif以下に注目する。「売上報告書」のことである。 No.4 男性のHow以下はいわゆる「本日のおすすめコーヒー」である。 No.5 女性のbutからeveningまでに「メールをくれれば折り返し返信する」と言っている。 PART 2 No.1 女性の1回目と2回目の発言で船旅に関する企業のスタッフであることがわかる。 No.2 女性の2回目の発言のincluding以下「日本人20名を含んで」と言っている。 No.3 男性が2回目の発言で「現在は科学を専攻している」と言っている。 No.4 女性は2回目の発言で，ボランティアで仕事を手伝ってくれる大学生のインターンを探していると言っている。そして最後にこの男性に頼みたいと言っている。

PART 3 (1) ①・② 男性は1回目の発言の第3段落の1文目でin books and academic papersと述べている。 ③ 同第3段落3文目のeither以下でどちらか一方を一貫して使うように言っている。 ④ 男性の2回目の発言のsuggest以下「伝統的なほうを使うことを勧める」と述べている。 (2) 男性の1回目の発言の第1段落2文目のthat is以下と，同第2段落1文目の記述にしたがって，コンマを書き入れる。

## 【中学校】

【1】1 繰り返して 2 考え 3 コミュニケーション

〈解説〉問題文中に「第1学年及び第2学年における学習内容」とあるので，この文は第3学年に対応するものであることがわかる。また，空欄1の後に「定着を図る」とあるので，繰り返しの指導が想像できる。空欄2の前後には「様々な」と「や意見など」とあるので，「考え」が適切であると推測できる。さらに，空欄3の後は「が図れるような」と続いているので，「コミュニケーション」だとわかる。外国語科の指導においては，各学年での学習内容を，言語活動の中で繰り返し学習することで，言語材料の定着を図るとともに，それらを実際に活用させることが重要である。指導に当たっては特にこれらの点に留意する必要がある。いずれにしても，学習指導要領の当該の部分も含めて熟読することが解答には効果的である。

【2】(1)　greeting　(2)　term　(3)　school trip
〈解説〉(1)　greetingは，口頭・動作・書面によるあいさついずれにも使う。　(2)　解答例は，3学期制の1学期であり，2学期制の場合は，semesterと言う。　(3)　school excursionでもよい。

【3】(1)　Could you turn off the lights?　(2)　Classes are forty-five minutes long today.　(3)　Do you have any other questions?
(4)　Move your desks to the back.
〈解説〉(1)　Please switch off the lights.でもよい。　(2)　We have 45 minute lessons today.でもよい。なお，45という数字が形容詞の働きをしているので，minuteはsをつけない単数形である。　(3)　Do you haveを省略して簡単に言う場合もある。　(4)　Get your desks to the back.でもよい。

【4】(1)　is, pianist　(2)　What, you　(3)　had, been　(4)　only, to
〈解説〉(1)「上手にピアノを弾く」ので「上手なピアニスト」と考えればよい。1語という条件がなければShe is good at playing the piano.でもよい。　(2)「なぜあなたはここへ来たのか」は無生物主語を使えば，「何があなたをここへ来させたのか」と考えればよい。　(3)　仮定法過去完了形の条件節の代わりに句が使われた例である。「彼にもう少しの忍耐があったならば」と考えればよい。　(4)　不定詞の「結果」を表す副詞用法である。「～してその結果…」と考えればよい。次の文を覚えておくとよい。One morning I awoke to find myself famous.「ある朝，私は目を覚ますと有名になっていた」。

【5】(1)　番号…①　正しい表現…laughed at　(2)　番号…④
正しい表現…hers　(3)　番号…④　正しい表現…What
(4)　番号…③　正しい表現…Is
〈解説〉(1)「私は姉(妹)に笑われた」の意味なので前置詞のatが必要である。　(2)「彼女の物」の意味である。　(3)「感想は」の意味で考えればよい。 (4) 「皆，用意はいいか」の意味であり，everyは単数扱いである。

【6】(1) wrong, number (2) care, yourself [yourselves] (3) favor, of (4) hello, to

〈解説〉(1) 「間違い電話をかける」はhave [get] the wrong number。
(2) take careで「注意をする」の意味である。 (3) ask a favor of…「…に依頼をする」の意味である。 (4) say hello to…「…によろしく言う」の意味である。Say hello to Mary when you meet her.で「Maryに会ったらよろしく」。

【7】(1) a エ b イ (2) ① was raised in a large family with ten ④ encouraged her to publish a book based on (3) 黒人にメインフロア席を与えること。 (4) メインフロア席と隔離席の税金差の1セントを支払わなかったこと。 (5) カナダ銀行が，2018年にヴィオラの肖像を新しい10ドル紙幣に起用することを発表し，彼女をエリザベス女王以外で紙幣に登場するカナダで初めての女性とした。
(6) B (7) a × b ○ c ×

〈解説〉(1) a 第1段落3文目のViola'sからcommunityまでに述べている「ヴィオラの両親が黒人のコミュニティに受け入れられたこと」は，20世紀初頭はまれなことであった。 b 空欄に続く文意は「ヴィオラを起訴したことについて」なので，イの「謝罪した」が適切。
(2) ① 「ヴィオラは大家族の中で10人の兄弟とともに育った」の意味である。 ② 「彼女を励ましてヴィオラの経験に基づいた1冊の本を出版させた」の意味である。 (3) 下線部②のitは形式主語。to give以下を訳せばよい。 (4) 下線部③の直後のfor以下は「メインフロアとの差額が脱税である」と言っているのである。 (5) making以下は現在分詞の分詞構文の用法であり，and madeと考えればよい。
(6) 「ヴィオラと弁護士は法廷闘争で負けた」という文なので，第4段落1文目のto fight以下「法廷で争うことを決意した」の後のBに入れるのが適切である。　(7)　aは誤り。第1段落2文目によれば，父親が黒人で母親が白人である。bは正しい。第2段落2文目のpeople以下の内容と一致する。cは誤り。第4段落にあるように，ヴィオラは法廷で差別と戦っている。第6段落1文目には，ヴィオラの活動を世に知らしめたのは妹のワンダであったと述べられている。

【8】(1)　My teacher told me to speak English more without being afraid of making mistakes.　(2)　It's good that the number of foreign tourists to Kagawa Prefecture has been increasing.

〈解説〉(1)　解答例は「tell＋人＋to不定詞」の構文を使っている。また，without以下の句の部分は，節を使ってeven if you make mistakesとすることも可能である。　(2)　解答例はIt～that…の形式主語の構文であるが，that以下をmore and more foreign tourists have come to Kagawa Prefectureとすることも可能である。

【9】①　I agree to the opinion. Junior high school students should experience the activities according to their interests in school education, especially in extracurricular activities. If students take part in those activities, they will be more interested in them and will be able to improve their skills better. Also, they will create good friendship with team members. As a result, students will enjoy their school lives much more. That's why I'm for the opinion. (73語)

②　I don't agree to the opinion. Junior high school students should not to be restricted. If they are required to belong to one of extracurricular activities, they will be completely tied up with them and can't live a free life after school. If they don't participate in it, they have more free time to develop their abilities in their school lives. That's why I disagree to the opinion. (68語)

〈解説〉文法的な誤りをしないことと，論理的な展開にすることが重要である。解答例の①は賛成の場合，②は反対の場合の意見をまとめたものである。

## 【高等学校】

【1】1　コミュニケーション能力　2　使用場面　3　音声指導　4　辞書　5　グループ・ワーク　6　ネイティブ・スピーカー

〈解説〉本問は，現行の高等学校学習指導要領「第8節　外国語　第4款　各科目にわたる指導計画の作成と内容の取扱い」のうち，内容の取扱いに当たっての配慮事項からの出題である。問題文の空欄1，2及び5，6が「英語」についてであり，空欄3，4は「外国語」に関するものである。高等学校学習指導要領については必ず同解説を参照のうえ熟読しておくことが必要である。

【2】(1)　Could you turn off the lights?　(2)　Classes are forty-five minutes long today.　(3)　Say that again in a louder voice.　(4)　Make pairs and put your desks together.

〈解説〉(1) Please switch off the lights.でもよい。　(2)　We have 45 minute lessons today.でもよい。なお，45という数字が形容詞の働きをしているので，minuteはsをつけない単数形である。　(3)　in a louder voiceはlouderの1語でもよい。　(4)　andをthenに変えてもよいし，andをはずして2文にしてもよい。

【3】(1)　is, pianist　(2)　What, you　(3)　had, been　(4)　only, to

〈解説〉(1)「上手にピアノを弾く」ので「上手なピアニスト」と考えればよい。1語という条件がなければShe is good at playing the piano.でもよい。　(2)「なぜあなたはここへ来たのか」は無生物主語を使えば，「何があなたをここへ来させたのか」と考えればよい。　(3)　仮定法過去完了形の条件節の代わりに句が使われた例である。「彼にもう少しの忍耐があったならば」と考えればよい。　(4)　不定詞の「結果」を表す副詞用法である。「～してその結果…」と考えればよい。次の文を覚えておくとよい。One morning I awoke to find myself famous.「ある朝，私は目を覚ますと有名になっていた」。

【4】(1)　番号…①　　正しい表現…laughed at　　(2)　番号…④　　正しい表現…hers　　(3)　番号…④　　正しい表現…What　　(4)　番号…③　　正しい表現…Is

〈解説〉(1)　「私は姉(妹)に笑われた」の意味なので前置詞のatが必要である。　(2)「彼女の物」の意味である。　(3)「感想は」の意味で考えればよい。　(4)「皆，用意はいいか」の意味であり，everyは単数扱いである。

【5】(1)　wrong, number　　(2)　care, yourself [yourselves]　　(3)　favor, of　　(4)　hello, to

〈解説〉(1)「間違い電話をかける」はhave [get] the wrong number。
(2)　take careで「注意をする」の意味である。　(3)　ask a favor of…「…に依頼をする」の意味である。　(4)　say hello to…「…によろしく言う」の意味である。Say hello to Mary when you meet her.で「Maryに会ったらよろしく」。

【6】(1)　①　日本の芸術品　　②　日本　　(2)　They have actively　　(3)　ウ　　(4)　③　ウ　　④　エ　　⑤　ア　　(5)　ホクサイ自身，かつて娘のすばらしい才能を認め，女性を描くことにおける自分の腕前は，エイのそれには及ばないと言った。　　(6)　⑦　Oui [Ei]　　⑧　Hokusai's　　(7)　Oui's existing works are owned by foreign organizations such as

〈解説〉(1)　第1段落2文目のcollected以下が答えである。　(2)「この疑問は長い間ヨーロッパの学者たちの興味を引いてきた」の意味なので，「この疑問」の該当箇所を探せばよい。第4段落の3文目Whyからpalsy?までが「疑問」である。この後ろに入れればよい。　(3)　第2段落3文目の最初からany printまでは「最初はどんな作品でも買う」。続く空欄にはその理由を述べるウが入るのが適切である。　(4)　③　第3段落1文目のand soon以下は「インスピレーションの源となった」。したがって，熱狂的に迎えられたのである。　④　空欄の直前のflatに注目する。

いわゆる平面画法のことである。 ⑤ 第4段落1文目のthe artist'sからsealまでは，作品が本物であると証明する手段について述べている。(5) superb「非常に優れた」。後半のsayingは現在分詞で，分詞構文の用法であり，and saidの意味で考えればよい。 (6) ⑦ 第6段落2文目に注目する。北斎のサインは一派のブランドと品質を保証するものであることが述べられている。 ⑧ Hokusaiでは不可である。ここでは彼の作品のことを言っているので，所有格にしないと誤りである。(7) 直後に美術館名があるので，最後にはsuch asがきて，「…のような」の意味になる。したがって，最初にはOui's existing worksがくる。

【7】① However depressed he is, you should be strict with him. ② Be kind to others, and someone will help you when you are in trouble.

〈解説〉① 「厳しく」はsevereでもよい。「彼に対して」の意味なので，前置詞はsevereの場合はwithまたはonである。また，解答例のisはmay beでもよい。 ② 「命令文＋and」を用いて書けばよい。解答例のsomeoneからhelp youの部分は受け身でyou will be helped by someoneでもよい。また，when以下を句で書けば，in case of your being in troubleとなる。

【8】① An electronic dictionary is good for students to use in their English study. First, they can access a word faster than a paper dictionary with it, so they can look up more words during their English study. Second, it can contain some kinds of dictionaries within itself, so students can use an English-Japanese dictionary and a Japanese-English one at a time. Third, it is portable and students can use it everywhere. That's why I agree to the opinion. (78語) ② I disagree to the theme. First, an electronic dictionary is generally more expensive than a paper dictionary, so some students can buy it, but others can't. Second, an electronic one works by battery, so students can't use it without battery. Third, it is hard to overlook both meaning of a word and it's example sentences on a small-screen at the same time. That's why I don't agree to the opinion. (70語)

〈解説〉まずは主題に対して賛成か反対かを明らかにすることで，論点が明確になり書きやすくなる。また，文法的な誤りをしないことと，論理的な展開にすることが重要である。解答例では，①に賛成意見，②に反対意見の両方を挙げている。

# 2017年度　実施問題

## 【中高共通】

【1】Lisitening Comprehension

There are three parts to this section, with special directions for each part. You may take notes while you are listening.

【PART1】

Now, let's begin Part 1. In this part, you will hear five conversations between two people. After each conversation, a third person will ask a question about what was said. Read the four possible answers on your test paper, choose the best answer to each question, and write it on your answer sheet. You will hear each conversation and question about it just one time.

No.1

(M) Tomorrow's sales meeting starts at 11, right?

(W) Oh, haven't you heard? It got changed to 3 because the manager has an appointment at 10:30.

Question: What time will the meeting begin?

(A) At 10;30.

(B) At 11:00.

(C) At 3:00.

(D) Undecided.

No.2

(M) Excuse me ... I'm looking for a bookshop. I thought there was one around here.

(W) It closed last year. The nearest bookshop is on Main Street. It's about five minutes' walk from here.

Question: Why is the man talking to the woman?

(A) To know when the bookshop was closed.

(B) To show the way to nearest bookshop.

(C) To walk with the woman on Main Street.

(D) To know the location of a bookshop.

No.3

(M) Mike invited us to see a movie tonight. It's the new comedy set in a sports gym.

(W) Oh, I've already seen it. I watched it on the plane during my business trip last week. It was good.

Question: What does Mike want the man and the woman to do?

(A) To play sports in a gym.

(B) To see a comedy.

(C) To talk about the woman's business trip.

(D) To enjoy a mobie on the plane.

No.4

(M) Got any plans for the long weekend? I'm going snowboarding. Do you want to come?

(W) Sorry, I can't. It's my parents' 40th wedding anniversary. The whole family is gathering in Boston.

Question: What is the woman going to do on the long weekend?

(A) To go snowboarding.

(B) To attend a wedding.

(C) To see the woman's family.

(D) To leave Boston.

No.5

(M) Does this train go to the airport?

(W) Yes, but it stops at Central Station on the way. The Airport Liner would be better. It costs a little more, but you'll get there faster.

Question: What does the woman want to say?

(A) The man should use the Airport Liner.

(B) The man should save the money.

(C) Central Station is worth visiting.

(D) The Airport Liner would get better.

【PART2】

Now, let's go on to Part 2. In this part, you will hear a conversation. After that, you will be asked four questions. Read the four possible answers on your test paper, decide which one is the best answer to the question you hear, and write it on your answer sheet. You will hear the conversation and questions about it two times.

(M) Thank you for coming in today, Ms. Takano. As you know, we are looking for a Japanese tutor here at Global Language Academy. Why do you think you're the right person for this job?

(W) Well, for one thing, I am fully bilingual. I lived in Australia until I was 12, then from junior high school on, I lived in Japan. I think my Japanese and English skills would be a big advantage.

(M) I understand that you studied International Communications at university.

(W) Yes, that's right. I found it fascinating. In my senior year, I worked part-time as a teaching assistant in the Japanese department. That's when I became interested in the idea of teaching Japanese as a career.

(M) Most of our clients are business people. Have you ever taught adults before?

(W) Yes, I helped to run a beginner's Japanese course for adults at a community college last year.

(M) I see. Do you have any questions about the position?

(W) Would there be any weekend and evening work?

(M) Yes, we would need you to work until 8 p.m. two nights a week, and from 9 to 12 on Saturdays. Would that be a problem?

(W) Not at all.

(M) Thank you, Ms. Takano. We'll let you know about the job soon.

Question No.1: What is the main purpose of this interview?

(A) To know how many languages Ms. Takano speaks.

(B) To know when Ms. Takano returned to Japan.

(C) To know if Ms. Takano is good for the job or not.

(D) To know why Ms. Takano has come to see the man.

Question No.2: What made Ms. Takano get interested in the job of teaching Japanese?

(A) The experience of living in Australia.

(B) The part-time job at the university.

(C) Studying International Communications.

(D) Teaching business people at a language school.

Question No.3: Where did Ms. Takano teach adults?

(A) In Australia.

(B) At the university.

(C) At Global Language Academy.

(D) At the community college.

Question No.4: Which is true about Ms. Takano?

(A) She graduated from junior high school in Australia.

(B) She worked at a department store in Japan.

(C) She speaks English as if it were her mother tongue.

(D) She doesn't think she can work on weekends.

【PART3】

Part3. In this part, you will hear one lecture about a certain kind of children. Summarize the lecture by filling in the blanks from one to five and write the answers on your answer sheet. You'll hear the lecture two times.

Part3. In this part, you will hear one lecture about a certain kind of children. Summarize the lecture by filling in the blanks from one to five and write the answers on your answer sheet. You'll hear the lecture two times.

Now, listen.

Have you ever heard a term "Third Culture Kid," also known as TCK? It refers to children who spent a significant part of their childhood in settings that are outside of their parents' cultures. Imagine children of foreign expats, for example. The first culture refers to their parents'; the second culture refers to that of the place in which they currently live; and the third culture refers to something in-between.

As a result of globalization or migration etcetera, the population of such children has been increasing over the years. Sure, there are many assets in being exposed to different cultures at their young ages; most of them are bilingual or multilingual, they tend to be open to new cultures, and be able to freely go into and out of the cultural gray zone — but there are challenges as well.

Some families move from one country to another every few years. It's not always easy for children to adjust to new cultures. As they don't know which culture they really belong to, children may develop confused loyalties in values, which could eventually cause them an identity crisis.

Now, the reason why I brought up this issue today is that some Japanese parents ask me my opinion about putting their children in international schools even though they live in Japan and have no plans to move to another country. As a sociologist and educator, I must urge them to think twice before doing so. I am all for the idea of experiencing diversity, but they must ponder what their children would endure in such a setting and what it would bring to their later lives.

述べられている内容について，次の1～5の(　　)内に入る日本語を書け。

| 導　入 | TCKとは（　1　）の大部分を（　2　）の文化圏外で育った子ども |
|---|---|
| 良い点 | 外国語に堪能で，（　3　）を受け入れやすい |
| 悪い点 | 自分が（　4　）がわかっていないことが原因で，問題が生じることがある |
| 結　論 | （　5　）が全くないのに子どもをインターナショナルスクールに入れるのは慎重にすべき |

This is the end of the Listening Comprehension Section.

(☆☆☆☆◎◎◎◎)

【2】次の(1)～(3)の各組において，a)とb)がほぼ同じ意味になるように，b)の(　　)内にあてはまる最も適切な一語をそれぞれ書け。

(1)　a)　It seems that she was happy.

　　b)　She seems to (　　) (　　) happy.

(2)　a)　Some students like English, and others don't like it.

　　b)　(　　) (　　) student likes English.

(3)　a)　Although I was sad, I felt hungry.

　　b)　In (　　) (　　) my sadness, I felt hungry.

(☆☆☆◎◎◎◎◎)

【3】次の(1)～(4)のそれぞれについて，下線部の①～④のいずれかに一箇所誤りがある。その箇所の番号と正しい表現に直したものを書け。

(1)　①It is ②necessary ③that she ④takes a rest.

(2)　I have two sisters. ①One lives in Tokyo, ②and ③other ④lives in Osaka.

(3)　The new island was ①found ②in ③the afternoon ④of June 30.

(4)　I had ①just ②finished my lunch ③when the baby ④has begun crying.

(☆☆☆◎◎◎◎)

【4】次の(1)～(3)のそれぞれについて，日本文の意味になるように，(　　)内にあてはまる最も適切な一語を書け。

(1)　きっと彼女は試験に合格すると思う。

I'm sure (　　) her (　　) the examination.

(2)　A : コーヒーが好きではないのですか。―B : はい，好きではありません。

A : Don't you like coffee? － B : (　　), I (　　).

(3)　彼女は私より3才年上だ。

She is senior (　　) me (　　) three years.

(☆☆☆◎◎◎◎)

## 【中学校】

【1】次の文は，中学校学習指導要領(平成20年3月告示，平成27年3月一部改正)「第2章　第9節　外国語　第2　各言語の目標及び内容等」の「3　指導計画の作成と内容の取扱い」の一部を示そうとしたものである。次の1～3の(　　)内にあてはまる語句を書け。

> 教材は，聞くこと，話すこと，読むこと，書くことなどのコミュニケーション能力を(　1　)に育成するため，実際の言語の(　2　)や(　3　)に十分配慮したものを取り上げるものとする。

(☆☆☆◎◎◎◎◎)

【2】次の(1)～(3)の日本語を英語に直して書け。ただし，(3)は小学校学習指導要領(平成20年3月告示，平成27年3月一部改正)第4章に示されている外国語活動のことである。

(1)　主語　　(2)　制服　　(3)　外国語活動

(☆☆☆◎◎◎)

【3】英語の授業で，次の(1)～(4)のとき，授業者が英語でどのように話すかを書け。

(1)　席に戻るよう指示するとき。
(2)　黒板を消すよう指示するとき。
(3)　その考えに賛成か反対かを尋ねるとき。
(4)　5人グループを作るよう指示するとき。

(☆☆☆◎◎◎◎)

【4】次の英文を読み，あとの(1)～(7)の問いに答えよ。なお，文中のGymnasium(ギムナジウム)，*Realschule*(レアルシューレ)，*Mittelschule*(ミッテルシューレ)はドイツの中等教育機関の名称である。

Germany is ①<u>know</u> for its unique school system. It is complicated even for

German people to understand, and details vary by federal state, but one distinctive characteristic of it is its secondary education.

Most German children attend primary school from the age of six or seven to ten. During the fourth grade, they receive final grades, which determine which secondary school they may enter. ②( other / a / are / that / given / there / few ) options, most children go either to Gymnasium, *Realschule* or *Mittelschule*.

③Children who receive highest grades at primary school usually move on to Gymnasium; however, only about 60% of them graduate from it without any issues. Gymnasium is designed to prepare children to finish with the final exam called *Abitur*, ④( advanced / enables / receive / which / education / to / them ).

In principle, students may take *Abitur* only once, and if a student's ⑤behavior has not been satisfactory at school, he or she may not be allowed to take the test. Therefore, going to Gymnasium does not automatically guarantee students higher education. [ A ]

*Realschule* and *Mittelschule* are vocational schools. Intermediate children usually go to *Realschule* and continue further professional education in office and administrative support occupations, such as bookkeeping and accounting, at vocational universities. At *Mittelschule*, students aim to ( a ) a degree called Meister through apprenticeship in about 170 different categories such as handcraft, construction and farming. [ B ]

This Meister system is said to be the backbone of Germany's strong industries, especially in manufacturing. It attracts some other countries' ( b ) and admiration; nevertheless, it is also controversial ⑥to determine children's future at such an early stage of life.

Many children at the age of nine or ten are still uncertain of what they would like to do in their future, and yet they are forced to decide which way to go, only according to their grades. Moreover, at around these ages, girls tend to be more matured and demonstrate better performances at school than boys. [ C ]

Some argue that apprentices still have a chance to switch their courses of study later on and take *Abitur*. ⑦However, according to the 2011 German census, only 22% of those who had started vocational training that year qualified for higher education.

(1) 下線部①の語を適切な形に直して書け。

(2) 下線部②，④の(　　)内の語を，本文の内容に即して並べかえ，英語で書け。

(3) 下線部③，⑦を日本語に直して書け。

(4) 下線部⑤について，この文脈で置き換えられる最も適切なものを，次のア～エから一つ選んで，その記号を書け。

ア environment　イ conduct　ウ chance　エ benefit

(5) 文中のa，bの(　　)内にあてはまる最も適切な語を，次のア～エからそれぞれ一つずつ選んで，その記号を書け。

a　ア work　イ give　ウ earn
　エ teach

b　ア attention　イ determination　ウ demonstration
　エ animation

(6) 下線部⑥に関する否定的な見解の根拠として，その年頃の子どもについて述べられていることを2つ日本語で書け。

(7) 次の文は，本文中のA～Cの[　　]のいずれかに入る。最も適切な箇所を一つ選んで，その記号を書け。

Furthermore, the level of difficulty of *Abitur* varies by state; in order to fix this unfairness, unified exams will be employed in some subjects in 2017.

(☆☆☆◎◎◎◎)

【5】次の(1)，(2)の日本語を英語に直して書け。

(1) 私は，彼が文化祭で一生懸命に働いているのを見て感動した。

(2) 私は，これらの単語をもう一度発音するよう生徒たちに頼まれた。

(☆☆☆◎◎◎◎)

【6】中学生の修学旅行の行き先として適切なのは，国内と国外どちらだと思うか。理由を添えて，自分の意見を30語以上の英語で書け。

(☆☆☆☆◎◎◎◎)

## 【高等学校】

【1】次の各文は，高等学校学習指導要領(平成21年3月告示)の「第8節　外国語　第2款　各科目　第5　英語表現Ⅰ　2　内容」を示そうとしたものである。次の1～6の(　　)内にあてはまる語句を書け。

(1)　生徒が情報や考えなどを理解したり伝えたりすることを実践するように具体的な言語の使用場面を設定して，次のような言語活動を英語で行う。

ア　与えられた話題について，(　1　)で話す。また，聞き手や目的に応じて簡潔に話す。

イ　読み手や目的に応じて，簡潔に書く。

ウ　聞いたり読んだりしたこと，学んだことや経験したことに基づき，情報や考えなどをまとめ，(　2　)する。

(2)　(1)に示す言語活動を効果的に行うために，次のような事項について指導するよう配慮するものとする。

ア　リズムやイントネーションなどの英語の音声的な特徴，話す速度，声の(　3　)などに注意しながら話すこと。

イ　内容の(　4　)を示す語句や文，つながりを示す語句などに注意しながら書くこと。また，書いた内容を読み返すこと。

ウ　発表の仕方や発表のために必要な表現などを学習し，実際に(　5　)すること。

エ　聞いたり読んだりした内容について，そこに示されている意見を他の意見と(　6　)して共通点や相違点を整理したり，自分の考えをまとめたりすること。

(☆☆☆☆◎◎◎◎◎)

【2】英語の授業で，次の(1)～(4)のとき，授業者が英語でどのように話すかを書け。

(1) ワークシートなどを一枚取って，後ろの席の生徒に回してほしいとき。

(2) 正しい答えを丸で囲ませたいとき。

(3) 5人グループを作らせたいとき。

(4) ペアでお互いの意見を交換させたいとき。

(☆☆☆◎◎◎◎)

【3】次の英文を読み，あとの(1)～(7)の問いに答えよ。

Humans' art activities can be traced back thousands of years. From prehistoric cave paintings and cult images to aboriginal arts ···· arts have always been integrated into our daily lives. In the modern society, however, arts are considered to be something high and sophisticated, and ①( a / education / to / artists / are / have / expected / formal) at established institutions. What, then, makes us think we could separate everyday arts from "official" arts?

During the early 1920's, some artists in Europe started to explore this question. In 1947, a French artist named Jean Dubuffet coined a term *art brut* (its literal translation into English is "raw art" or "rough art"), and started to celebrate artists who were untouched by and free from conventional art cultures and education, as well as ②their works created from their own spirits and instincts, outside the boundaries of mainstream arts. The central characteristic and the true spirit of *art brut* was, in a sense, refusal of elitism or snobbism that dominated the established art scene.

It was not until 1972 that the English equivalent of *art brut* was introduced; a British writer and art critic named Roger Cardinal first used the term "outsider art" in his book. Since then, the concept of outsider art has become a ( ③ ) movement that challenges and redefines the limits of what we call art.

④<u>While the interpretation of the original French term was rather specific and strict, the concept of the English term "outsider art" has expanded over the years to include a much greater range of marginal arts.</u> This transformation was particularly important in the United States, where the existence of the indigenous or vernacular cultures had been greatly ignored upon its constitution, and where cultural, racial, or religious diversity has become a key component of the modern society. From "primitive art" and "folk art" to "self-taught art" or "naïve art" …. the concept has grown independently from *art brut* to recognize any forms of ⑤<u>arts that have never been "inside."</u> [ A ]

Outsider artists are from all cultural background, all sexual orientation and age groups, and barely have had a formal training or education at established art institutions. ⑥<u>During the past decades, the term began to include children as well as artists with some kind of mental health illness or physical disabilities.</u> It must not be overlooked that even some established artists with formal art education are not always immune from mental illness either. [ B ]

The relationship between arts and mental issues has long been discussed. The method so-called "art therapy" emerged in 2005 right after Hurricane Katrina had hit the United States and some therapists began to use arts to treat traumatized children to help them regain their strength and resilience. Although there is some criticism against the casual association between art therapy and outsider art, there certainly is a therapeutic effect for arts to address mental health issues in modern education. [ C ]

(1)　下線部①の(　　)内の語を本文の内容に即して並べかえ，英語で書け。

(2)　下線部②が指すものを本文の内容に即して，具体的に日本語で書け。

(3)　本文中の③の(　　)内にあてはまる最も適切な語を，次のア～エから選んで，その記号を書け。

ア　martial　　イ　global　　ウ　artificial　　エ　political

(4)　下線部④，⑥を日本語に直して書け。

(5)　下線部⑤に当てはまらない語句を，次のア～エから一つ選んで，その記号を書け。

ア　rough arts　　イ　marginal arts　　ウ　mainstream arts

エ　everyday arts

(6)　次の文は，本文中A～Cの［　　］のいずれかに入る。最も適切な箇所を一つ選んで，その記号を書け。

In New Yor City, for instance, there are some art galleries that exclusively feature works by blind artists, or by artists with autism or Down syndrome.

(7)　本文の内容と一致するものを次のア～オから2つ選んで，その記号を書け。

ア　人は何千年もの間，芸術活動を続けており，芸術は常に人の日常生活に統合されてきた。

イ　フランス語の「アール・ブリュット」という用語と正反対の意味を持つ「アウトサイダー・アート」という用語がイギリスで使われ始めた。

ウ　先住民や土着の文化が建国時にことごとく無視され，また文化・民族・宗教の多様性が現代の社会の重要な構成要素となっているアメリカでは，正式な芸術教育が見直されるようになった。

エ　ハリケーン・カトリーナがアメリカを襲った後，心が傷ついた子どもたちを芸術の力を借りて治療しようとした専門家がいたことには批判があった。

オ　現代教育において，芸術には確かに精神疾患上の問題を抱えた人を癒す効果があると認められている。

(☆☆☆◎◎◎◎)

【4】次の文中の下線部①，②を英語に直して書け。

①急速な技術革新は私たちの生活を質的に変化させてきている。将

来就くことになる職業についても，技術革新により大きく変化すると予測されている。②今後10年から20年で半数近くの仕事が自動化されると言う人もいる。

(☆☆☆◎◎◎◎)

【5】「外国語を習得するには，留学する方がよい」という意見に対するあなたの考えを，30語以上の英語で書け。

(☆☆☆☆◎◎◎◎)

# 解答・解説

## 【中高共通】

【1】PART1　No.1　(C)　No.2　(D)　No.3　(B)　No.4　(C)　No.5　(A)　PART2　No.1　(C)　No.2　(B)　No.3　(D)　No.4　(C)　Part3　1　子ども時代　2　親　3　新しい文化　4　属する文化　5　海外に引っ越す計画

〈解説〉PART1　2人の会話を聞いて質問に答える形式である。放送は1回のみである。　No.1　会議の時間は当初11時に予定されていたが，変更されて3時になった。　No.2　男性は「探している」と言っていることに注意しよう。　No.3　男性は最初に「マイクが映画に誘ってくれた」と言っている。　No.4　女性は両親の結婚40周年記念に家族全員が集まると言っている。　No.5　「ライナーのほうが早く着く」と言っている。　PART2　2人の会話を聞いて，内容に関する質問に答える形式である。放送は2回である。　No.1　最初に男性が「日本語を教える者を探している」と言っている。　No.2　女性は「パートタイムで大学の講座の助手をした」と言っている。　No.3　女性は「去年，コミュニティー・カレッジで教えた」と言っている。
No.4　女性は「バイリンガルだ」と言っている。　PART3　講義を聞いて概要をまとめ，空欄に日本語で解答する問題である。

(1)・(2)　第1段落のchildrenからculturesまでを参照すること。なお，Spend A in Bは「AをBで費やす」という意味である。　(3)　第2段落3行目theyからculturesまでで「新たな文化に開放的」と記述されている。(4)　第3段落のAs以降に「どの文化に属するかわからないので，価値観の混乱を起こして結果的にアイデンティティの危機になる」と書かれている。　(5)　第4段落のevenからdoing soまでで「外国へ転居する計画がないにもかかわらず，子どもをインターナショナル・スクールに入れようとするのはよく考えるべきだ」と書かれている。

【2】(1)　have been　　(2)　Not every　　(3)　spite of

〈解説〉(1)　完了形不定詞の時制の問題である。It seemed that she was happy.ならば，She seemed to be happy.となる。　(2)「英語が好きな生徒もいれば，そうでない生徒もいる。」という意味なので，「全員が英語を好きではない。」という部分否定で考えればよい。　(3)「…にもかかわらず」の意味である。他には，despite ofやfor all，with allなどがある。

【3】(番号 : 正しい表現　の順)　(1)　④ : should take(take)

(2)　③ : the other　　(3)　② : on　　(4)　④ : began

〈解説〉(1)　特定の形容詞の用法で感情的な意味合いがある。このような形式主語の構文では，that以下で助動詞のshouldまたはそれが省略された表現が用いられる。「彼女は休むことがぜひ必要である。」と考えればよい。このような用法の形容詞は他に，absurd，curious，strange，amazingなどがある。　(2)　2人のうちの1人がone，残りは特定できるのでthe otherである。　(3)　特定の日の午前や午後の場合には，前置詞はinではなくてonである。　(4)　文全体の意味は，「私が昼食を済ませるやいなや，赤ん坊が泣き始めた」である。なお，問題文はAs soon as I just finished my lunch, the baby began crying.，またはOn my just finishing my lunch, the baby began crying.と書き換えることができる。

【４】(1)　of, passing　　(2)　No, don't　　(3)　to, by
〈解説〉(1)　be sure of …で「…は確実である」の意味である。複文では，I'm sure that she will pass the examination.と書くことができる。　(2)　日本語の応答と一致しないので注意すること。「好きか，否かにまず答える」と考えればよい。　(3)　逆に「年下」であればseniorではなくjuniorを使えばよい。なお，問題文はShe is three years older than I.と書き換えられる。

## 【中学校】

【１】1　総合的　　2　使用場面　　3　言語の働き
〈解説〉教材選定について，学習指導要領解説では「生徒の発達の段階，興味・関心について十分に配慮しつつ，英語の目標に照らして適切であり，学習段階に応じた言語材料で構成されているような適切な題材を変化をもたせて取り上げるように配慮する必要がある」としている。ここでいう「英語の目標」とは「聞くこと，話すこと，読むこと，書くことなどのコミュニケーション能力の基礎を総合的に育成」することなので，以上2点を踏まえた選定が必要であることがうかがえる。

【２】(1)　subject　　(2)　uniform　　(3)　Foreign Language Activities
〈解説〉(1)　文法指導などでよく使われる用語であるため，基本的なものはおさえておきたい。特に，動詞(verb)，形容詞(adjective)，副詞(adverb)は頻出である。　(3)　小学校から高等学校まで「外国語」は英語を扱うことを原則としており，学習内容等も英語を学習することを前提として示されている。ただし，他の外国語を学習することを否定しておらず，その場合は「英語の目標及び内容等に準じて行うものとする」としている。以上から，外国語活動(中学では「外国語」)は意訳してEnglishとしないことが求められている。

【３】(1)　Go back to your seat.　　(2)　Clean the blackboard.　　(3)　Are you for or against the idea?　　(4)　Make groups of five people.

〈解説〉(1) Go backの代わりにReturnでもよい。 (2) この場合の「消す」は「きれいにする」と考えればよい。Cleanの代わりにEraseでもよい。なお,「黒板ふき」はeraserである。 (3) ここでは前置詞を用いているが,Do you agree to the idea or not?でもよい。 (4) 授業中の活動でよく使う表現である。たとえば,「黒板の右列上隅の絵を見なさい。」ならば,Look at the picture on the blackboard in the right column uppermost.と言えばよい。

【4】(1) known (2) ② Given that there are a few other ④ which enables them to receive advanced education (3) ③ 小学校での成績が最も良い子どもたちはふつうギムナジウムに進むが,問題なく卒業するのはそのうちのわずか60パーセント程度である。 ⑦ しかしながら,2011年のドイツの国勢調査によると,その年に職業訓練を始めていた子どものうち22％しか高等教育を受ける資格を得られなかった。 (4) イ (5) a ウ b ア (6) ・9歳,10歳くらいの多くの子どもたちは将来何をしたいのかまだ明確でないが,学校の成績だけでどの方向に進むか決めさせられるため。 ・これくらいの年齢では,女子の方が男子より早く成熟し,学校の成績も良い傾向にあるため。 (7) A

〈解説〉(1) be known for …で「…で知られている」という意味になる。 (2) ② 直後にoptionsがあるので,この前に来るのはa few otherが考えられる。 ④ 直前にコンマ,カッコ内にwhichがあるので継続用法と考えればよい。さらに,enablesがあるので,enables them to receiveと考える。 (3) ③ 主語はschoolまでで動詞はmove onである。however以下では,主語がonlyからthemまでで,動詞はgraduateである。 (4) ⑤は「学校での行動」という意味である。 (5) aは「マイスターの単位を取る」,bは「他国の注目と称賛を得ている」という意味になる。 (6) 下線部を受けて,第7段落で2つの内容が述べられている。Manyからgradesまでで,「9歳から10歳の年齢の時に,成績だけで将来を決めねばならないこと」とMoreoverからboysまでで,「この年頃では,一般的に男子よりも女子のほうが，成績がよい傾向があること」が記述されている。　(7)　それぞれの空欄の前部の内容を考えればよい。Aは進学の仕組みについて，Bはミッテルシューレの説明，Cは男女の差異について述べている。提示された文はアビトゥーアについての記述である。

【5】(1)　I was moved to see him working very hard at the school festival.
(2)　I was asked to pronounce these words again by the students.

〈解説〉(1)　wasからhardまでは，was impressed with his very hard workingでも可能である。　(2)　askedはrequestedでもよい。

【6】I agree to the opinion that a school excursion in Japan should be prepared for junior high schools. Japan has historical and traditional cultures and places, and knowing such domestic cultures and nature will make the students recognize our own cultures and difference from overseas'.
So, a school excursion in our domestic places and cultures will be much effective to make those students recognize what our own culture is in this world.

〈解説〉解答例は，「国内の修学旅行に賛成」の立場で書いている。第1文のa school以下は直訳すれば，「日本での修学旅行は中学校で行われるべきだ」なので，「中学校の修学旅行は国内で」となる。第2文のknowing以下は「国内の文化や自然を知ることで自国の文化理解と海外との違いを理解できる」という意味である。

## 【高等学校】

【1】1　即興　　2　発表　　3　大きさ　　4　要点　　5　活用
6　比較

〈解説〉本科目は中学校で学習した内容を踏まえ，「話したり書いたりする言語活動を中心に，情報や考えなどを伝える能力の向上を図る」ことを目的とした選択履修科目である。学習内容については，空欄を中心におさえておくとよい。当然，他の科目も出題される可能性があるため，学習指導要領，および学習指導要領解説は必ず学習しておきたい。

【2】(1) Take one and pass them on. (2) Circle the right answers.
(3) Make groups of five people. (4) Share your ideas with your partner.

〈解説〉(1) pass on「移す，伝える」の意味であり，passはhandでもよい。
(2) in a circleは「輪になって」の意味である。 (4) 意見の交換とは，ここでは「考えを共有する」の意味なのでshareが適切である。

【3】(1) artists are expected to have a formal education (2) 慣習的な芸術文化や教育の影響を受けず，とらわれてもいない芸術家 (3) イ
(4) ④ 元のフランス語の用語の解釈がかなり明確で厳密である一方で，英語の「アウトサイダー・アート」という用語の概念は年々広がり，傍流の芸術のはるかに多くの範囲を含むようになった。
⑥ 過去数十年の間に，その用語は何らかの精神疾患や身体的な障害がある芸術家だけでなく，子どもも含み始めた。 (5) ウ
(6) B (7) ア，オ

〈解説〉(1) 第1段落でartsの様子とartistsの様子が対比されていることに注意する。arts are considered to beの部分がヒントになる。 (2) 第2段落にあるartists who … educationを考えればよい。 (3) 空欄後ろにあるthat以下は「我々が芸術と呼ぶものに挑戦し再定義する」という意味である。 (4) ④ Whileからstrictまでが従属節で「…する一方で」という意味であり，the concept以下が主節で「アウトサイダー・アートは周辺的芸術にまで拡大した」である。over the yearsは挿入句である。 ⑥ children as well as artistsは「芸術家だけでなく子どもまでも」であり，not only artists but also childrenと書き換えられる。physical disabilitiesは「身体障害」の意味である。 (5) 下線部は「今まで決して『内側』にならなかった芸術」，つまり「アウトサイダー」であ

る。　(6)　提示文の中にfor instance「例えば」がある点に注意。この語句以下で具体的な芸術の内容が書かれているので，さまざまな芸術内容の記述の後が適切である。　(7)　イ　第3段落最初のItから始まる文で両者は「同等の」と述べられている。　ウ　第4段落のto recognize以下で「アウトサイダーのどんな芸術でもその価値を認める」とある。エ　第6段落で専門家が治療したが，批判があったとは記述されていない。

【４】①　Rapid innovation in technology has been changing the quality of our lives.　②　Some people say that nearly half of the jobs will be automated in 10 to 20 years.

〈解説〉①「生活を質的に変化させ」は，「生活の質を変化させ」と考えればよい。文章を「急速な技術革新が原因で，私たちの生活は質的に変化してきている」と捉える場合は，On account of rapid innovation, our lives has been changing in quality. となるだろう。　②「…と言う人もいる」は，「何人かの人は…と言う」と考えればよい。

【５】I don't always agree to go abroad for the purpose of learning a foreign language. We can learn it even in Japan because we are in good circumstances for studying a foreign language. Through TV, radio, cinema, papers, and so on, we can really learn it. But the levels of learning it depends on people, so for some people, learning it overseas will be effective. On the other hand, it may not be effective for others.

〈解説〉英作文のポイントは，問題の条件を踏まえているか，意見に一貫性があるか，英単語や文法が正確かであり，意見の中身が採点されることはまずない。語数も比較的少なく，表現方法に制限もないので，「正確に・端的に」を心がけ，まとめるとよいだろう。

# 2016年度　実施問題

## 【中高共通】

【1】Listening Comprehension

There are three parts to this section, with special directions for each part. You may take notes while you are listening.

Now, let's begin Part1. In this part, you will hear five conversations between two people. After each conversation, a third person will ask a question about what was said. Read the four possible answers on your test paper, choose the best answer to each question,and write it on your answer sheet. You will hear each conversation and question about it just one time.

No.1

(M)　Look, eggs are on sale today.

(W)　Really? That's too bad. I just bought some yesterday! We only need bread and lettuce now.

Question: What will the woman probably buy?

No.2

(M)　Excuse me. Did you see a little girl around here?

(W)　I saw a girl with brown hair enter that building a few minutes ago.

Question: What is the man doing?

No.3

(M)　Excuse me, but I think you might be sitting in my seat. I'm in 27 A.

(W)　This is 27 B. You have the window seat.

Question: What will the woman probably do next?

No.4

(M)　We missed you at the party yesterday. What happened?

(W)　I wanted to go but I had to finish a big project for work. I didn't leave the office until 8.

Question: What happened on the day of the party?

No.5

(M)　Does this yellow bus go to the Central Library?

(W)　Yes, but it will take about 30 minutes because the bus goes to the City Hall first. That green bus over there will be quicker.

Question: Where are the speakers talking?

PART1(記号で書け。)

No.1

(A)　Only bread.

(B)　Only lettuce.

(C)　Only eggs.

(D)　Both bread and lettuce.

No.2

(A)　He is looking for a little girl.

(B)　He is looking at a little boy.

(C)　He is entering a building.

(D)　He is cutting a girl's brown hair.

No.3

(A)　She will move to 27A.

(B)　She will remain seated in 27B.

(C)　She will sit in the window seat.

(D)　She will take a wrong seat.

No.4

(A) The man saw the woman at the party.

(B) The man missed the party.

(C) The woman didn't go to the office.

(D) The woman didn't attend the party.

No.5

(A) At the City Hall.

(B) In the Central Library.

(C) At a bus stop.

(D) In the green bus.

Now, let's go on to Part 2. In this part, you will hear a conversation. After that, you will be asked four questions. Read the four possible answers on your test paper, decide which one is the best answer to the question you hear, and write it on your answer sheet. You will hear the conversation and questions about it two times.

(M) Professor King, may I speak with you for a moment?

(W) Sure. How can I help you, Daiki?

(M) I'm thinking of applying for the program to spend a year abroad in Canada.

(W) Oh, the program where you study at a university in Toronto, right? It would be a wonderful opportunity for you.

(M) I know. Do you have any advice?

(W) I think your conversation skills are already quite good. And you write English well. However, you need to learn to speak up more.

(M) What do you mean exactly?

(W) Well, you tend to be quiet in my English classes. You only speak when I ask you a question.

(M) I'm always worried about making a mistake.

(W) Everyone makes mistakes. It's how we learn! In Canada, college students are expected to share their opinions freely. There is usually more discussion than in classes here in Japan.

(M) I see. I'll try to be more confident. Thank you for your help.

(W) You're welcome. Let me know if you need any more help.

(M) Thank you. I will bring my application form with me tomorrow. Would you read it and give me some advice?

Question 1:Why does Daiki speak to Professor King? (6 seconds)

Question 2:According to Professor King, how should Daiki speak English? (6 seconds)

Question 3:What are university students in Canada expected to do? (6 seconds)

Question 4:What will Daiki probably do the next day? (6 seconds)

Listen again.

PART2(記号で書け。)

No.1

(A) To get a job in Toronto.

(B) To apply for her lecture.

(C) To ask for advice.

(D) To practice speaking English.

No.2

(A) With a little more fluency.

(B) More freely.

(C) More politely.

(D) Without making mistakes.

No.3

(A) To reject other's opinions.

(B) To exchange their opinions frankly.

(C) To keep silent in classes.

(D) To worry about making mistakes.

No.4

(A) He will help the professor.

(B) He will give up the program.

(C) He will leave for Canada.

(D) He will consult with the professor again.

Part3. In this part, you will hear one lecture about the education system in a certain country. Summarize the lecture by filling in the blanks from one to seven and write the answers on your answer sheet. You'll hear the lecture two times.

Now, listen.

The education system in this country is one of the best in the world. Here are some reasons.

Firstly I'll talk about teachers and schools. Being a teacher is a respected job here. And, a three-year undergraduate degree plus a two-year Master's degree are required to become a teacher. Each school can design its own curriculum. Teachers and students are involved in educational planning.

Secondly I'll tell you about the teaching method. Children start school at the age of seven, when they are old enough to study. In the first 2 years, students attend a school for 4 to 5 hours a day.Until the sixth grade, children usually have the same teacher for most subjects.Moreover, a number grading system is not used until the fifth grade. And, schools don't give homework until the students are teenagers. Students learn in the classroom. The relationship with the teacher is very close. Each class is limited to 20 students. Students spend time exploring, creating and experimenting, rather than memorizing. Teachers listen to feedback from their students, and also from other experienced teachers. So, teachers take good care of students who fall behind and who are ahead.

Finally I will share education culture and policy. In this country, 80% of families visit a library on weekends.And parents generally believe they, rather than the school, are responsible for the education of their kids. And, in 2009, the government spent 6.8% of its GDP on education. And public education is free.

Listen again.

This is the end of the Listening Comprehension Section.

PART3 (述べられている内容について，次の1～7の(　　)内に入る数字または日本語を書け。)

・教師になるためには，(　1　)年の学士課程修了と(　2　)年の修士課程修了が必要である。
・7歳で子どもは(　3　)する。
・5年生になるまで，教師は(　4　)による評価をしない。
・1クラスあたりの子どもの数は(　5　)人を超えない。
・学習の重点は(　6　)よりも探究や創作，実験に置く。
・親は，子どもの教育の責任は(　7　)にあると考えている。

(☆☆☆◎◎◎◎◎)

【２】次の(1)～(4)の各組において，a)とb)がほぼ同じ意味になるように，b)の(　　)内にあてはまる最も適切な一語をそれぞれ書け。

(1)　a)　Kanamaruza is the oldest theater in Japan.
　　b)　(　　) other theater in Japan is as old as Kanamaruza.

(2)　a)　A lot of people live in Takamatsu.
　　b)　The (　　) of Takamatsu is very large.

(3)　a)　You are so kind as to help me.
　　b)　It is kind (　　) you to help me.

(4) a) Anyone who leaves the room last should turn off the light.

b) (　　) leaves the room last should turn off the light.

(☆☆☆◎◎)

【3】次の(1)～(3)のそれぞれについて，下線部の①～④のいずれかに一箇所誤りがある。その箇所の番号と正しい表現に直したものを書け。

(1) ①Considered his ②age, Mr.Suzuki ③looks very ④young.

(2) The results ①of the examination ②should arrive ③until the end ④of the month.

(3) The guide asked ①us ②to observe the rule about ③not ④to walk on the grass.

(☆☆☆◎◎◎◎◎)

【4】次の(1)～(3)のそれぞれについて，日本文の意味になるように，(　　)内にあてはまる最も適切な一語を書け。

(1) この薬を飲んだらよく効くよ。

This medicine will do you (　　).

(2) どうぞくつろいでください。

Please make yourself at (　　).

(3) ごめんなさい。この辺りのことはよく知らないのです。

Sorry. I am a (　　) here.

(☆☆☆◎◎◎◎◎)

【5】次の英文は，米国のロケット開発者であるロバート・ゴダード博士が，病気がちでありながらも，細々と研究を続けていた時代の後の話である。次の英文を読み，あとの(1)～(5)の問いに答えよ。

It was the famous American aviator Charles Lindbergh who eventually persuaded millionaires to provide the financial support for Goddard. In 1929, Lindbergh heard about Goddard's experiments,visited him and was quickly convinced of the great importance of Goddard's rocket research.

Years later in 1959, as Lindbergh watched the United States' first satellite being launched into space, he said: "In 1929 I listened to Goddard discuss his ideas for the future development of rockets. Thirty years later, watching a giant rocket rise above the Air Force test base at Cape Canaveral, I ①(whether, he, then, wondered, dreaming, was) or I was dreaming now."

Having enough financial support, Goddard ②(make, dream, to, his, true, worked, come). Almost fifty years old, he moved to the dry and sunny southwest, near Roswell, New Mexico. [ A ] There, he developed and experimented with guided and stabilized rocket flights. He was the first to launch a rocket that flew faster than sound.

Then in 1939, World War Ⅱ began.A year later he left his New Mexico laboratory, went back East, and started working with America's defense forces. [ B ] Among these was the basic idea of the rocket launcher. Most of his other efforts, however, were politely ( a ).

Gradually, under pressure of work and worry, Goddard's health again began to fail. His old illness reappeared, but there was another far more deadly enemy—cancer. [ C ] ③If Goddard had lived seventeen years longer, he would have seen his life's work crowned with success.

In February 1962 America's first manned spacecraft to orbit the earth was launched at Cape Canaveral, Florida. Seven years later three Americans became the first men to land on the moon. ④Such achievements were possible only by the amazing power of liquid fuel rockets. And it is Robert Goddard's research and his ( b ) that have made these and every other modern rocket possible.

Today at the Goddard Space Flight Center in Maryland, which is dedicated to the memory of this great space pioneer and scientist, a small sign displays this statement he once made: "⑤It is difficult to say what is impossible, for the dream of yesterday is the hope of today and reality of tomorrow."

(1)　文中のA～Cの[　　]内にあてはまる最も適切な文を，次のア～ウからそれぞれ一つずつ選んで，その記号を書け。ただし，同じ選択肢を2回以上選ぶことはできない。

ア　On August 10, 1945, Robert Goddard died.

イ　He contributed many advanced ideas to help the war effort.

ウ　It was an ideal place for his workshop and rocket launching tower.

(2)　下線部①，②の(　　)内の語を，本文の内容に則して並べかえ，英語で書け。

(3)　下線部③，⑤を日本語に直して書け。

(4)　下線部④の指す内容を日本語で書け。

(5)　文中のa，bの(　　)内にあてはまる最も適切な語を，次のア～エからそれぞれ一つずつ選んで，その記号を書け。

a　ア　examined　　イ　continued　　ウ　ignored
　　エ　made

b　ア　penalties　　イ　parents　　ウ　invitations
　　エ　inventions

(☆☆☆◎◎◎◎◎)

## 【中学校】

【1】次の文は，中学校学習指導要領(平成20年3月告示，平成27年3月一部改正)第2章第9節外国語の「言語材料の取扱い」の一部を示そうとしたものである。次の1～3の(　　)内にあてはまる語を書け。

ア　(　1　)と綴(つづ)りとを関連付けて指導すること。

イ　文法については，(　2　)を支えるものであることを踏まえ，(　3　)と効果的に関連付けて指導すること。

(☆☆☆◎◎◎◎◎)

【2】次の(1)～(3)の日本語を英語で書け。

(1)　復習　　(2)　暗唱　　(3)　評価

(☆☆☆◎◎◎◎◎)

【3】英語の授業で，次の(1)～(4)のとき，授業者が英語でどのように話すかを書け。

(1)　グループで話し合いをするよう，生徒に指示するとき。

(2)　ワークシートに名前を書くよう，生徒に指示するとき。

(3)　「うどん」を英語でどう言うかをALTに尋ねるとき。

(4)　自分の国の有名な場所を一つ紹介するよう，ALTに頼むとき。

(☆☆☆◎◎)

【4】次の(1)，(2)の日本語を英語に直して書け。

(1)　本校のALTは，来日して1年半になる。

(2)　生徒たちは，私が学生時代に留学したことがあるかどうかをしばしば尋ねる。

(☆☆☆◎◎◎◎◎)

【5】中学校の運動会を行うのに適切なのは，春と秋どちらだと思うか。理由を添えて，自分の意見を30語以上の英語で書け。

(☆☆☆☆◎◎◎)

## 【高等学校】

【1】次の各文は，高等学校学習指導要領(平成21年3月告示)の「総則　第2款　各教科・科目及び単位数等」,「総則　第3款　各教科・科目の履修等」,「第8節　外国語　第3款　英語に関する各科目に共通する内容等」に基づき,「コミュニケーション英語Ⅰ」について述べたものである。あとの(1)，(2)の問いに答えよ。

・外国語として英語を履修させる学校においては，①(　すべての　/　選択させて　/　「英語会話」の履修後に　)生徒に履修させる科目である。また，標準単位数は，②(　2　/　3　/　4　)単位とする。

・次の(ア)～(ク)に示すすべての事項を，③(　既習事項　/　演習問題　/　言語活動　)と効果的に関連付けながら適切に取り扱う。

(ア)　不定詞の用法

(イ) 関係代名詞の用法
(ウ) 関係副詞の用法
(エ) 助動詞の用法
(オ) 代名詞のうち，itが名詞用法の句及び節を指すもの
(カ) 動詞の時制など
(キ) 仮定法
(ク) 分詞構文

(1) ①～③の(　　)内の語句または数字から最も適切なものを，それぞれ一つ選んで書け。

(2) (ア)～(ク)の文法事項のうち，中学校学習指導要領(平成20年3月告示，平成27年3月一部改正)と比較した際，高等学校で初めて取り扱う事項として示されているのはどれか。3つ選んで，その記号を書け。

(☆☆☆◎◎◎◎◎)

【2】英語の授業で，次の(1)～(4)のとき，授業者が英語でどのように話すかを書け。

(1) グループで話し合いをするよう，生徒に指示するとき。

(2) ワークシートに名前を書くよう，生徒に指示するとき。

(3) 生徒の言った答えが正解に非常に近いので，それに対して「惜しいね」と言うとき。

(4) 生徒たちにペアワークをさせる際，「この列の人たちは，たけしさんの役をしてください」と言うとき。

(☆☆☆◎◎◎◎)

【3】次の英文を読み，あとの(1)～(7)の問いに答えよ。

Quick quiz! Advice, information, (　①　), permission, equipment, luggage, garbage—what do these words all have in common? Perhaps many English teachers in Japan will swiftly recognize these words as mass nouns ②<u>(learners/that/particularly tricky/find/may)</u> to remember not to add an "s" to.

Dividing up the world into countable and uncountable nouns may be very difficult for English learners, but research suggests that ③it may have an impact on how English speakers view objects, compared to their Japanese counterparts.

Cognitive psychologists Mutsumi Imai and Dedre Gentner showed American and Japanese people objects that were of both a specific shape and material. Some of the objects were complex, such as a plastic lemon juicer, while others were simple, like a cork pyramid.

④For each object, two other alternatives were created, one with the same shape but a different material, and the other with a different shape but the same material. In the experiment, the researchers pointed to the main object, saying, "Look at this (made-up name). Can you point to the tray that also has the (made-up name) on it?"

Imai and Gentner found that almost all American and Japanese adults in the study chose shape alternatives rather than material for complex objects. However, regarding the simple objects, the Americans were much more likely to choose the object that had the same shape over the material alternative than the Japanese were.

[　A　] The researchers also administered the same test to 2-year-olds, 2 1/2-year-olds, and 4-year-olds of both countries. From age 2 the American children also exhibited a clear tendency to choose shape over material in identifying equivalent terms for simple objects. For the Japanese children, on the other hand, a preference for material equivalences emerged from age 2 1/2.

[　B　] Imai and Gentner suggest that the results may indicate that English speakers first classify objects according to whether they are countable or not, which leads to a preference for shape. ⑤Japanese speakers, on the other hand, are not focused on whether what they are seeing is countable and are therefore more likely to pay attention to other aspects like material.

[　C　] Applied linguist Vivian Cook and a team of researchers carried out an experiment similar to that of Imai and Gentner, examining the choices made by adult Japanese speakers who had lived in English-speaking countries a short time—from six months to two years and 11 months — with those who had stayed between three and eight years. They found that those Japanese speakers in the long-stay group were more likely to select the shape alternative than the short-stay speakers for the simple shapes tests.

⑥What we view as natural may depend on the language we use to identify objects. That this may also change as we learn other languages is one of the "countless" fascinations of cultural difference.

(1) 本文中の①の(　　)内にあてはまる最も適切な語を，次のア～エから一つ選んで，その記号を書け。

ア child　イ dish　ウ homework　エ book

(2) 下線部②の(　　)内の語句を，本文の内容に即して並べかえ，英語で書け。

(3) 下線部③が指す内容を日本語で書け。

(4) 下線部④に関して，プラスチックのレモン絞り器と対比させるために作られた物の例として，考えられる適切なものを，次のア～エから2つ選んで，その記号を書け。

ア 陶器のレモン絞り器

イ 金属の大根おろし器

ウ プラスチックの大根おろし器

エ コルクのピラミッド型の置物

(5) 下線部⑤，⑥を日本語に直して書け。

(6) 次の文は，本文中のA～Cの[　　]のいずれかに入る。最も適切な箇所を一つ選んで，その記号を書け。

It seems clear that a language you learn as a young child determines the way you view the world. But what about the influence of languages learned later?

(7) 本文の内容と一致するものを次のア～オから2つ選んで，その記号を書け。

ア　アメリカ人と日本人の成人は異なる3つの物を見せられ，それぞれに名前をつけるよう指示された。

イ　単純な形の物を分類するときの判断の傾向は，アメリカ人と日本人の成人の間で異なった。

ウ　アメリカ人の2歳児は，単純な形の物の分類に関して，素材を優先する傾向があった。

エ　成人の日本語話者は，英語圏での滞在期間が長い人の方が，滞在前後で，単純な形の物の分類の仕方が変わらない傾向が顕著であった。

オ　人の物の見方は，幼児期に身につけた言語だけでなく，後に学んだ言語によっても影響を受ける。

(☆☆☆☆◎◎◎◎)

【4】次の文中の下線部①，②を英語に直して書け。

①丸亀うちわ(Marugame fans)は江戸時代に金比羅(こんぴら)さん(Konpira Shrine)のおみやげとして最初に作られたと言われています。現在の生産量は年間約8,300万本，全国シェアの90％を誇り，平成9年5月，国の伝統的工芸品に指定されました。②約60年前には多くの人がうちわを使っていましたが，私たちの生活様式の変化とともにその需要は減少しました。しかしながら，風情あふれるうちわは，日本の夏に欠かせない風物詩として，根強い人気を保っています。

(☆☆☆◎◎◎◎◎)

【5】「高校生のスマートフォンの使用について，学校等が制限を設けるべきである」という意見に対するあなたの考えを30語以上の英語で書け。

(☆☆☆☆◎◎◎◎◎)

# 解答・解説

## 【中高共通】

【1】PART1　No.1　(D)　　No.2　(A)　　No.3　(B)　　No.4　(D)　　No.5　(C)　　PART2　No.1　(C)　　No.2　(B)　　No.3　(B)　　No.4　(D)　　PART3　1　3　　2　2　　3　就学　　4　数値　　5　20　　6　暗記　　7　親自身

〈解説〉PART1　放送は1回だけであるが，焦らずに落ち着いて聞けば，内容としては難しくはないだろう。　No.1　女性がそのとき買う予定のものは，発言の最後の1文にある。　No.2　男性は女性に「この辺りで小さな女の子を見ませんでしたか」と尋ねている。　No.3　女性は席を間違っていないので，そのまま27Bの席に座っていればよい。No.4　女性は仕事の大きなプロジェクトを終わらせるため8時まで退社できなかったため，パーティーに行けなかったのである。男性の発言のmissはこの場合「見つけそこなう」の意。　No.5　this yellow busやThat green busという発言から，乗ろうとするバスを目で見て確認できる位置で会話をしていることが推測できる。　PART2　No.1　カナダのトロント大学への1年間の留学に応募しようと考えているDaikiからKing教授がアドバイスを請われ，それに答えているという会話の流れである。　No.2　King教授の3つ目の発言にあるspeak upは「自分の意見を自由に話す」という意味である。　No.3　King教授の5つ目の発言に「カナダでは学生たちは互いに自由に意見を分かち合うことを望みます」とある。　No.4　Daikiの最後の発言に「次の日に申請書を持ってまいりますので，ご一読のうえアドバイスをいただけませんか」とある。　PART3　英文は2回放送されるので，1回目で聞き取れなかった部分を2回目で集中して聞くようにするとよいだろう。1回目のとき聞き取れなかった部分を補おうと考えるあまり，それ以降の部分を聞き逃すような事態は避けたい。

【2】(1)　No　(2)　population　(3)　of　(4)　Whoever

〈解説〉(1)　a)は「金丸座は日本で一番古い劇場です」なので，「金丸座ほど古い劇場は他にない」と言い換える。　(2)　a)は「高松にはたくさんの人が住んでいます」なので，「高松の人口はとても多い」と言い換える。　(3)　be kind of＋(人)で「(人)は親切だ」という意味になる。　(4)　whoever，whatever，wheneverなどの表現に慣れておこう。

【3】(1)　番号…①　正しい表現…Considering　(2)　番号…③　正しい表現…by　(3)　番号…④　正しい表現…walking

〈解説〉(1)「～を考慮すると」は，considering ～で表す。「考慮する」の主語は話し手なので，受身形にする理由がないからである。

(2)　untilは「～まで」の意味で，特定の時期まである動作が続く，という場合に使われる(例：This ticket is valid until 30 September.「この券は9月30日まで有効です」すなわち，9月30日まで「券が有効」という状況がずっと継続する)。問題文のように「～までに」という期限を表す言い方をしたい場合は，untilの代わりにbyやbeforeを使う。

(3)　aboutのような前置詞の後に動詞を続けたい場合は，必ず動名詞(～ing)の形に動詞を変形させなければならない。前置詞と動詞の間にnotが挟まれていても，惑わされないように。

【4】(1)　good　(2)　home　(3)　stranger

〈解説〉英語の日常会話やくだけた文章で使われる慣用表現については，日々の学習の中で着実に知識を増やしておこう。　(1)　do＋人＋goodで「(人)によく効く」の意味。　(2)　make oneself at homeはmake oneself comfortableと同様の意味。　(3)　I'm a stranger here「この辺りに対しては，私は新参者なのです」という表現。

【5】(1)　A　ウ　B　イ　C　ア　(2)　①　wondered whether he was dreaming then　②　worked to make his dream come true

(3)　③　もしあと17年長くゴダードが生きていたならば，彼は生涯の仕事が成功という栄冠を得るのを見たであろう。　⑤　何が不可能か述べることは難しい。というのも，昨日の夢が今日の希望であり，明日の現実であるからだ。　(4)　1962年2月，フロリダ州ケープ・カナベラルで，地球の軌道上に乗る米国初の有人宇宙船が飛び立ったこと。7年後，米国人3人が最初の月面に上陸した人となったこと。

(5)　a　ウ　　b　エ

〈解説〉(1)　A　直前の文が「ニューメキシコに移住した」なので，「それは研究所とロケット発射機を設置するのに最適な場所だった」を入れるのが適切。　B「その中にはロケット発射機の基礎となるようなアイディアもあった」という文が続いているので，「戦争のためにたくさんの先進的なアイディアを提供した」が入る。　C　cancer「がん」という言葉が登場しており，次に「彼があと17年長生きしていたら」という文が来ているので，空欄に入るのは「ロバートが亡くなった」という文であることがわかる。　(2)　①　空欄の後にor I was dreaming nowという表現があるので，これと対比するようにhe was dreaming thenという構文を作ることができれば，あとはI wondered whetherという語順で残りの語を並べることで，whether he was dreaming then or I was dreaming nowというwhether節を完成させることができる。

②「ゴダードは夢を叶えるために働いた」という意味。make one's dream come true「自分の夢を叶える」という表現。

(3)　③　過去の内容を仮定して，「もしあの時～だったら，～しただろう」という表現。　⑤　ここでのforは理由を表すbecauseと同じ意味で使われている。for以前の部分と「昨日夢だったことが今日の希望になり，明日の現実になる」という部分は切り離して2つの日本文として訳すと収まりがいいだろう。　(4)　such achievementsと複数形になっているので，この「達成」が意味する内容を複数挙げなければならない。指示語の指す内容は通常その直前に書かれている。

(5)　a「その中にはロケット発射機の基礎となるようなアイデアもあった。しかしながら彼のその他の功績は，丁重に(　a　)」という文脈なので，ignored「無視された」がふさわしい。　b「近代的ロケットを実現したのは，ロバート・ゴダードの研究と( b )」なので，inventions「発明」を入れるのが適切。

## 【中学校】

【1】1　発音　2　コミュニケーション　3　言語活動

〈解説〉中学校学習指導要領(平成20年3月告示，平成27年3月一部改正)第2章第9節外国語で掲げられる目標や指導内容の目指す究極のねらいは「聞くこと，話すこと，読むこと，書くことなどのコミュニケーション能力の基礎を養う」ことである。いずれかの言語活動に偏重することなく，コミュニケーション能力を総合的に育成できるようにする。

【2】(1)　review　(2)　recitation　(3)　evaluation

〈解説〉(1)　reviewの他に，recapやrevisionなどがある。　(2)　recitationの他に，repeating from memoryなどがある。memorizingは「記憶する」の意味なので少し違ってくる。　(3)　evaluationの他に，assessmentなどがある。

【3】(1)　Talk in your group.　(2)　Write your name on the worksheet.
(3)　How do you say *udon* in English?　(4)　Could you introduce a famous place in your country?

〈解説〉解答例以外には，次のような表現も考えられる。　(1)　Discuss in groups. / I would like you to consider this in groups.　(2)　Put your names on the handout.　(3)　What is the English word for *udon*? / How do you call *udon* in English?　(4)　Would you tell us about one famous place in your country?

【4】(1)　It is one and a half years since our ALT came to Japan.
(2)　My students often ask me whether I studied abroad while I was at university.

〈解説〉(1)　過去に開始した動作が現在まで続いていることを示すには，

現在完了形を使って作文しなければならない。「本校の」は単にourと表現してもよい。　(2)「生徒たちはしばしば尋ねる」が一番大切な枠組み。その後に目的語として，「私が学生時代に留学したことがあるかどうか」を置く。「～かどうか」はifまたはwhether節で表すことができる。「留学する」はstudy abroadで覚えておこう。

【5】I think spring is better for a sports festival at junior high schools. Spring is warmer and the weather is more predictable. Cherry blossoms also enhance the atmosphere and fun of the festival. (33 words)

〈解説〉春と秋のどちらを選んでもよいが，理にかなった理由付けができているか，語数を満たしているか，英語の表現として正しいかどうかが問われる。

## 【高等学校】

【1】(1)　①　すべての　②　3　③　言語活動　(2)　(ウ)，(キ)，(ク)

〈解説〉(1)　問題文にもあるように，「コミュニケーション英語Ⅰ」は必履修科目となっているので，その目標や指導事項，取扱いなどに関してはしっかりおさえておきたい。なお，英語以外の外国語を履修する場合は，学校設定科目として設ける1科目をこれにあてる。

(2)　他の選択肢はいずれも中学校においてその全部または一部を取り扱う。なお，「代名詞のうち，itが名詞用法の句及び節を指すもの」について，中学校ではitを名詞用法の句として用いるものを指導する。

【2】(1)　Talk in your group.　(2)　Write your name on the worksheet.　(3)　That's very close!　(4)　Students in this row, play the role of Takeshi.

〈解説〉解答例以外には，次のような表現も考えられる。　(1)　Discuss in groups. / I would like you to consider this in groups.　(2)　Put your names on the handout.　(3)　That was so close! / You almost got it!　(4)　I would like those in this row to play the role of Takeshi.

【3】(1)　ウ　(2)　that learners may find particularly tricky　(3)　世界を，数えられる名詞と数えられない名詞に分類すること

(4)　ア，ウ　(5)　⑤　一方，日本語話者は，自分が見ている物が数えられるかどうかを重視することはなく，したがって，素材のような他の面に注意を払う傾向が強い。　⑥　私たちが何を当り前だとみなすかは，物を識別するために私たちが使う言語で決まるのかもしれない。　(6)　C　(7)　イ，オ

〈解説〉(1)　この段落の後半部分を読むと，これらの単語は複数形になった時に-sをつけるべきでない単語，ということが分かる。childはchildrenと変化するので，他にあげられている単語が複数形になった時に特別な変化をしないことから，ここに同列にするのは不適切。

(2)　mass nounsを修飾するthat節。節の主語になれるのはlearnersしかない。その後には助動詞＋動詞の語順でmay findと続ける。

(3)　指示語の指す内容は通常その直前に出てくる。ここでは，dividing up the world into countable and uncountable nounsである。これは英語の学習者にとっては難しいことかも知れないが，英語話者の物の見方に影響を及ぼす可能性がある，というのである。　(4)　下線部④で述べられている，「同じ形で違う材質」「違う形で同じ材質」に当てはまるものを選ぶ。　(5)　⑤　少し複雑な構文だが，最初の部分はJapanese speakers are not focused on whether what they are seeing is countableというのが基本的な文。後半部分は，主語はそのままのJapanese speakersである。more likely to ～「より～する傾向にある」という意味。　⑥　主語はwhat we view as natural。depend on ～は「～に左右される」の意味。we ～ objectsまでが，the languageを修飾している。　(6)「幼児期に学習する言語が，その人の世界観を決定するというのは明らかと言えそうだ。しかし，その後に(大人になってから)学んだ言語に関してはどうだろうか？」という文。Cから始まる段落では，「英語圏に住んだことのある成人日本語話者」に対する実験につ

いて述べられているので，ここに挿入するのが適切と分かる。

(7) ア　第4段落で，実験実施者が「この(made-up name)を見てください。(made-up name)が載っているトレイを他にも見つけることができますか？」と被験者に質問した，と書かれていることに反する。

ウ　第6段落2文目のAmerican children also exhibited a clear tendency to choose shape over materialに反する。　エ　Cから始まる段落の最後の文，Japanese speakers in the long-stay group were more likely to select the shape alternative than ～に反する。

【4】① It is said that Marugame fans were first made in the Edo period as a souvenir from Konpira Shrine.　② A lot of people used fans about 60 years ago, but the demand for them has declined with the change of our lifestyle.

〈解説〉①「～と言われています」はit is said that …で表現する。「作られた」は過去の受身形で表現するのを忘れないように。madeはcreatedで，periodはeraで言い換えてもよい。　② While many people used to use fans about 60 years ago, the demand decreased as our lifestyle changed.などの表現でもよい。butの代わりにhoweverを使うとより改まった表現になる。

【5】I think that high schools should put some restriction on the students' use of smartphones. If they don't, the students may end up getting harmed from visiting malicious or unsuitable websites. / While the students have certain freedom and right to privacy, the school is responsible for protecting them. (49 words)

〈解説〉肯定と否定のどちらを選んでもよいが，理にかなった理由付けができているか，語数を満たしているか，英語の表現として正しいかどうかが問われる。

# 2015年度　実施問題

## 【中高共通】

【1】Listening Comprehension

There are three parts to this section, with special directions for each part. You may take notes while you are listening.

Now, let's begin Part 1. In this part, you will hear four conversations between two people. After each conversation, a third person will ask a question about what was said. Read the four possible answers on your test paper, choose the best answer to each question, and write it on your answer sheet. You will hear each conversation and question about it just one time.

No.1

(M) Are you really sure you had your purse when we came to this theater? Didn't you leave it at home?

(W) I'm positive I had it when we got here. I paid for the tickets, didn't I?

Question: Where does the woman think she lost her purse?

No.2

(M) Excuse me. Do you mind showing me where the Asian history books are?

(W) No, I don't mind. Follow me.

Question: What is the woman going to do?

No.3

(M) Why did you come late for class? Did you oversleep again this morning?

(W) I didn't today. This is what happened: I felt tired this morning from staying up late last night, so I took a seat in the train. That was a mistake.

I slept through the station.

Question: Why was the woman late for class?

No.4

(M) The new manager is different. He's more relaxed and friendlier.

(W) Time will tell. He's had no experience running a company. I'll wait before making my decision.

Question: What does the woman imply?

PART 1 (記号で書け。)

No.1

(A) On the way to the theater.

(B) In the station.

(C) In the theater.

(D) At home.

No.2

(A) Ask the man to find another person's help.

(B) Lead the man to the Asian history books.

(C) Send the man to the information desk.

(D) Refuse to show the man the books.

No.3

(A) She missed her usual train.

(B) Her train didn't arrive on time.

(C) She fell asleep in the station.

(D) She failed to get off at the right station.

No.4

(A) She's not sure if the manager will be good or not.

(B) She agrees with the man's opinion that the manager will be good.

(C) She thinks the manager should run the company differently.

(D) She's not sure who the manager really is.

Now, let's go on to Part 2. In this part, you will hear a conversation. After that, you will be asked four questions. Read the four possible answers on your test paper, decide which one is the best answer to the question you heard, and write it on your answer sheet. You will hear the conversation and questions about it two times.

(M) I've decided to change the topic for my paper. At first I wanted to write about Renaissance women, but my advisor told me the topic was too general.
(W) What did you finally decide to choose as a topic?
(M) I'm going to write about the popular culture of Paris in the 1920s.
(W) That sounds like a challenging topic.
(M) Well, I discussed it with my advisor. He suggested that I focus on something more specific, like the music or theater of the period.
(W) Have you started doing the research?
(M) I'm afraid I don't know where to start. I plan to go to the library later today and get some help in the reference section.

Question 1: What are the man and woman talking about?
Question 2: What topic did the man finally choose to write about?
Question 3: What suggestion did the advisor give?
Question 4: What is the man going to do after this conversation?

Listen again.

PART 2　(記号で書け。)

No.1

(A)　His paper about Renaissance women.
(B)　His problem with his advisor.
(C)　The music in the 1920s.

(D) The topic for his paper.

No.2

(A) Renaissance women and their culture.

(B) How to research a paper on music.

(C) The popular culture of Paris.

(D) Where to start his research.

No.3

(A) Discuss the topic with a librarian.

(B) Choose a topic that is less general.

(C) Write about Renaissance women.

(D) Do some research before choosing a topic.

No.4

(A) Find a new topic.

(B) Get some research material.

(C) Meet his advisor.

(D) Call the reference section.

Part 3. In this part, you will hear one lecture two times. Before listening, you should read the three questions carefully so that you can write the answers on the answer sheet. You have 20 seconds to read.

Now, listen.

Probably the first thing people weighed was gold. About six thousand years ago, the ancient Egyptians used weights made of cut and polished stones. Later, they made fancy bronze weights in the form of oxen and ducks.

One reason the Egyptians weighed gold was to keep people from cheating. Only the pharaoh and a few great nobles could own gold. When the pharaoh wanted to have a ring or necklace made, gold was taken from the royal treasury and given to the goldsmiths.

But there was always a risk. The goldsmiths might try to keep a little of the gold instead of using it all. So, before the gold was given to the goldsmiths, it was always weighed on a balance.

The gold was put into one of the pans of the balance. One or more small weights, shaped like animals, were then put into the other pan until the weights and the gold balanced. And, after the ornament was made, it was weighed − to make sure that the goldsmiths hadn't kept any of the gold.

After a while, someone came up with the idea of making small pieces of gold or silver that were marked to show their weight. And these weights were the beginning of money - the first coins. That is why some money names were originally the names for units of weight.

Listen again.

PART 3　(述べられている内容についての(1)～(3)の問いに対する答えを，日本語で書け。)

Questions

(1)　When did the ancient Egyptians use weights made of stones?

(2)　What did it mean that the ornament the goldsmiths had made and the weights balanced?

(3)　What kind of weights became the first coins?

This is the end of the Listening Comprehension Section.

(☆☆☆◎◎◎)

【２】次の(1)～(4)の各組において，a)とb)がほぼ同じ意味になるように，b)の(　　)内にあてはまる最も適切な一語をそれぞれ書け。

(1)　a)　Bill was so kind that he picked me up at the station.

b)　Bill was kind (　　) (　　) pick me up at the station.

(2)　a)　I didn't want to hear her hard-luck story, for I had heard it many times before.

b) (　　) (　　) it many times before, I didn't want to hear her hard-luck story.

(3) a) Needless to say, honesty is the best policy.

b) It goes (　　) (　　) that honesty is the best policy.

(4) a) He made us write an essay on environmental pollution.

b) We (　　) (　　) (　　) (　　) an essay on environmental pollution.

(☆☆☆◎◎◎)

【3】次の(1)～(3)のそれぞれについて，下線部の①～④のいずれかに一箇所誤りがある。その箇所の番号と，正しい表現に直したものを書け。

(1) ①<u>Due to</u> ②<u>poor eyesight</u>, he always has to ③<u>put on</u> ④<u>contact lenses</u> while driving.

(2) Wind power is ①<u>one of</u> ②<u>the most</u> promising types of energy, ③<u>and</u> so ④<u>does</u> solar power.

(3) I am very ①<u>sorry for</u> any ②<u>inconvenient</u> this ③unexpected delay ④<u>has caused</u> you.

(☆☆☆☆◎◎◎)

【4】次の(1)～(3)のそれぞれについて，(　　)内にあてはまる最も適切なものをア～エから一つ選んで，その記号を書け。

(1) A: Oh, Mary! Come right in. Would you like something to drink?

B: (　　) I've just had a cup of coffee.

ア Yes, thank you.　　イ Certainly.

ウ No, thank you.　　エ I don't drink.

(2) A: I have an appointment with Doctor Smith for this afternoon but I'd like to change it if possible.

B: (　　) What time would be convenient?

ア No, I'm afraid you can't.　　イ Certainly.

ウ How about this afternoon?　　エ You're welcome.

(3)　A: Would you like some help with those bags?

B: Yes. Could you put them in the car for me?

A: Sure. I'll be glad to.

B: (　　)

ア　Don't mention it.　　イ　It's very kind of you.

ウ　Thank you just the same.　　エ　You are most welcome.

(☆☆☆☆◎◎◎)

## 【中学校】

【1】次の文は，中学校学習指導要領(平成20年3月告示)「第2章　第9節　外国語　第1　目標」を示そうとしたものである。次の1～3の(　　)内にあてはまる語句を書け。

外国語を通じて，(　1　)に対する理解を深め，積極的にコミュニケーションを図ろうとする(　2　)を図り，聞くこと，話すこと，読むこと，書くことなどのコミュニケーション能力の(　3　)を養う。

(☆☆◎◎◎)

【2】次の(1)～(3)の日本語を英語で書け。

(1)　学習指導要領　　(2)　過去時制　　(3)　道徳教育

(☆☆◎◎◎)

【3】次の(1)～(4)のとき，英語でどのように話すかを書け。

(1)　生徒に，自分の後に続いて英文を音読させたいとき。

(2)　生徒に，CDを聴かせて空欄を埋めさせたいとき。

(3)　ALTに，指導案を見せてアイデアを求めたいとき。

(4)　ALTに，自分の国と日本との違いを生徒に話してもらいたいとき。

(☆☆◎◎◎)

【4】次の英文を読み，あとの(1)～(5)の問いに答えよ。

Since the late 1970s, the world has increasingly (　1　) interdependent in several ways. First of all, the amount and speed of economic exchange between different nations has increased dramatically. This has created a global economy where trade and finances are ever expanding. Secondly, technological advances in communication have fundamentally changed the way we interact with the rest of the world. Mutual exchange between different societies and cultures has increased to the extent that we ①(living, one, village, were, if, to, global, we, in, feel, tend, as). Finally, the progress in transportation has enabled more and more people to visit other countries and regions. For many living in developed nations, traveling abroad is no longer a luxury to enjoy.

It is important to note that the deepening of interdependence among nations ②(values, created, common, and, only, has, not) interests but also common problems. Today, many problems do not respect national borders. Against this background, a new term has been made : *Global Issues*. Indeed, when viewed more broadly, the term Global Issues is more than just a catchphrase, but a shift in perspective.

Basically, there are two different views on Global Issues. Optimists tend to believe that we will overcome ③the current problems with future progress in science and technology, coupled with increased international cooperation among countries. Thus, for them there is hope for our future. On the other hand, for pessimists, the picture looks very different. Such issues as global warming, food shortages, and natural disasters have ( 2 ) pessimists to argue that if it were not for fundamental shifts in our way of thinking, the fate of our planet would be quite dark. ④In contrast to the optimists' view, pessimists believe that global issues are so serious that we must fundamentally change our current lifestyle.

It is up to each person to decide his / her perspective of Global Issues. But, from the historical point of view, one thing I can assure you is that the rising attention to Global Issues represents ⑤a paradox. The existence of Global Issues itself requires a fundamental change in a traditional perspective. On the other hand, we cannot solve these issues without looking back on our past experience. The term Global Issues seems to indicate the importance of rediscovering the valuable lessons of the past in order to cope with these newly emerging problems. If we do this, the future of our planet, and indeed all our fellow inhabitants, will be (　3　).

(「平成20年度福島大学経済経営学類(前期)試験問題」による)

(1)　文中の1～3の(　　)内にあてはまる最も適切な語を，次のア～エからそれぞれ一つずつ選んで，その記号を書け。

ア　forced　　イ　secured　　ウ　lost　　エ　become

(2)　下線部①，②の(　　)内の語を，本文の内容に即して並べかえ，英語で書け。

(3)　下線部③の具体例を文中より3つ抜き出して，それぞれ日本語に直して書け。

(4)　下線部④を日本語に直して書け。

(5)　下線部⑤の内容を日本語で書け。

(☆☆☆☆☆◎◎◎)

【5】次の文中の下線部①，②を英語に直して書け。

①全国で最も面積の小さい県である香川県は，四国の北東に位置しています。県庁所在地は高松市です。②うどんの消費量が多い県で，「讃岐うどん」で知られています。

(☆☆☆☆◎◎◎)

【6】車を運転することに比べ，自転車に乗ることの利点について，あなたの意見を30語以上の英語で書け。

(☆☆☆☆☆◎◎◎)

## 【高等学校】

【1】次の各文は，高等学校学習指導要領(平成21年3月告示)「第2章　第8節　外国語　第2款　各科目」における，ある科目の目標を示したも

のである。次の(1)～(5)の各目標にそれぞれ対応する科目名を書け。

(1) 英語を通じて，積極的にコミュニケーションを図ろうとする態度を育成するとともに，身近な話題について会話する能力を養う。

(2) 英語を通じて，積極的にコミュニケーションを図ろうとする態度を育成するとともに，事実や意見などを多様な観点から考察し，論理の展開や表現の方法を工夫しながら伝える能力を養う。

(3) 英語を通じて，積極的にコミュニケーションを図ろうとする態度を育成するとともに，聞くこと，話すこと，読むこと，書くことなどの基礎的な能力を養う。

(4) 英語を通じて，積極的にコミュニケーションを図ろうとする態度を育成するとともに，情報や考えなどを的確に理解したり適切に伝えたりする基礎的な能力を養う。

(5) 英語を通じて，積極的にコミュニケーションを図ろうとする態度を育成するとともに，情報や考えなどを的確に理解したり適切に伝えたりする能力を更に伸ばし，社会生活において活用できるようにする。

(☆☆☆◎◎◎)

【2】次の(1)～(5)のとき，生徒に英語でどのように話すかを書け。

(1) 自分の後に続いて英文を音読させたいとき。

(2) 教科書の10ページを開かせたいとき。

(3) プリントを後ろから前に送らせたいとき。

(4) CDを聴かせて空欄を埋めさせたいとき。

(5) 授業を終えることを告げたいとき。

(☆☆◎◎◎)

【3】次の英文は，2005年に書かれたアメリカの新聞記事の一部である。英文を読み，あとの(1)～(8)の問いに答えよ。ただし，英文の前の[1]～[9]の数字は段落番号を示している。

[1] There was a time when Americans thought they understood class. The

upper crust vacationed in Europe and worshiped an Episcopal God. The middle class drove Ford Fairlanes, settled the San Fernando Valley and enlisted as company men. The working class belonged to the A.F.L.-C.I.O., voted Democratic and did not take cruises to the Caribbean.

2 Today, the country has gone a long way toward an appearance of classlessness. Americans of all sorts are awash in luxuries that would have dazzled their grandparents. Social diversity has erased many of ①the old markers. It has become harder to read people's status in the clothes they wear, the cars they drive, the votes they cast, the god they worship, the color of their skin. The contours of class have blurred; some say they have disappeared.

3 But class is still a powerful force in American life. Over the past three decades, it has come to play a greater, not lesser, role in important ways. At a time when education ( ② ) more than ever, success in school remains linked tightly to class. At a time when the country is increasingly integrated racially, the rich are isolating themselves more and more. At a time of extraordinary advances in medicine, class differences in health and lifespan are wide and appear to be widening.

4 One difficulty in talking about class is that the word means different things to different people. Class is rank, it is tribe, it is culture and taste. It is attitudes and assumptions, a source of identity, a system of exclusion. To some, it is just money. It is an accident of birth ③[a life / influence / that / of / can / outcome / the ]. Some Americans barely notice it; others feel its weight in powerful ways.

5 At its most basic, class is one way societies sort themselves out. ④Even societies built on the idea of eliminating class have had stark differences in rank. Classes are groups of people of similar economic and social position; people who, for that reason, may share political attitudes, lifestyles, consumption patterns, cultural interests and opportunities to get ahead. Put 10 people in a room and a pecking order soon emerges.

6 When societies were simpler, the class landscape was easier to read. Marx divided 19th-century societies into just two classes; Max Weber added a few more. ⑤<u>As</u> societies grew increasingly complex, the old classes became more ⑥<u>heterogeneous</u>. As some sociologists and marketing consultants see it, the commonly ( ⑦ ) big three - the upper, middle and working classes - have broken down into dozens of microclasses, defined by occupations or lifestyles.

7 A few sociologists go so far as to say that social complexity has made the concept of class meaningless. Conventional big classes have become so diverse - in income, lifestyle, political views - ⑧<u>that</u> they have ceased to be classes at all, said Paul W.Kingston, a professor of sociology at the University of Virginia. To him, American society is a "ladder with lots and lots of ⑨<u>rungs</u>."

8 "There is not one decisive break saying that the people below ⑩<u>this</u> all have this common experience," Professor Kingston said. "Each step is equal-sized. Sure, for the people higher up this ladder, their kids are more apt to get more education, better health insurance, But ⑪<u>that</u> doesn't mean there are classes."

9 Many other researchers disagree. "Class awareness and the class language is receding at the very moment that class has reorganized American society," said Michael Hout, a professor of sociology at the University of California, Berkeley. "I find these 'end of class' discussions naive and ironic, because we are at a time of booming inequality and this massive reorganization of where we live and how we feel, even in the dynamics of our politics. Yet people say, 'Well, the era of class is over.'"

(1) 下線部①の例を 2 段落の中より探し，<u>一つ</u>抜き出して書け。

(2) 文中の②，⑦の(　　)内には，次の[　　]内の語を適切な形に直したものが入る。それぞれ適切な形に直した一語を書け。

[accept　cultivate　matter　reserve]

(3)　下線部③の[　　]内の語句を，本文の内容に即して並べかえ，英語で書け。

(4)　下線部④を日本語に直して書け。

(5)　下線部⑤，⑧について，同じ用法を用いている英文を，次のア～エからそれぞれ一つ選んで，その記号を書け。

⑤　ア　If you are not sure how to behave, do <u>as</u> I do.

　　イ　<u>As</u> it was getting late, I decided to stop at a hotel.

　　ウ　<u>As</u> you know, I'll be leaving tomorrow.

　　エ　<u>As</u> he grew older, he grew more obstinate.

⑧　ア　So great was my surprise <u>that</u> I could not utter a word.

　　イ　Please speak louder so <u>that</u> everyone can hear you.

　　ウ　There was no hope <u>that</u> he would recover his health.

　　エ　He was glad <u>that</u> his wife succeeded in the test.

(6)　下線部⑥，⑨とほぼ同じ意味で使われている単語を[7]～[9]段落の中よりそれぞれ抜き出して書け。

(7)　下線部⑩が指すものを本文から抜き出して書け。

(8)　下線部⑪が指す内容を日本語で書け。

(☆☆☆☆☆◎◎◎)

【4】次の文中の下線部①，②を英語に直して書け。

①<u>NEETというのは，1990年代後半，イギリスで最初に現れた言葉である</u>。それは仕事をせず，教育や職業訓練を受けていない若者を意味している。②<u>日本では，働きも学びもしていない若者が60万人ほどいると推定されており，日本政府はそのような人々に対する支援を行っている</u>。

(☆☆☆☆◎◎◎)

【5】働くことの大切さや喜びを生徒に教えるためにどのような取り組みをすればよいか。あなたの意見を30語以上の英語で書け。

(☆☆☆☆☆◎◎◎)

# 解答・解説

## 【中高共通】

【1】PART 1　No.1　(C)　　No.2　(B)　　No.3　(D)　　No.4　(A)
PART 2　No.1　(D)　　No.2　(C)　　No.3　(B)　　No.4　(B)
PART 3　(1)　約6000年前　　(2)　金細工職人が与えられた金を全て使った　　(3)　重さが刻印された金や銀の小片

〈解説〉リスニング問題では，放送が始まる前に選択肢に一通り目を通しておくとよい。　PART 1　No.1　質問は「女性はどこで財布をなくしたと思っていますか」。女性のセリフにI'm positive I had it when we got here.とあり，会話の流れを追って，it(＝purse)とhere(＝to this theater)の指しているものを正しく把握しているかが問われている。女性は「私が劇場に着いたとき，財布を持っていたのは確かです」とあり，劇場までは財布があったと思っているので，(C)「劇場の中」が正解。positive「確信している」。　No.2　Do you mind doing ～?は「～することを気にかけますか」→「(気にかけないなら)～してくれませんか」という依頼の表現。男性はアジアの歴史の本がどこにあるのか教えてくれるように女性に頼んでいる。女性はNo, I don't mind.「いいえ，(教えることを)気にかけません」→「いいですよ」と応じているので，(B)「男性をアジアの歴史の本に案内する」が正解。lead＋人＋to ～「人を～へ案内する」。　No.3　男性が授業に遅れた理由を女性に尋ね，This is what happened.「こういうことなんです」と女性が応えている。sleep throughは「～に気づかず寝続ける」という意味。I slept through the station「駅を寝過ごす」と同じ内容の(D)「正しい駅で降りそこなう」が正解。　No.4　質問文は「女性は何を暗に示していますか」。男性が新しいマネージャーをほめているのに対して，女性はTime will tell.「時間が経てばわかる」やI'll wait before making my decision.「待ってから判断するわ」と言って決めかねていることから，(A)「マネージャーがいいのかそうでないのかわからない」が正解。imply「暗に示す」。

PART 2　No.1　会話の流れは，「論文のテーマを変更することに決めた」→「最初はルネサンス期の女性」→「1920年代のパリの大衆文化」→「もっと限定して1920年代のパリの音楽や演劇」→「図書館に行って調査する」となり，一貫して男性の論文のテーマ(topic for his paper)をどうするか，という話をしているので(D)が正解。　No.2　女性の1つ目のセリフで，What did you finally decide to choose as a topic?「最終的にテーマとして何を選ぶことに決めましたか」とたずね，男性はI'm going to write about the popular culture of Paris in the 1920s.「1920年代のパリの大衆文化について書くつもりです」と応えているので，(C)が正解。　No.3　男性の3つ目のセリフで，I discussed it with my advisor. ….「指導教官と話し合いました。彼はもっと限定したものに焦点を絞るべきだと提案しました」とあることから(B)が正解。more specific「より限定した」をほぼ同じ意味のless general「あまり一般的でない」に言い換えている。　No.4　男性の最後のセリフで，I plan to go to the library later today ….「今日このあと図書館に行って，参考図書室で役立つもの(資料)を手に入れる」とあるので，(B)「調査資料を手に入れる」が正解。　PART 3　(1)　第1段落2文目に「約6,000年前，古代エジプト人は研磨された切石の重りを使用した」とある。　(2)　質問文は「金細工職人が作った装飾品(指輪やネックレス)と重りが釣り合うとはどういう意味だったか」。第3段落に「金細工職人は金を全部使う代わりに，少しとっておこうとするかもしれないので，金細工職人に渡す前に，はかりで重さを測る」とあり，第4段落では「金が天秤の皿の1つに置かれ，1つ以上の動物の形の小さな重りが，金と釣り合うまでもう1つの皿に置かれた。装飾品が作られたあと，金細工職人が金をとっておかないことを確かめるために重さを測った」とあることから，装飾品と重りが釣り合うということは，金細工職人が金をとっておかずに全て使ったことを意味する。goldsmith「金細工職人」，balance「天秤；釣り合う」，pan「天秤の皿」，ornament「装飾品」。(3)　第5段落に「しばらくして，だれかが重さを示す刻印のある金や銀の小片を作ることを考え出した。そしてこれらの重りがお金の始まり―最初の硬貨であった」とある。

【2】(1) enough to　(2) Having heard　(3) without saying　(4) were made to write

〈解説〉(1)　a)は〈so＋形容詞［副詞］＋that ～〉「とても～なので…」を用いた「ビルはとても親切なので，駅で私を車に乗せてくれた」という意味の文。b)はkind(形容詞)の後に空欄があるので，〈形容詞［副詞］＋enough to do ～〉「～するのに十分…」を使って表す。

(2)　a)は「私は彼女の不運な話を聞きたくなかった。というわけは，私は以前それを何度も聞いていたから」。forはここでは接続詞で，「というわけは」の意味。b)は「以前何度も聞いていたので，私は彼女の不運な話を聞きたくなかった」と考え，Because I had heard it many times before, I didn't want to hear her hard-luck story.とする。これを(　)の数に合わせて接続詞を省いた分詞構文の文にする。従位節はhad＋過去分詞(過去完了)で，主節の動詞(didn't want，過去形)の表す時よりも前の時を表しているので，Having heard ～の分詞構文を作る。

(3)　a)のneedless to sayは「言うまでもなく」という意味。b)はこれと同じ意味のIt goes without saying that ～「～は言うまでもない」。

(4)　a)は使役動詞makeを用いた，「彼は私たちに環境汚染についての論文を書かせた」という意味。b)はその使役動詞の受け身の文。usを主語のweにし，madeをwere madeにする。原形のwriteをto writeにすることを忘れずに，We were made to write ～とする。

【3】(1)　番号　③　　正しい表現　wear　(2)　番号　④　　正しい表現　is　(3)　番号　②　　正しい表現　inconvenience

〈解説〉(1)　put on contact lensesは「コンタクトレンズをつける」という動作を表す。問題文は「視力が悪いので，いつもコンタクトレンズをつけている」という状態を表すのでput on → wearにする。　(2)　前半は「風力は最も有望なエネルギーの1つ」とあり，and 以下は「太陽光発電も最も有望なエネルギーの1つ」であると考え，solar power is one of the most promising types of energyとbe動詞のisを用いて表す。そのあと下線部をso「そう」にして，前に出して倒置構文で表す。つまり動詞はdoes→isにする。　(3)　②は前置詞forの目的語で，目的語は品詞でいうと基本的に名詞なので，convenient(形容詞)→ convenience(名詞)にする。

【4】(1)　ウ　　(2)　イ　　(3)　イ

〈解説〉(1)　AがWould you like something to drink?「何か飲み物はいかがですか」と申し出ていて，Bは空欄のあとでI've just had a cup of coffee.「ちょうどコーヒーを飲んだところです」とある。このやりとりから申し出を断っていると考え，ウ No, thank you.「いいえ，結構です」が正解。　(2)　AがI'd like to change it if possible.「可能ならそれ(スミス先生との今日の午後の予約)を変えたい」と依頼していて，Bは空欄のあとでWhat time would be convenient?「何時が都合がいいですか」と時間を決めようとしている。Bが依頼を受け入れたと考え，イ Certainly.「もちろん」が正解。　(3)　BがCould you put them in the car for me?「私のためにそれら(バッグ)を車に入れてくれませんか」と依頼している。AはSure. I'll be glad to (put them in the car for you).「もちろん。喜んで」と依頼を受け入れてくれたので，Bはそれに対し，イ It's very kind of you.「あなたはとても親切です」とお礼を述べる流れとなる。

## 【中学校】

【1】1　言語や文化　　2　態度の育成　　3　基礎

〈解説〉中学生が中学校で外国語を学ぶ目標を問われている。学習する言語と，その言語を通じていろいろな国の文化への理解を深める。また，外国人と話した経験がなく，物怖じする中学生に積極的にコミュニケーションを図ろうという態度を身につけさせる。中学校の3年間という期間を通じて，4技能(聞くこと，話すこと，読むこと，書くこと)を用いたコミュニケーション能力の基礎を養うことが目標となる。

【2】(1) the Course of Study (2) past tense (3) moral education

〈解説〉(1) 「学習指導要領」は，全国のどの地域で教育を受けても，同じような水準の教育を受けられるように，文部科学省が学習(study)の進むべき進路(course)を定めたもの。日本の学校は学習指導要領に沿って指導を行っている。 (2) 現在時制はpresent tense，未来時制はfuture tenseという。 (3) moral「道徳」，education「教育」。

【3】(1) Repeat after me. (2) Listen to the CD and fill in the blanks. (3) This is my lesson plan. Do you have any ideas? (4) Could you tell the students about the differences between your country and Japan?

〈解説〉(1) 自分のあとについて，英語を繰り返してもらいたい時の定番表現。 (2) 多くの場合，空欄は1つでないので，blanksと複数形になっている。 (3) 「指導案」はlesson plan。Do you have ～?のかわりにCould you suggest ～?なども可。 (4) Could you tell the students about ～?で「～について生徒に話してもらえますか」という意味。about以下に話してもらいたいことを言う。

【4】(1) 1 エ 2 ア 3 イ (2) ① tend to feel as if we were living in one global village ② has created not only common values and (3) ・地球温暖化 ・食糧不足 ・自然災害 (4) 楽観主義者たちの考え方とは対照的に，悲観主義者たちは，地球規模問題はとても深刻なので，私たちは今の生活様式を根本的に変えなければならないと信じている。 (5) 地球規模問題が存在することで，従来のものの見方の根本的な変革が求められる一方で，この問題の解決には過去の経験を振り返ることが不可欠であるということ。

〈解説〉(1) 1 become interdependentで「相互依存する」という意味になる。 2 to argueがあるのでforce＋目的語(人)＋to do「人に～するように強いる」を使って，地球温暖化や食糧不足や自然災害といった問題が「悲観論者に(無理矢理)～を主張させる」とする。 3 第4段落の最後の文のthisは直前の文の「新しく生じている問題に対処するために，過去の価値ある教訓を再発見すること」を指す。「もしこれをすると，私たちの惑星，つまり私たちの仲間の住民は」～とあるので，教訓を再発見して地球規模の問題が解決されれば「守られる」と考え，secure「守る，安全にする」の過去分詞securedのイが正解。

(2)　①　第1段落は，1970年代以来，世界は相互依存が加速し，経済交流や通信技術の進歩で，世界の人たちと交流できるようになったとある。その結果，「異なる社会や文化の人たちが国境を越えて容易に交わり～」，という文脈なのでone global village「ひとつの地球村」になっていくと考える。feel as ifは「まるで～のように感じる」という意味。従位接続詞if以下はS＋V ～にし，仮定法なので動詞は過去形になって，as if we were living in one global village「まるでひとつの地球村に住んでいるよう」でまとめる。tend to＋動詞の原形で「～しがちである」なのでtend to feel as if ～.「まるで～と感じがちである」にする。②　下線部②を含む第2段落1文目は，It is important to note that ～.「that以下に注意することが重要である」という構文であり，that以下の意味は「国々の間の相互依存を深めることは，共通の価値観や関心ばかりでなく，共通の問題もまた生み出してきた」となる。not only ～ but also …「～ばかりか…も」。　(3)　第3段落では，楽観主義者と悲観主義者が同じ現代の地球規模の問題をどう考えているかを述べたもの。5文目のSuch issues as ～以下に具体的にどんな問題があるのか3つ言われている。　(4)　in contrast to ～は「～と対照的に」で，believe that S ＋ V ～は「～を信じる」という意味。この文の骨格はIn contrast to ～, pessimists believe that ～. で，「～と対照的に，悲観主義者たちは～を信じている」となる。that以下のso ～ that S ＋ V …は「とても～なので…」という構文で，結果を表す副詞節を導く。「地球規模の問題はとても深刻なので(その結果)私たちは～」となる。

(5)　第4段落の2文目のhistorical point of view「歴史的視点」とは，過去の出来事から得られた教訓からものを見るということ。新しく生じている問題は従来のものの見方では対処できないので根本的にそれを変革するという考えと，過去の出来事から学んだ，現在にも通じる教訓を活かすという視点が矛盾(paradox)する。その矛盾が3文目と4文目に書かれている。

【5】① Kagawa Prefecture, the smallest Japanese prefecture in land area, is located in north-eastern Shikoku. ② Kagawa is a large consumer of *udon* noodles and is famous for its Sanuki *udon*.

〈解説〉①「香川県は四国の北東に位置しています」→ Kagawa Prefecture is located in north-eastern Shikoku. が文の骨格。Kagawa Prefectureの後ろに「全国で最も面積の小さい」という修飾部を置く。英語になるように「土地面積で一番小さい日本の県である」→ the smallest Japanese prefecture in land areaとして同格でつなげる。 ② この文を前半の「(香川は)うどんの～」と，後半の「(香川は)「讃岐うどん」で～」に分けて，andでつなげる。前半の「うどんの消費量が多い県」は「うどんの大量消費者」に言い換え，Kagawa is a large consumer of *udon* noodlesにする。後半は「～で知られている」を「～で有名な」にしてand の次にis famous for its Sanuki *udon*. にする。

【6】(解答例) Riding a bicycle is a cheaper and more environmentally-friendly way to travel than driving a car, which needs gasoline to run and emits exhaust gas. Bicycling also helps you keep in shape, so these days more and more people ride a bicycle to school or work. (46語)

〈解説〉まず「燃料費がかからない」,「環境に優しい」,「健康によい」など車を運転することよりも自転車に乗ることの利点を2，3点あげる。前提として車を運転することに比べ，とあるので比較級で書き表すほうがよい。

## 【高等学校】

【1】(1) 英語会話 (2) 英語表現Ⅰ (3) コミュニケーション英語基礎 (4) コミュニケーション英語Ⅰ (5) コミュニケーション英語Ⅲ

〈解説〉(1)　後半に「身近な話題について会話する能力を養う」とあることから，「英語会話」が正解。　(2)　英語を聞いたり読んだりして得た事実や意見を，聞き手や読み手の目的に応じて適切に表現(話したり書いたり)しながら，情報や考えを伝える能力の向上を図るのが「英語表現Ⅰ」の目的。　(3)　後半に「聞くこと，話すこと，読むこと，書くことなどの基礎的な能力を養う」とあり，中学校における基礎的な学習内容の定着をはかり，高校で英語を履修するすべての生徒が学ぶ「コミュニケーション英語Ⅰ」へ円滑に移行することが目的なので，「コミュニケーション英語基礎」が正解。　(4)　事物に関する紹介や対話などを聞いて，または説明や物語などを読んで，情報や考えなどを理解したり，概要や要点をとらえ，話し合ったり意見の交換をしたり，簡潔に書けるようにすることが，「コミュニケーション英語Ⅰ」の目的。　(5)　後半の「情報や考えなどを的確に理解したり適切に伝えたりする能力」は，「コミュニケーション英語Ⅱ」で伸ばすとしている事項。これを「更に伸ばし，社会生活において活用できるようにすること」が，「コミュニケーション英語Ⅲ」の目的。

【２】(1)　Repeat after me.　(2)　Open your textbook to page ten.　(3)　Pass the papers forward.　(4)　Listen to the CD and fill in the blanks.　(5)　That's all for today.

〈解説〉(1)　自分のあとについて，英語を繰り返してもらいたいときの定番表現。　(2)　Open your textbook to page ～. ～のところにページ数を入れる。特定のページを開かせたいときの決まった言い方。
(3)　pass ～ forwardで「前に～を送る，手渡す」。　(4)　「CDを聴く」はlisten to the CD. 多くの場合，空欄は1つではないので，blanksと複数形になる。　(5)　「これで授業を終わります」というときの決まった言い方。

【３】(1)　the clothes they wear　(2)　②　matters　⑦　accepted　(3)　that can influence the outcome of a life　(4)　階級をなくそうとい

う考えに基づく社会にも，地位の違いは厳然と存在する。

(5) ⑤ エ ⑧ ア (6) ⑥ diverse ⑨ step

(7) one decisive break (8) 社会的により高い地位にある人の子どもの方が，より高度な教育や，よりよい健康保険を手にする可能性が高いということ

〈解説〉(1) 第1段落では上流，中流，労働者階級ごとに旅行先や住む場所，乗る車などに違いがあると述べられ，第2段落ではすべてのアメリカ人がぜいたく品で満たされ，階級差がなくなったとある。その結果，社会が多様になって，昔の特徴を示すもの(the old markers)が消え，具体例としてはthe clothes they wearやthe cars they drive，the votes they cast，the god they worship，the color of their skinなどに階級ごとの特徴が消えて，人々の社会的地位を読み取ることが難しくなった，とあることから，これらのいずれかを書けばよい。 (2) ② 空欄を含む文の主節で「～のときは，学校の成功(学歴での成功)が階級と密接に関係したままである」とあることから，「教育がますます重要だと思われているとき」と考え，matter「重要である」を選ぶ。主語はeducationで三人称単数，時制は現在なのでmattersが正解。more than ever「ますます」。 ⑦ 空欄を含む文の前の文で「社会がますます複雑になると，古い階級はもっと多くの異なる成分(異なる階級)からなる」とあり，問題の文ではそれをもう少し細かく述べている。(古くから)一般に「受け入れられていた」階級が，新しい小さな階級に分かれたと考え，acceptを選ぶ。階級は人々に「受け入れられていた」ので受け身を表す過去分詞のacceptedにする。 (3) 第4段落1～4文目では，classの意味を，人それぞれ「地位」だったり，「部族」，「文化」や「趣味」，「アイデンティティ」，「お金」などと理解していると述べられている。これらはどこの国や地域，家庭に生まれるかで決まることが多く，すなわちAn accident of birth can influence the outcome of a life.「生まれ合わせは人生の結果に影響を及ぼす可能性がある」と見当をつけて英文を作る。文頭にIt is とあり，[ ]内にthatがあるので，It is ～ that …の強調構文にして，an accident of birthをIt is と that の間に

入れて強調する。　(4)　第5段落の1文目で「階級は社会を落ち着かせる(安定させる)方法である」とあるが，2文目で「その階級がない社会でさえ」厳然とした地位の相違があると見当をつける。そして，そのような意味になるようにbuiltを形容詞用法の過去分詞で直前のsocietiesを修飾しているととらえ，built on the idea of eliminating class「階級をなくそうという考えに基づかれた社会でさえ」とする。stark「厳然とした」，difference in「～における相違」。　(5)　⑤　下線部⑤のasは「社会がますます複雑になるにつれて」と比例を表す。選択肢のasは4つとも接続詞だが，エが「彼は年を取るにつれ頑固になった」と「～するにつれて」という意味なので正解。　⑧　下線部⑧のthatは，so ～ that …「とても～なので…」のthatである。したがって，アの「私はとても驚いたので，一言も発することができなかった」が正解。なお，イのso thatは「～するように」という用法。

(6)　⑥　heterogeneousは「異成分からなる」という意味。「社会がますます複雑になると，古い階級はもっと多くの異なる成分(異なる階級)になる→もっと多様になる」となる。第7段落2文目にConventional big classes have become so diverse …「従来の大きな階級はとても多様になったので…」とありdiverse「多様な」がほぼ同じ意味で正解。

⑨　rungは「梯子の横木，段」という意味。「アメリカ社会はたくさんの横木のあるはしごだ」と，階級が細分化したものを横木にたとえて述べている。第8段落2～3文目にEach step is equal-sized. Sure, for the people higher up this ladder, …「それぞれの横木は同じサイズだ。社会的により高い地位にある人，…」とあり，ladderを身分や地位の段階に，stepを階級が細分化したものに喩えていることからrungとstepをほぼ同じ意味で使っている。　(7)　下線部⑩を含む文は「きっぱりと別れることに至っていない(きっぱりとは別れない)人びとはみんな，共有する経験をもっていると言いながら，きっぱりと別れるようなことはない」という意味。その後の文で，「社会的により高い地位にある人の子どもはより高度な教育やよりよい健康保険を手にする可能性が高いが，はしごの横木はみんな同じサイズで，同じような経験を持っ

ているので別れずにいる。ただそのグループは階級と呼べるものではない」と続く。　(8)　下線部⑪を含む文の直前の文で,「確かに社会的により高い地位にある人の子どもはより高度な教育やよりよい健康保険を手にする可能性が高い」とあり,これがひとつの階級になっていそうだが,「そのことが,階級が存在するということを意味してはいない」と続いているので,thatは直前の文の内容を指す。

【4】①　NEET is a term that first appeared in Britain in the late 1990s.

②　In Japan, it is estimated that there are about six hundred thousand young people who are neither working nor studying, and the Japanese Government is giving support to such people.

〈解説〉(1)　①「NEETは言葉である」→ NEET is the term.というのがこの文の骨格になる。termは「言葉(特に術語,用語を指す)」という意味。次にどういう言葉かというと「イギリスで最初に現れた」言葉なのでthe termのあとに関係代名詞that[which]でつなげる。→ the term that first appeared in Britain. 最後に,いつ現れたかというと「1990年代後半に」現れたとあるのでin the late 1990sを続ける。「～年代」は年号の後に複数形のsをつける。　②　まずこの文を,前半の「日本では～」と,後半の「日本政府は～」の部分に分けandでつなげる。前半はIt is estimated that S ＋ V ～「～と推定される」で始めて,何が推定されるのかをthat以下に述べる。that以下は「若者が60万人ほどいる」→there are about six hundred thousand young peopleを骨格にする。「～ほど」は数字の前にaboutをつける。次に「働きも学びもしてない」若者とあるので,関係代名詞のwho(又はthat)でpeopleの後に続ける。時制は,現在,働きも学びもしていないと考え進行形にする。「AもBも～ない」はneither A nor Bで表せるので,最終的にwho are neither working nor studyingにする。後半は単純な第3文型の文。時制は「現在支援を行っている」と考え進行形にする。

【5】(解答例) I think students should be encouraged to join an internship program or a volunteer activity. It gives them an opportunity to get practical work experience, develop professional consciousness and to realize happiness at work through working together with other workers. (40語)

〈解説〉まず「インターンシップ」や「ボランティア」など，取り組む手段を2，3点あげる。その手段を通して生徒が何を得るのかを書くことで，なぜその取り組みをすることが生徒にとって効果的なのかを説明する。

# 2014年度　実施問題

## 【中高共通】

【1】Listening Comprehension

PART 1 (記号で書け。)

No. 1

(A) Butter.

(B) Eggs.

(C) Butter and eggs.

(D) Milk.

No. 2

(A) In a clothing store.

(B) In a department store.

(C) In someone's home.

(D) On the fifth floor.

No. 3

(A) How long does it take to the coffee shop?

(B) Where is the coffee shop?

(C) Let's meet at the coffee shop on College Street.

(D) I don't like the coffee shop on College Street.

No. 4

(A) The man painted the woman's house.

(B) Someone painted the man's house.

(C) Someone painted the woman's house.

(D) The man painted his own house.

No. 5

(A) Cathy didn't quit her job because of her boss.

(B) Cathy wondered why her boss didn't like her.

(C) Many people knew Cathy left because of her boss.

(D) Cathy quit because she didn't like her boss's secret.

PART 2 (記号で書け。)

No. 1

(A) She was unhappy with her grade.

(B) She had some questions about grammar.

(C) She wanted to thank him for her grade.

(D) She wanted to talk about the topic of her next essay.

No. 2

(A) A.

(B) A minus.

(C) B minus.

(D) D minus.

No.3

(A) It needed more supporting details.

(B) It had no careless grammar errors.

(C) It was long overdue.

(D) It was poorly organized.

No.4

(A) She has poor potential.

(B) She is lazy.

(C) She is careless.

(D) She has good writing ability.

No. 5

(A) To study the form of the essay.

(B) To finish her essay earlier.

(C) To give herself time to study grammar.

(D) To do more research.

PART3 (述べられている内容についての(1)～(4)の問いに対する答えを，日本語で書け。)

Questions

(1) What were the students expected to do in preparation for the discussion?

(2) Who did the first insurance contracts protect? And when were the contracts made?

(3) What determined the cost of early insurance policies?

(4) When was the basic form of a current insurance policy made?

(☆☆☆◎◎◎)

【2】次の(1)～(5)のそれぞれについて，下線部の①～④のいずれかに一箇所誤りがある。その箇所の番号と，正しい表現に直したものを書け。

(1) ①Some parents ②need ③to be taught how to ④grow their children.

(2) ①Won't you tell him ②I'm out if he ③will call me up ④later?

(3) The teacher objected to ①let the students ②go ③home ④in such a bad weather.

(4) Carol was ①upset last week ②because she ③had to do too ④many homeworks.

(5) The number of ①politicians who ②have been questioned ③on this issue ④are quite large.

(☆◎◎◎)

【3】次の(1)～(3)の各組において，a)とb)がほぼ同じ意味になるように，b)の(　　)内にそれぞれ適切な一語を書け。

(1) a) It is three years since the war broke out.

b) Three years have(　　) since the war broke out.

(2) a) The older he grew, the more obstinate he became.

b) (　　) he grew older, he became more obstinate.

(3) a) I don't know the distance from here to the college.

b)　I don’t know how (　　) it is from here to the college.

(☆◎◎◎)

【4】次の(1)～(5)のそれぞれについて，日本文の意味になるように(　　)内に適切な一語を書け。

(1)　残念ながら，私の英語は通じなかった。

Unfortunately, I couldn’t make myself(　　) in English.

(2)　このコンピュータはどこかおかしい。

Something is wrong (　　) this computer.

(3)　あなたはこの計画に賛成ですか，反対ですか。

Are you for or (　　) this plan?

(4)　その地図がなければ，私たちは道に迷ってしまっただろう。

(　　) for the map,we would have got lost.

(5)　成功への道はいくつもあると私は信じる。

I am sure of there (　　) so many ways to success.

(☆☆☆◎◎◎)

【5】次の，Markと上司の会話文の1～5の(　　)内には，あとのア～クのいずれかが入る。それぞれにあてはまる最も適切なものを一つずつ選んで，その記号を書け。ただし，同じ選択肢を2回以上選ぶことはできない。

Mark :　Excuse me. May I come in?

Boss :　Sure. (　1　)

Mark :　Can you check this draft of our poster for the Compact Unmanned Aircraft Contest?

Boss :　(　2　)

Mark :　Oh, it shouldn’t take that long.

Boss :　All right. So, what kind of contest is it?

Mark :　(　3　)

Boss :　Sounds interesting. Can I see your poster? .... So, what exactly do you want to show in this poster?

Mark : We want to highlight the best features of our aircraft's design.

Boss : ( 4 )

Mark : Right here, under the title.

Boss : Oh, I see. .... Well, this is OK, but it'll have more impact if there's a picture for each point. ( 5 )

Mark : OK, I'll add some pictures. Thank you for your advice.

ア Do you know who won the contest last year?

イ This is the fifth annual contest.

ウ OK, but I have a meeting in thirty minutes.

エ That'll make it easier for people to understand your plane's features.

オ The poster is too big.

カ How can I help you?

キ Well, where do you describe them?

ク We're supposed to design an unmanned plane that can transport objects.

(☆☆◎◎◎)

【6】次の(1)～(3)のそれぞれについて，下のア～クを並べかえて日本文と同じ意味の英文を作る。その際，( ① )，( ② )内にあてはまる語を，ア～クからそれぞれ選んで，その記号を書け。(文頭に来る語も小文字で表記している。)

(1) 彼女に言われたとおりにはしないほうがいいよ。

You ( )( )( ① )( )( )( )( ② )( ) to.

ア she　イ you　ウ had　エ as　オ not

カ do　キ tells　ク better

(2) パーティーの準備をするのに何時間かかると思いますか

( )( )( ① )( )( )( )( ② )( ) to prepare for the party?

ア do　イ how　ウ it　エ long　オ take

カ think　キ will　ク you

(3)　彼女が私たちに見せたかったものは何だったのですか。

(　　)(　　)(　①　)(　　)(　　)(　　)(　②　)(　　) us?

ア　it　　イ　she　　ウ　show　　エ　that　　オ　to

カ　wanted　　キ　was　　ク　what

(☆☆☆◎◎◎)

## 【中学校】

【1】次の文は，中学校学習指導要領(平成20年3月告示)第2章第9節外国語の「言語活動の取扱い」の一部を示そうとしたものである。次の1～5の(　　)内にあてはまる語句を書け。

イ　生徒の学習段階を考慮して各学年の指導に当たっては，次のような点に配慮するものとする。

(ア)　第1学年における言語活動

小学校における外国語活動を通じて(　1　)面を中心としたコミュニケーションに対する(　2　)な態度などの一定の(　3　)が育成されることを踏まえ，身近な言語の使用(　4　)や言語の働きに配慮した言語活動を行わせること。その際，自分の(　5　)や身の回りの出来事などの中から簡単な表現を用いてコミュニケーションを図れるような話題を取り上げること。

(☆☆☆◎◎◎◎)

【2】英語の授業で次の(1)～(5)のことをALTに伝えたいとき，英語でどのように話すかを書け。

(1)　ゲームのルールを説明してください。

(2)　生徒の間をまわってアドバイスしてください。

(3)　生徒に対話のモデルをやって見せましょう。

(4)　あなたが自分の国でおこなったボランティア活動について話してくれませんか。

(5)　数字を使ったゲームを知っていますか。

(☆☆☆◎◎◎)

【3】中学生に，言語材料としてto不定詞(副詞としての用法)を導入する際にJTLとALTが行う，対話形式のオーラル・イントロダクションを考え，英語で書け。ただし，英文は10文以上とし，追加の部分が必要であれば，付け足してもよい。

(☆☆☆☆◎◎◎)

【4】次の英文を読み，あとの(1)～(4)の問いに答えよ。

Stefan Ottomanski is a rare educator: he enjoys uncertainty and views obstacles as opportunities to teach both his students and himself lessons that were never part of the curriculum. Ottomanski works for the Japan Wildlife Research Center (JWRC) in the Uguisudani district of Tokyo's Taito Ward, where for the past five years he has been developing and leading JWRC overseas training tours. Though the tours run by the nonprofit research foundation offer Japanese young people a chance to experience marine and forest preservation projects in ①( developing / developed) countries, what they learn there goes far beyond *coral reefs and forest regeneration.

Ottomanski, 46, gives the example of a recent program he conducted on the island of Leyte in the Philippines. Youths from a village ②<u>were to join</u> Japanese students for a study program, but the community was anxious because a previous group of German students had *intimidated the villagers with their excellent English and polite *inattention. For months before the Japanese came, there was concern about how they would adapt and how the shy local youths would communicate.

"When the Japanese came," Ottomanski recalled, "the local youths were surprised, and ( ③ ), to find that they also spoke poor English. The two sides formed such a close bond that it was hard to pull them apart at the end of the program. God only knows what they were talking about, but there was communication, and it was rich." To date, more than 120 Japanese have taken part in JWRC tours.

The training tours are not cheap, ④( boasts / regrets ) Ottomanski, a professional photographer-turned-educator with 16 years' experience in Japan. Two-week programs in the Philippines or Indonesia range from 170,000 yen to 250,000 yen. But they are also not simply study tours, since a key feature of each trip is one-to-one participation with local youth. "If there are 15 Japanese participants, there will be 15 local students joining the program on an equal basis," he explains. "In this sense, our programs are as much about cultural exchange as they are about preservation."

The one-to-one approach is ideally suited to Japanese, says Ottomanski, and he would like to see more such programs developed because of the various benefits they bring to both sides. For the Japanese, there is a rare chance to work and live with people of the ⑤( different / same) generation in a country of the Third World. The programs have fixed themes and objectives, so, says Ottomanski, the students not only learn for themselves, but also see how locals approach similar challenges.

*coral reefs : サンゴ礁　　*intimidate : 萎縮(いしゅく)させる
*inattention : 無愛想

(1) 文中の①，④，⑤の(　　)内の語のうち，文脈に合う適切な方をそれぞれ選んで書け。

(2) 下線部②とほぼ同じ意味を表しているものを，次のア～エから一つ選んで，その記号を書け。

ア　were forbidden to join　　イ　were unwilling to join
ウ　were scheduled to join　　エ　were pleased to join

(3) 本文の内容と一致するように，次の(a)～(c)の書き出しに続く最も適切なものを，下のア～エから一つずつ選んで，その記号を書け。

(a) Stefan Ottomanski is a rare educator because he
ア　avoids uncertainty.
イ　follows a fixed curriculum.
ウ　sees obstacles as chances to learn.
エ　is a foreign teacher in Japan.

(b) Stefan Ottomanski has been working for JWRC

ア for more than twenty years.

イ developing training programs.

ウ teaching young people marine sports.

エ as a professional photographer to provide pictures.

(c) Ottomanski believes the JWRC training programs are particularly well-suited to Japanese youths because of the

ア variety of themes offered.

イ one-to-one approach they use.

ウ marine and forest preservation.

エ opportunity to practice English.

(4) 本文の内容について，次の(a)～(c)の問いの答えとして最も適切なものを，下のア～エから一つずつ撰んで，その記号を書け。

(a) Which of the following is true about recent programs conducted in Leyte?

ア The German youths turned out to be shy and poor in English.

イ The local youths from Leyte communicated easily with the German youths.

ウ The German youths participated in the program after the Japanese youths.

エ For months before the Japanese youths came, the villagers were worried about their shy youths.

(b) According to Ottomanski, which of the following is true?

ア The local youths from Leyte spoke better English than the Japanese youths.

イ Both the Japanese youths and the local youths from Leyte would not talk with each other.

ウ The Japanese youths had difficulty adapting themselves to the new environment.

エ The local youths from Leyte enjoyed communicating with the

Japanese youths.

(c) Which of the following best fits in ( ③ )?

ア respected　イ determined　ウ relieved　エ suited

(☆☆☆☆◎◎◎)

【5】次の英文を読み，あとの(1)～(5)の問いに答えよ。

Finland, according to a major international survey, has the best educational system in the world. This news comes after several other studies showing that Finland has the highest rate of teen literacy in the world, the highest percentage of '①regular readers,' and the most 'creatively competitive' economy, according to the World Economic Forum.

The Finnish education minister says that heavy investments in education are a matter of economic survival for a small, wealthy, high-tech-based nation. Finland spends more per elementary, middle, and high school student than any other nation on earth, and ranks second for higher-education spending. Schools are local, community-based affairs, with extremely low turnover in their teaching staff and strong expectations from parents. Students all study languages, math, and science. In short, the Finns ②go to great lengths to maintain an exceptionally successful education system.

On the other hand, maybe the secret is what they don't do; Finnish students spend ( 1 ) time in class than students in any other industrialized nation. While some kids in the United States begin preschool by age three, Finnish kids don't even start school until age six, and their formal schooling begins at age seven. Throughout their schooling, pupils spend the fewest hours in school of any Western country, with longer breaks and holidays. The result of this is strong emphasis on ③a family's role in educating kids. Finland scores remarkably high in reading comprehension, which can be attributed largely to an active tradition of reading at home and with family.

Clearly, the Finnish system amounts to a successful employment of quality over quantity. Time and money well spent means kids gain ( 2 ) from their schooling without having to spend too much time in the classroom. And free meals for all students mean kids' health and concentration improve.

On top of all this, Finnish schools do not pick out students who excel and separate them from students who struggle. From age seven to sixteen, all children receive the same education, eliminating the idea widespread in other countries of not expecting much from certain kids, and ultimately watching their performance decline. ④The behavioral issues that normally accompany troubled and failing pupils do not seem to affect Finland — parents or teachers give 'problem kids' a talking-to, and the issue is usually easily resolved.

Kids generally attend the ( 3 ) school from age seven to sixteen, making for a smoother ride than in other school systems where numerous transitions are the norm. Child-care services are available, and kids walk around barefoot, in an atmosphere that feels homey and intimate. The same freedom can be felt in the curriculum. Kids hold a great degree of control over their own course selections and schedules, choosing from numerous subjects that complement the core academic program.

At the end of the comprehensive nine-year basic academic period, sixteen-year-olds have a choice between vocational and secondary academic school. Almost all kids choose one or the other; dropout rates remain ( 4 ). Universities in Finland are free, and about 65 percent of Finnish young adults attend.

In Finland, education, literacy, school attendance, and multilingualism comprise some of the most important cultural values. ⑤It's no wonder that kids want to be in school — they are born into a system that makes school fun.

(1) 下線部①について，この文脈で置き換えられる最も適切なものを，次のア～エから一つ選んで，その記号を書け。

ア considerate　　イ easy　　ウ frequent　　エ silent

(2)　下線部②と最も近い意味をもつものを，次のア～エから一つ選んで，その記号を書け。

ア　spend a lot of time　　イ　go long distances

ウ　get into trouble　　エ　make every effort

(3)　文中の1～4の(　　)内にあてはまる最も適切な語を，次のア～カから一つずつ選んで，その記号を書け。ただし，同じ選択肢を2回以上選ぶことはできない。

ア　high　　イ　low　　ウ　more　　エ　less　　オ　different

カ　same

(4)　下線部③の具体例として，本文中に述べられていることと，その成果を日本語で書け。

(5)　下線部④，⑤を日本語に直して書け。

(☆☆◎◎◎)

【6】次の(1)，(2)を英語に直して書け。

(1)　公共の場所では，携帯電話の電源を切っておくのが礼儀です。

(2)　外国人とのコミュニケーションを通して日本人にはないものの考え方を発見したとき，私は最も幸せを感じます。

(☆☆☆◎◎◎)

【7】英語の授業におけるグループワークの利点について，あなたの意見を50語以上の英語で書け。

(☆☆☆◎◎◎)

## 【高等学校】

【1】次の各文は，高等学校学習指導要領(平成21年3月告示)第2章第8節外国語第4款の一部を示そうとしたものである。次の1～7の(　　)内にあてはまる語句を書け。

○　教材については，外国語を通じてコミュニケーション能力を(　1　)的に育成するため，各科目の目標に応じ，実際の言語の使用(　2　)

や言語の(　3　)に十分配慮したものを取り上げるものとすること。

○　音声指導の補助として，(　4　)表記を用いて指導することができること。

○　(　5　)の活用の指導などを通じ，生涯にわたって，自ら外国語を学び，使おうとする積極的な態度を育てるようにすること。

○　各科目の指導に当たっては，指導方法や指導体制を工夫し，ペア・ワーク，(　6　)などを適宜取り入れたり，(　7　)教材やコンピュータ，情報通信ネットワークなどを適宜指導に生かしたりすること。

(☆☆☆◎◎◎◎)

【2】英語の授業で次の(1)～(3)のことを生徒に伝えたいとき，英語でどのように話すかを書け。

(1)　この意見についてどう思いますか。

(2)　間違いをおそれないで。

(3)　この単語の意味がわからない人は辞書を引いてください。

(☆☆☆◎◎◎)

【3】次の(1)～(3)の文法事項を用いた英文を，それぞれ1文書け。

(1)　ifを含む仮定法過去

(2)　ifを含む仮定法過去完了

(3)　主語がif節の代わりに用いられている仮定法

(☆☆☆◎◎◎)

【4】次の英文を読み，あとの(1)～(5)の問いに答えよ。

Think back to the first time you rode a bike or the last time you had ice cream for dessert. Now, imagine a perfect summer day. What's going on in your brain that allows you to remember, dream and think?

Lots. And some of the world's smartest scientists are conducting experiments and doing research to figure out how ①it all works.

In recent years, brain-imaging techniques such as functional magnetic resonance imaging (fMRI) have allowed scientists to watch the brain in action. Studies using fMRI show how different parts of the brain do different things. For example, one part of the brain, called the *amygdala*, handles emotional information, and another part of the brain, the *prefrontal cortex*, makes plans [　A　] the future. Yet another brain system, the *cerebellum*, helps control your movements and balance, while the *hypothalamus* works to control your body's temperature. The *hippocampus*, meanwhile, has the job of transferring information between short-term and long-term memory. By working together, ②<u>these systems</u> let you think, remember, see, hear, smell, taste and touch.

Though the human brain is sometimes compared [　B　] a computer, it's not one. It's actually much more complex. Computers, for example, are designed to record everything perfectly. ③<u>Rather than recording everything, the brain sorts out all the information in through the senses and decides what to hold on to.</u> Because the brain does all this sorting, things such as the pattern in your carpet or the sound of birds singing outside your window don't constantly distract you.

Though your brain is not a computer, they do share something [　C　] common: Both brains and computers use electrical signals to transmit information. Your brain doesn't get its electrical energy from a socket in the wall, the way a computer does. Instead, it creates and sends electrical signals through specialized cells called neurons.

The human brain contains billions of neurons, and each individual neuron may receive information from thousands of other neurons. To keep the mental machinery running smoothly, the neurons specialize in doing certain tasks. Sensory neurons, for example, carry messages from your eyes, ears and other sensory organs to your brain. Motor neurons carry signals from your brain to your muscles and organs, enabling you to walk, talk, and breathe. Other types of neurons in the brain help in building social relationships. Mirror neurons, for example, are specialized cells that help you show empathy and understanding to others.

"Mirror neurons are active when I pick up a cup, and are also active when I watch someone else pick up a cup," says neuroscientist Sam Wang. "If you've ever thought 'ouch!' when you see someone cut themselves, you have your mirror neurons to thank."

Some neurons have very specific tasks. Things and people that you see regularly — your mother, your dog, even your favorite singer or actor — all have their own special group of neurons.

Figuring out how the mind gives rise to thoughts, actions and emotions isn't easy, and scientists are still working to get a complete picture. When it comes to learning new information, one thing is certain, however: Practice makes perfect. When messages travel [ D ] neuron to neuron, again and again, the brain creates a connection between the neurons to form a memory. Once this happens, processing and remembering information becomes easier. This is true whether you are trying to learn a new language [ E ] learn a new dance move, Wang says. Allowing time for rest breaks also aids learning. That's why spacing out your study time ④<u>works better</u> than trying to cram information all at once.

Now that's something to keep in mind.

(1) 次のア～エのうち，本文の表題として最も適切なものを一つ選んで，その記号を書け。

ア　The Technology of fMRI

イ　Why the Brain is Just Like a Computer

ウ　The Role of Mirror Neurons in the Brain

エ　How the Brain Works

(2) 下線部①，②，④について，(　　)内にあてはまる最も適切な語(句)を，それぞれア～エから一つずつ選んで，その記号を書け。

①　"it" refers to (　　).

ア　the human brain　　イ　the world　　ウ　research

エ　dreaming

② "these systems" means (　　).

ア　the *hippocampus* and *hypothalamus*

イ　short and long-term memory

ウ　the different parts of the brain

エ　your senses

④ "works better" means (　　).

ア　tries harder　　イ　has more time　　ウ　studies later

エ　is more successful

(3) 本文中のA～Eの[　　]内にあてはまる最も適切な語を，それぞれア～エから一つずつ選んで，その記号を書け。

| | | | | |
|---|---|---|---|---|
| A | ア　with | イ　on | ウ　for | エ　to |
| B | ア　to | イ　of | ウ　for | エ　from |
| C | ア　in | イ　by | ウ　on | エ　to |
| D | ア　away | イ　from | ウ　in | エ　for |
| E | ア　for | イ　with | ウ　so | エ　or |

(4) 下線部③からは，本来入るべ taken が削除されている。takenを本来の位置に戻したとき，その次の語を書け。

(5) 本文の内容と一致するものを，次のア～クから三つ選んで，その記号を書け。

ア　fMRI is a technique that allows scientists to create a human-like brain.

イ　If you damaged your *cerebellum*, you might have difficulty walking properly.

ウ　The brain gets its power from the *hippocampus*.

エ　Motor neurons are used to take information from your senses.

オ　Mirror neurons help us to feel sympathy for other people.

カ　The writer believes the scientists fully understand how the brain works.

キ　The more you practice something, the more easily neurons can connect with each other.

ク　If you want to learn better, you should study without pausing.

(☆☆☆◎◎◎)

【5】次の英文を読み，あとの(1)～(9)の英語の問いに答えよ。なお，英文の左の1～9の数字は段落番号を示している。

1　Many students believe that intelligence is fixed, that each person has a certain amount and that's that. We call this a *fixed mindset*, and, as you will see, students with this mindset worry about how much of this fixed intelligence they possess. A fixed mindset makes challenges threatening for students (because they believe that their fixed ability may not be up to the task) and it makes mistakes and failures demoralizing (because they believe that such setbacks reflect badly on their level of fixed intelligence).

2　Other students believe that intelligence is something that can be cultivated through effort and education. They don't necessarily believe that everyone has the same abilities or that anyone can be as smart as Einstein, but they do believe that everyone can improve their abilities. And they understand that even Einstein wasn't Einstein until he put in years of focused hard work. In short, students with this *growth mindset* believe that intelligence is a potential that can be realized through learning. As a result, confronting challenges, profiting from mistakes, and persevering in the face of setbacks become ways of getting smarter.

3　To understand the different worlds these mindsets create, we followed several hundred students across a difficult school transition — the transition to seventh grade. This is when the academic work often gets much harder, the grading gets stricter, and the school environment gets less personalized with students moving from class to class. As the students entered seventh grade, we measured their mindsets (along with a number of other things) and then we monitored their grades over the next two years.

4　The first thing we found was that students with different mindsets cared about different things in school. Those with a growth mindset were much more interested in learning than in just looking smart in school. This was not the case for students with a fixed mindset. In fact, in many of our studies with students from preschool age to college age, we find that students with a fixed mindset care so much about how smart they will appear that they often reject learning opportunities — even **ones** that are critical to their success (Cimpian, *et al.*, 2007; Hong, *et al.*, 1999; Nussbaum and Dweck, 2008; Mangels, *et al.*, 2006).

5 Next, we found that students with the two mindsets had radically different beliefs about effort. [ A ] Those with a growth mindset had a very straightforward (and correct) idea of effort — the idea that the harder you work, the more your ability will grow and that even geniuses have had to work hard for their accomplishments. [ B ] In contrast, the students with the fixed mindset believed that if you worked hard it meant that you didn't have ability, and that things would just come naturally to you if you did. [ C ] If they work hard at it that means that they aren't good at it, but if they don't work hard they won't do well. [ D ] Clearly, since just about every worthwhile pursuit involves effort over a long period of time, this is a potentially crippling belief, not only in school but also in life.

6 Students with different mindsets also had very different reactions to setbacks. Those with growth mindsets reported that, after a setback in school, they would simply study more or study differently the next time. But those with fixed mindsets were more likely to say that they would feel dumb, study *less* the next time, and seriously consider cheating. If you feel dumb — permanently dumb — in an academic area, there is no good way to bounce back and be successful in the future. In a growth mindset, however, you can make a plan of **positive action** that can remedy a deficiency. (Hong, *et al.*, 1999; Nussbaum and Dweck, 2008; Heyman, *et al.*, 1992)

7 Finally, when we looked at the math grades they went on to earn, we

found that the students with a growth mindset had pulled ahead. (　　) both groups had started seventh grade with equivalent achievement test scores, a growth mindset quickly propelled students ahead of their fixed-mindset peers, and this gap only increased over the two years of the study.

8 In short, the belief that intelligence is fixed dampened students' motivation to learn, made them afraid of effort, and made them want to quit after a setback. This is why so many bright students stop working when school becomes hard. Many bright students find grade school easy and coast to success early on. But later on, when they are challenged, they struggle. They don't want to make mistakes and feel dumb — and, most of all, they don't want to work hard and feel dumb. So they simply retire.

9 It is the belief that intelligence can be developed that opens students to a love of learning, a belief in the power of effort and constructive, determined reactions to setbacks.

(1) In paragraph 1, why do students with a fixed mindset find challenges threatening? Write the answer in English.

(2) In paragraph 2, what does "even Einstein wasn't Einstein" imply? Write the answer in English.

(3) In paragraph 3, to understand the different worlds the two mindsets create, why did the author and her colleagues choose the transition to seventh grade, not the transition to fifth or ninth grade, for their study? Write the answer in English.

(4) In paragraph 4, what does the word, **ones**, refer to? Write the answer in English.

(5) In paragraph 5, the four letters [ A ], [ B ], [ C ], and [ D ] indicate where the following sentence could be added to the passage. Where would the sentence best fit? Choose the place where the sentence fits best and write the letter from A, B, C, and D.

This means that every time something is hard for them and requires effort, it's both a threat and a bind.

(6) Give an example of **positive action** that can remedy a deficiency in paragraph 6. Write the answer in English.

(7) Fill in the blank space in paragraph 7 with an appropriate word. Write the answer in English.

(8) Summarize paragraph 8 by filling in the blank spaces A and B in the following with an appropriate word for each. Write the answers in English.

The students with the ( A ) mindset were discouraged to learn and suffered a setback, and this is why many bright students retire when ( B ) becomes hard.

(9) Read the following and choose three statements that describe the growth mindset. Write the three letters from A to F.

A. You have a certain amount of intelligence, and you can't really do much to change it.

B. No matter who you are, you can significantly change your intelligence level.

C. To be honest, you can't really change how intelligent you are.

D. You can learn new things, but you can't really change your basic intelligence.

E. No matter how much intelligence you have, you can always change it quite a bit.

F. You can change even your basic intelligence level considerably.

(☆☆☆◎◎◎)

【6】次の文中の下線部を英語に直して書け。

<u>いったんある子が級友たちの間で一定の評判を得ると，その初期のイメージを変えることは，不可能でないにしてもとても難しい。級友たちの普段の反応によって，その子は同じ役割を果たし続けることを強いられるからである。</u>教師はそのことを念頭において，生徒の指導

にあたらなければならない。

(☆☆☆☆◎◎◎)

【7】*オンラインショッピング(online shopping)を利用するメリットとデメリットの両方について，あなたの意見を50語以上の英語で書け。

*オンラインショッピング:インターネットを利用する通信販売

(☆☆☆☆◎◎◎)

# 解答・解説

## 【中高共通】

【1】PART 1　No. 1　(D)　No. 2　(B)　No.3　(C)　No. 4　(B)　No. 5　(C)　PART 2　No. 1　(A)　No. 2　(C)　No.3　(A)　No. 4　(D)　No. 5　(B)　PART 3　(1)　保険に関する章を読んでおくこと　(2)　商人 / 紀元前3000年　(3)　その商品の運搬に関わる危険度　(4)　中世

〈解説〉PART 1は，小問の内容がそれぞれ独立していることや登場人物が示されていることから，短い会話文を聴いて答える問題であると考えられる。No. 4のように詳細を問う質問がある一方で，No. 2の場面を推測する問題やNo. 3の(おそらく)次に発せられるであろう台詞を予想する問題も含まれている。そのため，選択肢を確認して，内容を厳密に聴くのかトップダウン的に場面を想像しながら聴くのか，見当をつけて聴き始めると解答しやすくなると考えられる。　PART 2は5つの小問を通して成績，文法やエッセイといったキーワードが含まれているため，やや長い英文を聴いて答える問題であると推測される。問題文が印字されていない状況で長い英文を聴くことから，選択肢に関連した内容が放送されたときに，適宜メモをするとよいであろう。PART 3は質問文が与えられているので，あらかじめ読んで頭に入れた上で，それに関連する本文箇所を集中して聴き取るようにする。

【２】(1)　④　raise　(2)　③　calls　(3)　①　letting
(4)　④　much homework　(5)　④　is

〈解説〉(1)　grow は育てるのではなく，自分が育つこと。　(2)　条件を示す if 節や時間を表す when 節の中では，未来形ではなく現在形を用いる。　(3)　objected to は不定詞ではなく前置詞のため，to の後ろは動名詞を用いる。似た表現に，oppose to もあり，こちらも前置詞。
(4)　homework は不可算名詞である。　(5)　この文の主語は The number であるため，単数に対応する is を用いる。

【３】(1)　passed　(2)　As　(3)　far

〈解説〉(1)「～年が過ぎた」の書き換えとしてよく見受けられるかたちである。The war has lasted for three years. とも言える。　(2)「年を重ねるほど」「年をとるにつれて」という意味になる接続詞として，asが適切である。　(3)　I don't knowの後ろに疑問詞が導く名詞節が続くかたちである。距離はhow far，時間はhow long，なども抑えておきたい。

【４】(1)　understood　(2)　with　(3)　against　(4)　But
(5)　being

〈解説〉(1)　使役動詞の make が用いられている。後続の myself は理解される側なので，過去分詞 understood を用いる。類似した表現に，make one / oneself heard「(人)の声 / 考えを聞いてもらう」がある。
(2)　Something is wrong with ～ で「～の調子が悪い」。　(3)　agree / disagree，for / againstのように意見を述べる表現は中高ともに，教科書でも用いられる。　(4)　But for ～ と同様の表現として，Without ～ と If it had not been for ～ も抑えておくとよいであろう。　(5)　of に続いているため，there 以下は名詞句である必要がある。

【5】1 カ　2 ウ　3 ク　4 キ　5 エ

〈解説〉会話やパッセージの中に空欄がある場合は，その前後で流れが一貫しているか，言語的な照応形や内容的な文脈を考慮する。 1 空欄のあとに Mark が上司に頼みごとをしているため，空欄では相手の用件を尋ねる内容がくると想定できる。 2 空欄のあとに時間について答えられているため，空欄も時間を気にする内容になる。
3 空欄の前でどのようなコンテストか尋ねられているため，それに答える内容となる。 4 空欄のあとが場所を示しているため，where で尋ねるのが適切である。 5 空欄の前後で写真を付け加えることが話されているため，内容の分かりやすさという点が文脈に沿う。

【6】(1) ① オ　② キ　(2) ① ア　② キ　(3) ① ア　② オ

〈解説〉(1) (You) had better not do as she tells you(to.) が正答。肯定形では had better ＋原型不定詞となる。not の位置に注意する。また，この表現を用いる場合には，押し付けがましいニュアンスを持ち目上の人に対しては失礼に当たる点に留意する。 (2) How long do you think it will take (to prepare for the party?) が正答。疑問詞を伴う疑問文に do you think がつく場合，疑問詞を先に述べ，think に続く節は肯定形になる。
(3) What was it that she wanted to show (us?)「何だったのか」という疑問の核となる部分を先に述べ，it を関係代名詞 that を用いて後置修飾で説明する。

## 【中学校】

【1】1 音声　2 積極的　3 素地　4 場面　5 気持ち

〈解説〉小学校学習指導要領第4章にある小学校の外国語活動の目標のポイントとして，「体験的に」理解を深めること，「音声や基本的な表現に慣れ親しませ」ること，「コミュニケーション能力の素地を養う」ことが挙げられる。問題では取り上げられていないが，小学校段階で音声を中心とした指導が行われていることから，中学校では「読むこと」「書くこと」が目標に取り込まれている点も抑えておきたい。

【2】(解答例) (1)　Please explain the rules of the game.　(2)　Will you walk around and give the students some advice?　(3)　Let's show the students a model of the dialogue.　(4)　Can you talk about volunteer activities you did in your country?　(5)　Do you know any games using numbers?

〈解説〉問題文中に「英語の授業で」とあり，職員室での会話でなく授業を想定すると，生徒へのインプットになることも頭に入れる必要がある。公式解答では Please，Will you，Let's，Can you など，中学1年生で学習する事項がほとんどであるが，学年の想定が2年生，3年生であれば，学習した事項を取り入れるために Could you の表現や，which you did in your country という関係代名詞などを意識的に用いることも大いに考えられる。いずれにせよ，できるだけ生徒にとっても理解可能な平易な表現を心がけたい。

【3】(解答例)

ALT: What did you do last weekend?

JTL : I went to Tokyo.

ALT: Really? Why did you go there? To do some shopping?

JTL : No. To see my aunt.

ALT: Oh, you have an aunt in Tokyo. What did you do with her?

JTL : We went to Tokyo Sky Tree to enjoy the view.

〈解説〉会話の中で to 不定詞(「～のため」という副詞的用法)が何度も出現するという条件はもちろんであるが，to 不定詞の導入であることを踏まえ，2年生の前半までの語彙・文法レベルを想定できるとよい。2人でのコミュニケーションであるため，片方が長く話すことなく適度に発言の交代ができている必要もある。

【4】(1) ① developing ④ regrets ⑤ same (2) ウ
(3) (a) ウ (b) イ (c) イ (4) (a) エ (b) エ
(c) ウ

〈解説〉(1) ① 次の段落で具体例を見るとフィリピンでの活動が挙げられており，最終段落でthe Third World ともあることから，途上国を選択する方が適切だといえる。 ④ 良いプロジェクトである一方で参加費が安くないという事実は，自慢することではないと考えられる。⑤ 日本と現地の参加者両方が若者である。 (2) be to の用法のうち「予定」の意味で用いられている。 (3) (a) 第1段落1文目に記述がある。 (b) 2文目に記述がある。 (c) 最終段落の1文目に記述がある。 (4) (a) 選択肢はすべて第2段落より正誤が判断できる。アはドイツ人の学生が英語で村民を萎縮させたとあるため違う。それにより村民は次にくる日本人のことを懸念していた点から，イとウも誤りである。 (b) 第3段落に，お互い英語はつたないながらも非常に強い絆を築いたことが書かれている。 (c) 空欄の前の段落で，日本人が来る前のドイツ人学生はすばらしい英語力で現地の人々を萎縮させたとあり，空欄のあとでは，日本人も英語が下手だったと述べられているため，現地民の心境として適切なものは「安心」であると考えられる。

【5】(1) ウ (2) エ (3) 1 エ 2 ウ 3 カ 4 イ
(4) 述べられていること… 家族が子どもと一緒に家で本を読むこと。成果…フィンランドが読解力で驚異的な高得点を記録していること。
(5) ④ 課題を抱え，落第しそうな生徒に通常伴う生活態度の問題は，フィンランドには影響を与えているようには思われない。 ⑤ 子どもたちが学校にいたがるのは当然である。彼らは学校を楽しい場としている制度の中に生まれるからだ。

〈解説〉(1) 文脈から，「コンスタントに読書をする人」であることが分かる。 (2) In shortでまとめられている前述の部分を見ると，様々な要因や努力，現状が示されている。 (3) 1 この段落は「フィンランドの人々がしないこと」に関して述べられており，空欄以降も，学校にいる期間や時間が短いことが示されている。　2「教室で過ごす時間がそれほど長くないなかで子どもが(　　　)を得られる」ので，多くを意味するウが正解である。　3 smoother ride のために考えられるのは，カ。　4 フィンランドの教育面での成功に関する内容であるため，dropout の割合は低いと考えるのが妥当である。　(4) 下線直後の文で，家庭の役割の具体例として家庭内の活発な読書の文化が触れられており，また，成果についても同じ文中に述べられている。(5) ④ 主語が ～ pupils までであることに注意すること。　⑤ no wonder や that makes school fun を日本語として不自然でないように訳すこと。

【6】(解答例) (1) It is good manners to turn off your cell phone in public places.　(2) I feel happiest when I find a way of thinking which the Japanese do not have through communication with people from abroad.

〈解説〉(1)「礼儀」の訳がうまくできるか「礼儀正しい」の意味だと polite も考えられるが，問題文の場合は礼儀正しいというよりも当然の行いとして述べられているため，manner を用いるのが適切であると言える。　(2) 1文が長いが，最上級の使用や，関係代名詞での後置修飾がきちんと抑えられているとよい。

【7】(解答例) The biggest advantage to include group works in classes would be the opportunity for students to use or communicate in English. When a task to be completed has a clear goal, language use can be more active. For example, if the target grammar is “there is / are”, a task such as “the picture-description competition” can motivate students to find words they know and use the target expression. (66 words)

〈解説〉学習指導要領の「3　指導計画の作成と内容の取り扱い」(1)のキにおいて，ペアワークやグループワークなどの学習形態が工夫されるべきであることが述べられている。これらの形態の利点としては，言語活動やコミュニケーション活動を行うことで，英語を手段として意味の伝達を行うことが一番に挙げられる。特に3名以上で行うグループワークでは，協同学習の観点から，個々に役割や責任のある相互協力的な活動が可能になる。

## 【高等学校】

【1】1　総合　　2　場面　　3　働き　　4　発音　　5　辞書　　6　グループ・ワーク　　7　視聴覚

〈解説〉問題文にあるように，高等学校学習指導要領の第2章第8節にすべて記載がある。また，問題にあがっている文言は，中学校学習指導要領の記述とも重複がかなりあり，中高を通じて重視されている観点であるため，しっかり抑えたい。　1については，平成21年3月告示の指導要領で，「総合的に」という文言が加えられた。高等学校学習指導要領解説の第1章第1節「2　改訂の趣旨」にも「4技能の総合的な指導を通して」と述べられているように，4つの領域の言語活動の統合は，内容の取り扱いにおいて重要な観点である。

【2】(解答例) (1)　What do you think about this opinion?　　(2)　Don't be afraid of making mistakes.　　(3)　If you don't know the meaning of this word, look it up in your dictionary.

〈解説〉学習指導要領解説の第3章において「教師が授業を英語で行うとともに，生徒も授業の中でできるだけ英語を使用することにより，英語による言語活動を行うことを授業の中心とする」とある。英語使用が目的ではなく手段であるということを念頭におき，授業内においても指示やフィードバックなど，英語をコミュニケーションツールとしたい。解答のポイントとしては，生徒にとって理解可能な平易な英語であるか，高等学校で学習する表現や文法事項が適切に用いられているかに注意するとよいであろう。

【３】(解答例) (1)　If I were you, I would accept his offer.　(2)　If I had had enough money, I could have bought the picture.　(3)　An honest man wouldn't do such a thing.

〈解説〉良質な例文の条件として，文が短いこと，生徒にとって身近なことなどが挙げられる。特に，仮定法は高等学校で初出の文法であるため，文法項目に意識を向かせるために語彙は難易度が高い必要はないであろう。　(1)　If I were you, ～「もしもわたしがあなただったら～」という分かりやすい例文を作っている。　(2)「もしわたしが(過去のある一時点で)十分なお金をもっていたら，その絵を買えたのに」と過去の非現実を表している。　(3)　主語がif節の代わりとして用いられる仮定法でも通常の仮定法と同じように「もし～だったら」という意味になる点に注意する。解答例では，「正直な人なら，そんなことはしないであろう」の意になる。

【４】(1)　エ　(2)　①　ア　②　ウ　④　エ　(3)　A　ウ　B　ア　C　ア　D　イ　E　エ　(4)　in　(5)　イ／オ／キ

〈解説〉(1)　全体を通して語られている内容はエのみ。　(2)　①　前の文で，「脳内で何が起こっているのだろうか」という疑問を投げかけており，研究がその働きを明らかにしたとあるので，答えは脳だと分かる。　②「一緒に働くことで考えたり思い出したり…することができる」とあるので，脳内のどこか1箇所ではなく，様々な部位をまとめたウが正解である。　④　勉強時間に間隔をあけることと詰め込むことを比較しているため，「勉強時間に間隔をあけることが効率的である」と考えるのが妥当である。　(3)　A　the future のコロケーションとして考えられるものは in the future や for the future があるが，for the future は特に plan や vision といった語を伴うことが多い。　B　compared と共に使われる前置詞は to と with が挙げられる。　C　「共通の」という意味の in common はセットで覚えたい。　D　「ニューロンからニューロンへ」という文脈であるため，from が適切である。　E　you are trying toの後ろに learn a new language と learn a new dance move が並列でつなげられている。 (4) information の後置修飾として taken in through the senses が続いている。 (5) イは第3段落4文目の the *cerebellum*, helps control your movements and balance から，オは第6段落最後の文 Mirror neurons, for example, are specialized cells that help you show empathy and understanding to others から，キは第9段落2文目の Practice makes perfect や後続の文章から分かる。

【5】(1) Because they believe that their fixed ability may not be up to the task. (2) It implies that someone who looks smart was not born smart but worked hard to become smart. (3) Because it is when the academic work often gets much harder, the grading gets stricter, and the school environment gets less personalized with students moving from class to class. (4) It refers to "learning opportunities." (5) C (6) Simply to study more or study differently the next time. (7) Although / Though (8) A fixed B school (9) B / E / F

〈解説〉英語で答える問題であるが，解答にあたる部分はほとんど本文中に記載されており，該当部分を見つけることができれば，それほど難しい問題ではないといえる。 (1) 質問は第1段落の3文目に対応しており，because 以降を書けば問題ない。 (2) even Einstein wasn't Einstein until he put in years of focused hard work と続いているので，Einstein(知能の高い人)であっても，一生懸命勉強しなければEinstein(知能が高い人)にはならないという内容が書けていればよい。
(3) 7年生がどのような時期であるのかということが This is when 以降で述べられている。 (4) 「自分たちの成功にとって重大であっても」と続いているので，これに合う既出の語句は直前の learning opportunities である。 (5) Cの直前の文，「fixed mindset の学生は，一生懸命にやるということは，自分には能力がないということを意味し，もしも能力があれば，事柄は自然に頭に浮かんでくるものだと信じている」から，問題文「このことは，なにか難しくて，努力を要するときはいつも，彼らにとってそれは脅威でありやっかいなものである」と続けるのが適切である。　(6)　同段落の2文目に，growth mindsetの生徒たちが学習を続けたり異なる方法を試したりする前向きな様子が述べられている。　(7)　節中は主語と動詞がそろっているが，節同士を結ぶ接続詞が見当たらない。文脈より，逆説の接続詞を入れる。　(8)　A　fixedかgrowthで，文脈に合うfixedを用いる。　B　2文目より引用。　(9)　growth mindset については本文全体を通して述べられているが，第2段落だけからでも，B，E，F を選ぶことが可能である。

【6】(解答例) Once a child has earned a certain reputation among his classmates, it is very difficult, if not impossible, to change the early image. This is because their usual responses force him to maintain the same role.

〈解説〉できるだけ厳密に訳していくことが望ましいが，その場で単語や構文が思いつかない場合，時には言い換えることも必要であろう。

【7】(解答例) Today online shopping has become a major shopping style for its convenient and accessible characteristics. The biggest advantage for customers is that they can buy anything — cloths foods and even furniture — at any time. While we can enjoy such convenience, we have to be more careful about some problems such as overspending and hacking on the Internet. (57 words)

〈解説〉1つの事象について，メリットとデメリットの両方を書く問題であるため，どちらかに偏った意見ではなく，中立的な立場から述べる必要がある。対照的なポイントを挙げるため，in contrast，on the other hand，while ～，などといった表現を用いながら，まとまりのある文章が書けるようにしたい。本問題はごく一般的なオンラインショッピングがトピックとして取り上げられているが，英語教育に関する話題についても自分の意見をまとめておくとよいであろう。

# 2013年度 実施問題

## 【中高共通】

【1】(Words in parentheses should not be read.)

Listening Comprehension Section

There are three parts to this section, with special directions for each part. You may take notes while you are listening.

Now, let's begin Part1. In this part, you will hear five conversations between two people. After each conversation, a third person will ask a question about what was said. Read the four possible answers on your test paper, choose the best answer to each question, and write it on your answer sheet. You will hear each conversation and question about it just one time.

PART 1 (記号で書け。)

No.1

(M) The concert starts at 8 : 00.

(F) We still have fifteen minutes.

Question : What time is it?

(A) 7 : 50.

(B) 8 : 15.

(C) 7 : 45.

(D) 8 : 00.

No.2

(M) Did you return the CD to the rental shop for me? I don't want to pay a late charge.

(F) Don't worry about it. I took care of it.

Question : What does the woman mean?

(A) She returned the CD.

(B) She's taking good care of the CD.

(C) She'll have to pay a late charge.

(D) She's worried about the CD.

No.3

(M) Would you like to go to the movies with Tom and me on Friday?

(F) I wish I could, but I'm having dinner at my sister's.

Question : What will the woman do on Friday?

(A) Go to the movies with the man.

(B) Take her sister to the movies.

(C) Eat at her sister's.

(D) Cook dinner with Tom.

No.4

(M) Driving at night always makes me tired. Let's stop for dinner.

(F) Fine! And let's find a motel, too — instead of continuing on, we can get an early start tomorrow.

Question : What will the speakers probably do?

(A) Drive on through the night.

(B) Check out of the motel.

(C) Cancel their motel reservation.

(D) Stop driving for the rest of the day.

No.5

(M) What a beautiful day it is! It's a perfect day for the football game.

(F) Indeed, you couldn't ask for better weather.

Question : What does the woman mean?

(A) Everyone will enjoy the game.

(B) It's nice weather.

(C) Tomorrow will be better weather.

(D) She expected better weather.

Now, let's go on to Part2. In this part, you will hear a conversation. After that, you will be asked five questions. Read the four possible answers on your test paper, decide which one is the best answer to the question you heard, and write it on your answer sheet. You will hear the conversation and questions about it two times.

PART 2

(F) Hi, John!

(M) Oh. Hi, Laura. What are you doing here?

(F) Uh ... this is my dad's shop. I'm usually here on weekends to help him. So ... you're looking for a bike?

(M) Yeah. Now that the weather's warming up, I thought I'd better get some exercise — instead of taking the bus all the time.

(F) Well, you came to the right place. Do you know what you'd like?

(M) Well, I dont want a racer or a touring bike or anything like that. Mostly I'll just be using it to get me back and forth from work.

(F) How far is that?

(M) About four miles.

(F) Are there a lot of hills on the way?

(M) Some, I guess. But ... uh ... maybe I should just tell you up front that I've only got a hundred and fifty dollars. Can I get anything decent for that?

(F) Well, you're not going to get anything top-of-the-line — but we do have a few trade-ins in the back that are in good condition.

(M) That sounds good.

(F) And you're right, for the kind of riding you're going to be doing, the most important thing is comfort. You want to make sure it's the right height for you. Follow me and I'll show you what we've got.

Question 1 : Why is Laura at the bicycle shop?

Question 2 : Why does John want to buy a bicycle?

Question 3 : What does Laura suggest that John do?

Question 4 : What does Laura say is the most important thing about John's bike?

Question 5 : What will they probably do?

Listen again.

PART 2(記号で書け。)

No.1

(A) She's getting some exercise.

(B) She's having her bicycle repaired.

(C) She wanted to surprise John.

(D) She's helping her father.

No.2

(A) To replace his stolen bicycle.

(B) To begin bicycling to work.

(C) To join a bicycle club.

(D) To train for a bicycle race.

No.3

(A) Buy a used bicycle.

(B) Buy a racing bicycle.

(C) Replace the tires on his bicycle.

(D) Sell his old bicycle to the shop.

No.4

(A) It must be the right height.

(B) It must have several gears.

(C) It must have good tires.

(D) It must be the right weight.

No.5

(A) Go to another bicycle shop together.

(B) Choose a bike.

(C) Ask Laura's father to hire John.

(D) Keep talking about Laura's bike.

Part3. In this part, you will hear one lecture about a bird two times. Before listening, you should read the four questions carefully so that you can write the answers on your answer sheet. You have 20 seconds to read.

Now, listen.

The hummingbird is nature's smallest bird. In addition to its size, it is also well-known for its skill in flying. Not only can it hover in mid-air with its wings beating up to 78 times per second, but it also can fly backwards and even upside down.

Since hummingbirds eat up to half the weight of their bodies each day and drink up to eight times their weight in water, they must migrate south to where food is plentiful as winter approaches.

For a long time it was a mystery how the tiny hummingbird could make a 500 mile trip from the United States to Central America. Some suggested that perhaps the birds stopped on islands in the Gulf of Mexico along the way to rest and eat. Another popular explanation was that hummingbirds made the trip on the backs of larger, stronger birds. It is now known that the tiny birds store up to several grams of fat before they start their trip.

The hummingbird has many enemies including other birds. Large frogs and even fish also feed on them. Because of their small size, spider webs and sharp grasses are also hazardous to them.

Listen again.

PART 3 (述べられている内容について，指示に従って答えよ。)

Questions

(1)　What are the hummingbird's we11-known skills in flying?　(適切な答えの番号を三つ○で囲め。)

(2)　How much does the hummingbird eat and drink every day?　(日本語で書け。)

(3)　Why can the hummingbird take a very long trip?　(適切な答えの番号を一つ○で囲め。)

(4)　Except for other birds, what are dangerous to the hummingbird? Give two examples of them.　(日本語で書け。)

| | | |
|---|---|---|
| (1) | 1　眠りながら飛べる　2　空中で停止できる　3　78時間連続して飛べる<br>4　後ろ向きに飛べる　5　仰向けになって飛べる | |
| (2) | 自分の体重の（　　　　）の餌を食べる | 自分の体重の（　　　　）の水を飲む |
| (3) | 1　途中の島で休んで食べるから<br>2　自分より大きく強い鳥の背中に乗るから<br>3　出発前に脂肪を体内に蓄えるから | |

This is the end of the Listening Comprehension Section.

(☆☆☆◎◎◎)

【2】次の(1)～(5)のそれぞれについて，下線部の①～④のいずれかに一箇所誤りがある。その箇所の番号と，正しい表現に直したものを書け。

(1)　The movie I ①saw last night ②was so ③excited ④to me.

(2)　Baseball ①is introduced and ②started to be played ③in Japan ④during the Meiji era.

(3)　After the ①owners rejected their demand, the players debated ②that they should go ③on ④strike or not.

(4)　Because she ①was a new actress, she was not ②used to ③having her photographs ④take in the street.

(5)　Among the friends ①you make at college, ②some will remain ③close to you all your life, while ④other will be only casual companions.

(☆☆☆◎◎◎)

【3】次の(1)～(3)の各組において，a)とb)がほぼ同じ意味になるように，b)の(　　)内にそれぞれ適切な一語を書け。

(1) a) My parents were born in Tokyo and still live there.

b) My parents have lived in Tokyo (　　) (　　) were born.

(2) a) I prefer working to sitting idle.

b) I would (　　) work than sit idle.

(3) a) Tired as she was, she did not give up her plan.

b) (　　) she was tired, she did not give up her plan.

(☆☆☆◎◎◎)

【4】次の(1)～(5)のそれぞれについて，日本文の意味になるように(　　)内に適切な一語を書け。

(1) 点字の発明は19世紀である。

Braille was (　　) in the 19th century.

(2) その知らせを聞いてとても驚いた。

The news (　　) us very surprised.

(3) どんなに一生懸命やってみても，彼女を満足させることはできません。

(　　) hard we may try, we cannot satisfy her.

(4) 彼は心ならずも計画をあきらめるほか仕方がなかった。

He could do (　　) but give up his plan against his wil1.

(5) 彼女は喜びのあまり我を忘れた。

She was (　　) herself with joy.

(☆☆☆◎◎◎)

【5】次の会話文の1～5の(　　)内には，あとのア～クのいずれかが入る。それぞれにあてはまる最も適切なものを一つずつ選んで，その記号を書け。ただし，同じ選択肢を2回以上選ぶことはできない。

Yuko : When I was at university, I stayed with an American family in Texas.

Helen : Did you have any interesting or funny experiences with your English?

Yuko : I had one experience, but for me it wasn't interesting or funny. ( 1 )

Helen : So you think it's funny now?

Yuko : Yes. ( 2 )

Helen : So what happened?

Yuko : My host family had a dog called Charlie. One day I took it for a walk.

Helen : And it didn't like you?

Yuko : ( 3 ) But I did not know how to give commands to it in English.

Helen : ( 4 )

Yuko : That's right. I got so tired running after it that I shouted, "I gave up."

Helen : ( 5 )

Yuko : No. It ran back to me and started jumping up and licking me.

Helen : Maybe the dog heard you say, "up," so it jumped up. Didn't your host family help you?

Yuko : They did after they stopped laughing. They gave me an immediate lesson in dog commands.

Helen : I'm sure you learned very quickly.

ア Actually, it was very friendly to me.
イ At least, not at the time.
ウ Did the dog stop when it heard you?
エ I fell over.
オ I often laugh about it.
カ I still feel unhappy about it.
キ Like saying, "sit" when you want it to sit?
ク We always went by car.

(☆☆◎◎◎)

【6】次の(1)～(3)のそれぞれについて，下のア～クを並べかえて日本文と同じ意味の英文を作る。その際，( ① )，( ② )内にあてはまる語(句)を，ア～クからそれぞれ選んで，その記号を書け。

(1) あの背の高い男の人の年齢を知っていますか。

Do ( )( )( ① )( )( )( ② )( )( )?

ア that　イ man　ウ know　エ is　オ you
カ o1d　キ tall　ク how

(2) ストレスは，起こっていることからではなくて起こったことに対する私たちの感じ方から生じる。

Stress ( )( )( ① )( )( )( ② )( )( ), not from the things that are happening.

ア has happened　イ from　ウ feel　エ what
オ the way　カ comes　キ we　ク about

(3) 同じ飛行機に乗り合わせるとは本当に偶然でした。

It was by ( )( )( ① )( )( )( ② )( ) ( ) same plane.

ア coincidence　イ we　ウ that　エ a　オ on
カ sheer　キ were　ク the

(☆☆◎◎◎)

## 【中学校】

【1】次の文は，中学校学習指導要領(平成20年3月告示)の外国語の目標を示そうとしたものである。次の1～5の( )内にあてはまる語句を書け。

( 1 )を通じて，言語や( 2 )に対する理解を深め，積極的に( 3 )を図ろうとする態度の育成を図り，聞くこと，( 4 )，読むこと，書くことなどの( 3 )能力の( 5 )を養う。

(☆☆◎◎◎◎◎)

【２】英語の授業で次の(1)～(5)のことを生徒に伝えたいとき，英語でどのように話すか。書け。

(1) 質問はありますか。

(2) 40ページの3行目の文を見なさい。

(3) ペアで読む練習をしなさい。

(4) 話をやめて，私の話を聞きなさい。

(5) 何枚カードを持っていますか。

(☆☆◎◎◎◎)

【３】中学生に，言語材料として現在完了形(経験)を導入する際にJTLとALTが行う，対話形式のオーラル・イントロダクションを考え，次の与えられた最初の一文に続けて英語で作成せよ。ただし，作成する英文は10文以上とし，追加の部分が必要であれば，付け足してもよい。

JTL : Do you have any plans for this weekend?

ALT :

JTL :

ALT :

JTL :

ALT :

JTL :

ALT :

(☆☆☆◎◎◎◎)

【４】次の英文は，アメリカの大学に勤めている NNES teacher (nonnative-English-speaking teacher)が書いたものの抜粋である。これを読み，あとの(1)～(6)の問いに答えよ。

①There are conflicting views in the literature about the benefits of NNES teachers revealing their nonnative status to students. The teachers themselves may not necessarily agree that doing so is beneficial. Some may feel that it is important to gain students' trust and respect first. At the beginning of each course, I build rapport with students by saying that I know what it is like to be an English learner, and I talk about my own language learning experiences. Revealing one's identity and nonnative status to students ②(may / may not) depend on one's teaching context and students, so NNES teachers should carefully consider whether to ③do so. I use the opportunities created by my nonnative status to reveal my firsthand experiences with learning English. This strategy brings me closer to students and usually serves to unify the class.

One example of a language learning experience I often share with students is using a monolingual dictionary. Some students may think that using a monolingual dictionary in one's first year of learning a language may be difficult because they may not have a basic understanding of the language. ( 1 ), I started using a monolingual dictionary during my first year learning English in Brazil. And I have to confess that it was ④(easy / hard) at first. As a reading strategy, I looked up a word in the dictionary, and I would find maybe three (or more) words within the definition that I didn't know. Forcing myself to check the meanings of so many words in ⑤the language of instruction actually helped me learn many new words. I would recommend monolingual dictionaries that provide sentences as examples to clarify what the main word means.

I also used a bilingual dictionary because it was helpful when I really needed to translate a word. ( 2 ), in my Portuguese-English dictionary, I would look up a Portuguese word that I wanted to know in English. The dictionary would list many words as options for the Portuguese word, so what would I do? I would go back to my monolingual dictionary and look up ⑥each option to see which nuance was the one I needed. That took a long time, but it was worth it. Now I use an online dictionary, ( 3 ) I have bookmarked in my web browser. The best aspect of many online dictionaries is that they give the pronunciation of words, so in addition to learning the meaning of the word, one can listen to the word being pronounced.

(1)　下線部①について，筆者の立場として最も適切なものを，次のア～エから一つ選んで，その記号を書け。

ア　Teachers should reveal their nonnative status to students.

イ　Teachers should not reveal their nonnative status to students.

ウ　Teachers should ask their students if they want to know their teachers' backgrounds.

エ　Teachers should ask their authority about revealing their nonnative status.

(2)　文中の②，④の(　　)内の語(句)のうち，文脈に合う適切な方をそれぞれ選んで書け。

(3)　下線部③の内容として最も適切なものを，次のア～エから一つ選んで，その記号を書け。

ア　talk about my own language learning experiences

イ　reveal one's identity and nonnative status to students

ウ　depend on one's teaching context and students

エ　use the opportunities created by my nonnative status

(4)　文中の1～3の(　　)内にあてはまる最も適切なものを，次のア～エからそれぞれ一つずつ選んで，その記号を書け。

( 1 )　ア　Therefore　イ　However　ウ　Similarly　エ　For example

( 2 )　ア　Therefore　イ　However　ウ　Similarly　エ　For example

( 3 )　ア　that　イ　which　ウ　and　エ　but

(5)　下線部⑤にあたるものを，次のア～エから一つ選んで，その記号を書け。

ア　English　イ　Portuguese　ウ　Spanish　エ　Japanese

(6)　下線部⑥の内容として最も適切なものを，次のア～エから一つ選んで，その記号を書け。

ア　language　イ　dictionary　ウ　word entry　エ　pronunciation

(☆☆☆◎◎◎)

【5】次の英文を読み，下の(1)～(6)の問いに答えよ。

Do you often talk about blood types with your friends? In Japan, blood types are often talked about in daily conversation. Why do the Japanese people like to talk about their blood types?

At student parties, for example, the conversation often begins with a question, "Hey, what's your blood type?" ①It works well to break the ice among people who have just met. If someone mentions casually that, "Type O women are really compatible with Type B men," then the people involved feel closer. ②〔to / the Japanese / as much as / about /few peoples / talk / blood types / like〕 do.

However, people who talk about blood types usually aren't very ( 1 ). Most people don't believe that ③it is really possible to classify personalities into only four categories.

Still, if there's somebody you don't like, it's often easy to get others to understand your feelings by saying, "That guy has Type A blood. I don't get along with people like that." ④Blood types provide a convenient excuse for people obsessed with relationships with others.

Even though there's no basis for claims like "Type 0 women are really compatible with Type B men," such statements create bonds that make people feel more ( 2 ). Rather than believing in blood-type fortunetelling, people feel relieved to put themselves and others into neat pigeonholes.

In fact, it is practically ( 3 ) to classify people's personalities according to four blood types. Perhaps the reason this blood-type fantasy was created is that, since the Japanese people are so similar to each other and difficult to tell apart, blood types help people maintain a sense of individual identity.

In other countries, blood types are thought about only for ( 4 ). ⑤Rarely are they ever discussed in relation to people's personalities.

(1) 文中の1～3の(　　)内にあてはまる最も適切な語を，次のア～オからそれぞれ一つずつ選んで，その記号を書け。ただし，同じ選択肢を2回以上選ぶことはできない。

ア　comfortable　　イ　complete　　ウ　amiable　　エ　impossible
オ　serious

(2)　下線部①，③の指す内容を，それぞれ日本語で書け。

(3)　下線部②が次の日本語に合うように〔　　〕内の語を並べかえ，英語で書け。(文頭に来る文字も小文字で表記している。)
「日本人ほど血液型の話題が好きな国民というのも珍しい。」

(4)　下線部④を日本語に直して書け。

(5)　下線部⑤を，theyの指すものを明らかにして，日本語に直して書け。

(6)　文中の4の(　　)内にあてはまる最も適切なものを，次のア～エから一つ選んで，その記号を書け。
ア　fortunetelling　　イ　a transfusion　　ウ　career　　エ　feelings

(☆☆☆◎◎◎)

【6】次の文中の下線部①，②を英語に直して書け。

①人と人がお互いの間にとる距離は文化によって異なっている。たとえば，日本人とアメリカ人とでは，二人の人が一つのベンチに座る時にとる距離は違っている。日本人の方が，距離をとることを好むようだ。

人と人との距離は普段，無意識のうちに保たれている。このため，②誰かが予想以上に近づいてくると，人は不快に感じるのだ。

(☆☆☆◎◎◎)

【7】中学生が部活動を通して得られるものについて，あなたの意見を50語以上の英語で書け。

(☆☆☆☆◎◎◎)

## 【高等学校】

【1】高等学校学習指導要領(平成21年3月告示)第2章第8節外国語第2款各科目に示された科目名を省略せずに，7つすべて書け。

(☆☆☆◎◎◎)

【2】英語の授業で次の(1)，(2)のことを生徒に伝えたいとき，英語でどのように話すか。書け。

(1) 4人グループを作り，机を合わせなさい。

(2) 質問があれば手を挙げなさい。

(☆☆◎◎◎◎)

【3】次の(1)～(5)の文構造の例文を，それぞれ1文書け。

(1) [主語＋動詞＋補語]のうち，主語＋be動詞以外の動詞＋現在分詞

(2) [主語＋動詞＋補語]のうち，主語＋be動詞以外の動詞＋過去分詞

(3) [主語＋動詞＋目的語]のうち，主語＋動詞＋ifで始まる節

(4) [主語＋動詞＋間接目的語＋直接目的語]のうち，主語＋動詞＋間接目的語＋thatで始まる節

(5) [主語＋動詞＋間接目的語＋直接目的語]のうち，主語＋動詞＋間接目的語＋whatで始まる節

(☆☆☆◎◎◎)

【4】1999年に書かれた次の英文を読み，あとの(1)～(8)の問いに答えよ。

Primary-school education was not made ①compulsory in Italy until many years later than in most other European countries. Because of the widespread poverty that prevailed in many parts of Italy then, relatively few people could afford to pay for education themselves. As a result, a substantial number of Italians in their sixties, seventies and eighties have had little or no schooling in their lives. [ A ]

One group of researchers was interested to find out whether the amount of education people had in early life had any effect on the state of their brains in old age. The results were very surprising: rates of Alzheimer's disease were fourteen times greater among illiterate people with no education than among those who had more than five years' education. Just over 7 percent of illiterate people had Alzheimer's disease, while just under 3 percent of those with less than five years of education suffered this ②dementia. [ B ]

Researchers have found the same result in many different countries. However, how education affects the brain's trembling web is not yet clear. One possibility is that the actual disease process in the brain tissue is stopped or delayed. Another is that education ③nurtures a better-connected network of neurons. [　C　] When this web is afflicted by the disease, so the argument goes, it keeps functioning better and longer than less well-connected webs because patterns of memories, skills and knowledge are stitched more densely into the connections, and hence are ④(ア more　イ less)easily lost.

Another possibility is that education fosters lifelong habits of mental activity. ⑤The more education you have, the more likely you are stimulate your brain with reading throughout a lifetime, and probably you will tend to debate, discuss and think more about the world around you. [　D　] ⑥It is also possible that this ongoing mental activity in old age offers protection to the old brain against the decay of Alzheimer's disease.

Researchers have actually measured the richness of connections among brain cells in people with ⑦(ア different　イ same) levels of education. While ⑧they could not prove which came first－complex brain neurons or relatively high education－the Italian research strongly supports the notion that education has effects in the brain which either delay the ⑨onset of disease or protect the brain against the disease when it does come on.

(1) 下線部①，②，⑨の本文中での意味と，最も近い意味を表す語を，次のア～エからそれぞれ一つずつ選んで，その記号を書け。

① ア introductory　イ obligatory　ウ supplementary　エ voluntary

② ア sprain　イ burn　ウ ability　エ illness

⑨ ア hold　イ move　ウ start　エ tremble

(2) 下線部③と最も近い意味で使われている語を，本文から抜き出して書け。

(3) ④，⑦の(　　)内から，適切な語を一つずつ選んで，その記号を書け。

(4) 下線部⑤からは，本来入るべきtoが削除されている。toを本来の位置に戻したとき，その前に来る語を書け。

(5) 下線部⑥を日本語に直して書け。

(6) 下線部⑧が指すものを本文から抜き出して書け。

(7) 次の文は，本文中の[ A ]～[ D ]のいずれかに入る。最も適切な箇所を一つ選んで，その記号を書け。

Among those who had more than five years' schooling, the rate of Alzheimer's disease was just half of l percent.

(8) 本文の内容と一致するものを，次のア～エから一つ選んで，その記号を書け。

ア 60歳代から80歳代のイタリア人の中で，ほとんど，あるいは全く学校教育を受けていない人はいない。

イ 若いときにどのくらい教育を受けたかによって，老人になってからの脳の状態に影響がでてくるかどうかを研究するグループがいた。

ウ 5年以上の教育を受けた人と，全く教育を受けていない人を比較すると，後者がアルツハイマー病にかかる割合は，前者の3%以下だった。

エ 高等教育を受けることで神経単位が複雑化し，アルツハイマー病の予防になることが，はっきり証明された。

(☆☆☆◎◎◎)

【5】次の英文を読み，あとの(1)～(6)の問いに答えよ。

What do you do? --- this is surely one of the oldest questions asked when getting to know others, but today we may want to add another: How do you work? ①<u>The way people work tells a lot about their values as well as the impact of globalization on our society.</u> According to an encyclopedia, globalization refers to "increasing global connectivity, integration, and interdependence in the economic, social, technological, cultural, political, and ecological spheres."

Indeed, thanks to various kinds of modern technology, an increasing number of people, products, and information are moving across countries. In such a world, an incident or an interest in one place affects lives in (　A　) places, and not only people's needs and desires but also work conditions are changing constantly and rapidly.

Facing this change in society, both workers and companies are now reconsidering the meaning of work in their life and society. Globalization, of course, means that you must work harder than ever, often competing with other people overseas. Jobs move to where the same quality of work is available at a cheaper cost. ②<u>This</u> is not just the case with factory workers. For example, as the August 20 and 27, 2007 issue of *Business Week* points out, today the U.S. sees even ③<u>white-collar jobs</u> being sent to emerging countries such as China and India. Since 2000, the number of positions for software programmers has decreased by 25.4 percent and that of call-center employees has decreased by 16.4 percent. In this situation, companies started rethinking the quality of their products or services. They are clarifying what can be done offshore and what should still be done face to face. As for workers, so-called "(　B　) skills" are becoming important. That is, in a changing workplace, they need to have basic communication skills and information literacy so that they can work anywhere, in addition to knowledge and experience in their field of specialty.

Furthermore, many workers and companies have asked themselves the question, "what do we work for?" and they now look to the notion of ④<u>work-life balance</u>. This is the idea that balancing one's work and private life leads to a higher quality of not just work but also life. Even working in a time of global competition, we, as human beings, want to live happily inside and outside of our workplace. Since companies also have recognized that happy workers are motivated and productive compared to less happy ones, many have made efforts to change their working environments. Some companies let their workers choose to work at home so that they can take care of their family. Others have banned their employees from working overtime.

It is difficult for an individual worker to change his or her work conditions. However, we still can make efforts to work better by understanding our values and the changes in our society, as well as by making decisions about the way we work. Making efforts to work better is a process of making our lives better in this era of (　C　).

(1)　下線部①を日本語に直して書け。

(2)　文中のA，Bの(　　)内にあてはまる最も適切な語を，次のア～エからそれぞれ一つずつ選んで，その記号を書け。

A　ア　distant　イ　intricate　ウ　dominant　エ　fertile

B　ア　domestic　イ　imaginary　ウ　portable　エ　physica1

(3)　下線部②の指す内容を日本語で書け。

(4)　下線部③の具体例を本文から二つ抜き出して書け。

(5)　下線部④を重視した会社の具体的な取り組みとして，本文中に述べられているものを，二つ日本語で書け。

(6)　文中のCの(　　)内にあてはまる最も適切な語を本文から抜き出して書け。

(☆☆☆◎◎◎)

【6】次の日本文を英語に直せ。

外国語を習得することは，ある年齢をすぎると不可能とは言わないまでも，極端に難しくなると主張する人々がいるが，この考えは現在では以前ほど広く受け入れられてはいない。

(☆☆☆☆◎◎◎)

【7】うそをつくのはどんな場合でも許されない」という意見について，賛成か反対のいずれかの立場から，あなたの考えを50語以上の英語で書け。

(☆☆☆◎◎◎)

# 解答・解説

## 【中高共通】

【1】Part 1　No.1　(C)　No.2　(A)　No.3　(C)　No.4　(D)　No.5　(B)　Part 2　No.1　(D)　No.2　(B)　No.3　(A)　No.4　(A)　No.5　(B)　Part 3　(1)　2，4，5　(2)　半分・8倍　(3)　3　(4)　大きなカエル/魚/クモの巣/鋭くとがった草　の中から二つ

〈解説〉Part 1　No.1　女性の「15分あるね」はコンサートが始まるまでを指す。　No.2　男性の会話から，女性のI took care of it.「ちゃんとやったよ」はレンタルCDを返却したことを指す。　No.3　having dinnerと言っている。at sister'sは「姉(妹)の家で」の意味。　No.4　Let's stop for dinner.にFine.と答えていること，let's find a motelから。No.5　女性のせりふを直訳すると「本当。これ以上よい天気はお願いできないわよね」となる。　Part 2　No.1　女性の2つ目の会話から。No.2　男性の3つ目の会話のto get me back and forth from work「職場から行ったり来たりするため」から，通勤に自転車を使うつもりとわかる。　No.3　女性が「良い状態の下取り品(trade-ins)ならあるわよ」と言っている。　No.4　最後のせりふで女性は，最も大事なのは心地よさ(comfort)で，そのためには高さ(height)がちょうどよくないといけないと述べている。　No.5　I'll show you what we've gotは「どんなものがあるか見せるわよ」の意味。つまりこれから購入のため実際の自転車を見せようとしている。　Part 3　(1)　以下の語句から。hover in mid-air「空中に浮かぶ」　fly backwards「後ろ向きに飛ぶ」　upside down「逆さまに」　(2)　eat up to half the weight of their bodies「体の重さの半分まで食べる」　drink up to eight times their weight in water「水を体重の8倍まで飲む」から。　(3)　store up to several grams of fat before they start their trip「旅を始める前に数グラムの脂肪を蓄える」から。　(4)　本文のLarge frogs，fish，spider webs「クモの巣」，sharp grassesから。

【2】(1) 番号 ③ 正しい表現 exciting (2) 番号 ① 正しい表現 was (3) 番号 ② 正しい表現 whether/if (4) 番号 ④ 正しい表現 taken (5) 番号 ④ 正しい表現 others

〈解説〉(1) excitedとexcitingはexcite「～を興奮させる」から派生した形容詞。Interested，interestingと同じように，人の心情を表すのは~edのほうで，そういう気持ちにさせるような事柄を説明するには~ingを用いる。訳「昨夜見た映画は私にとってとてもわくわくするものだった」 (2) 野球が日本に導入された(introduced)のは明治時代なので過去形が適切。訳「野球は明治時代に日本に導入され，プレーされるようになった」 (3) debateは通常matterやquestion，whether/if節を目的語にとり，that節はとらない。最後にor notがあるのでそれをヒントにするとよい。訳「オーナーが選手の要求を拒否した後，選手はストライキを続けるべきかどうか議論した」 (4) have＋O＋過去分詞は「Oを～してもらう」の意味の使役表現。よってtakeはtakenでなければならない。be used to の後は名詞(havingはここでは動名詞)がくる。訳「彼女は女優になったばかりだったので，通りで写真をとってもらうことに慣れていなかった」 (5) ここのotherはother friendsの略なので，othersと複数形でなければならない。訳「大学でできた友達のなかで，人生を通して身近な友達もいれば，うわべだけの仲間にしかならない友達もいる」

【3】(1) since, they (2) rather (3) Though/Although

〈解説〉(1) 過去に始まり現在まで続く事柄は現在完了時制(継続用法)で表す。sinceはその事柄の始点を表すのに用いる。 (2) prefer A to Bで「BよりAが好き(A・Bには名詞や動名詞が入る)」の意味。would rather A than Bは「BよりむしろAしたい(A・Bには動詞の原形が入る)」の意味。 (3) a)について，形容詞＋as S beで譲歩を表し「Sは～だけれども」の意味。「～だけれども」はthough/althoughで表せる。このas

の用法は文法書の接続詞の項目などで紹介されている。

【4】(1)　invented　(2)　made　(3)　However　(4)　nothing
(5)　beside

〈解説〉(1)「発明する」はinvent　(2)「驚く」は，人を主語にして「人 be surprised at 事柄」で表すか，無生物を主語にして「事柄 surprise 人」で表す。ここではsurprisedが文末にあるので，動詞のmadeを入れる。SVOCの型で，surprisedは形容詞的に使われている。　(3)「たとえ(何を・どこに・誰が・どんなに)～ても」は譲歩の表現で，「疑問詞＋ever ～ S V」または「no matter 疑問詞 ～ S V」で表す。ここは「どんなに一生懸命」とあって空欄が1つなので，前者の表現を使いHoweverが正解。　(4)　can/could do nothing but Vで「Vするほかなかった」の意味。　(5)　be beside oneself with ～ で「～で我を忘れる」の意味。

【5】(1)　イ　(2)　オ　(3)　ア　(4)　キ　(5)　ウ

〈解説〉(1)　空欄の後の会話で，HelenがSo you think it's funny now?と聞いていることから，Yukoがテキサスでの経験を今は面白いと思っていると判断できるようなせりふを選べばよい。イは「少なくとも，そのときはそうでなかった(＝面白くなかった)」という意味。　(2)　Helenが半ばせかすようにSo what happened?と話の詳細を求めていることから，YukoがHelenの興味を引くような一言を言ったと推測できる。
(3)　Helenが「犬があなたのこと嫌いだったの？」と聞いているので，犬がYukoを好きだったのかどうかわかるような1文を選ぶ必要がある。アは「実際は，犬は私にすごくなついていた」の意味。　(4)　空欄の直前のYukoのBut ～ の会話から始まる英語で，命令(commands)ができなかったという話をしていることがわかる。よって，キの「犬に座ってほしいときにsitって言うみたいに？」と，英語による命令の具体例が入る。　(5)　YukoがNoと答えていることから，Yes-No疑問文をHelenが尋ねたと推測できる。空欄の後に犬が飛びついたりなめてきたり(licking)したという話があるので，YukoがI gave upと叫んだ後も犬の行儀がよくなっていないことがわかる。ウは「犬がそれ(I gave up)を聞いたときおとなしくなったの？」という意味で，これらに合致する。

【6】(1) ① ク　② キ　(2) ① オ　② ク　(3) ① ア　② キ

〈解説〉(1)　並べ替え全文はDo you know how old that tall man is? である。間接疑問文は主語と述語が通常の語順になる。　(2)　並べ替え全文はStress comes from the way we feel about what has happened, not from the things that are happening.である。「(…についての)～の感じ方」はthe way S feel (about…)で表す。「起こったこと」はwhat has happenedで表せる。　(3)　並べ替え全文はIt was by a sheer coincidence that we were on the same plane.である。「偶然に」はby a coincidenceで，sheerは「全くの」の意味。文頭のItは形式主語で，真の主語，つまり何が偶然だったのかはthat以下で表す。

## 【中学校】

【1】1　外国語　2　文化　3　コミュニケーション　4　話すこと　5　基礎

〈解説〉学習指導要領において「教科の目標」は最初に書いてある最も重要な内容で，評価の観点とも直結する。必ず暗記すること。留意点としては，①言語だけでなく文化に対する理解も深めないといけない点，②一般的には会話能力と捉えられがちな「コミュニケーション能力」には読むことと書くことも含まれる点，③小学校で培われたコミュニケーション能力の「素地」をもとに，中学校ではコミュニケーション能力の「基礎」を養うことを目標としている点が挙げられる。

【2】(1)　(解答例)　Do you have any questions?　(2)　(解答例)　Look at the third line on page 40.　(3)　(解答例)　Practice reading in pairs.　(4)　(解答例)　Stop talking and listen to me.　(5)　(解答例)　How many cards do you have?

〈解説〉ここで出題された教室英語のほとんどが授業でよく使うもの。教室英語に関する書籍は多数あるので，1冊買って目を通しておくとよい。持っておけば教員になってからも役に立つ。

【3】(解答例)

(JTL)　Do you have any plans for this weekend?

(ALT)　Yes. I'm going to visit Hiroshima. Have you ever been to Hiroshima?

(JTL)　Yes, I have been there three times.

(ALT)　I have never visited there. Where did you visit in Hiroshima?

(JTL)　I visited Miyajima, Hiroshima Peace Memorial Park and many *okonomiyaki* shops.

(ALT)　Oh, you went to many *okonomiyaki* shops. I want to try Hiroshima-style *okonomiyaki.*

(JTL)　OK, then I'll tell you the best shop.

(ALT)　Thank you.

〈解説〉文法の口頭導入では，自然な場面を設定し，ALTと行うティームティーチングでは文法を対話のなかで何度も用いながら，その使用方法を生徒に気づかせていくようにする。現在完了の経験用法ではever/never，～timesといった表現も後に重要となるので，導入の段階から取り入れるといいだろう。また，日本や他国に関する文化(ここでは，宮島，広島平和記念館，広島風お好み焼き)への興味を喚起する内容にするとよい。

【4】(1)　ア　(2)　②　may　④　hard　(3)　イ　(4)　1　イ　2　エ　3イ　(5)　ア　(6)　ウ

〈解説〉(1)　①は「文献では，NNES教師が非母語話者であるという自らのステータスを生徒に明らかにすることの利益について，相対する見方がある」という意味。色々な考えがあってよいと認めながらも，4文目以降を読むとわかるように，筆者自身は原則ステータスを明かすことに賛成の立場。　(2)　②　このmayは「～かもしれない」の推量の意味。訳「身元と非母語話者のステータスを生徒に明かす(かどうかという)ことは，その先生の指導環境や生徒によるかもしれない」
④　that節の主語のitは「学習1年目からモノリンガル辞書(ここでは英英辞典を指す)を使うこと」を指す。常識で考えてもはじめのうちは(at first)難しいだろう。　(3)　文章の主旨からNNES教師が慎重に考える(carefully consider)べきことは，自分が非母語話者であることを明らかにするかどうかということ。　(4)　1　空欄の前で，学習1年目からモノリンガル辞書の使用は難しいという意見を紹介し，空欄後で自分は1年目から使用しているという反対の話をしている。逆接の接続詞を入れるのが適当。　2　空欄の後ではどういう場合にバイリンガル辞書(Portuguese-English dictionaryなど)が役立つか，具体例を示しているので，For exampleが入る。　3　I have bookmarked in my web browser (私のウェブブラウザにブックマーク保存している)はonline dictionaryを補足説明している。関係代名詞(非制限用法)を入れるのが適当。
(5)　下線部は直訳すると「指導用の言語」。筆者は英語を教えているのでEnglishが答え。　(6)　ここで紹介しているモノリンガル辞書の活用方法は，あるポルトガル語のニュアンスを持つ英単語を探す場合に，Portuguese-English dictionaryで英単語の候補(options)をいくつか見つけ，そのうちどれがもとのポルトガル語のニュアンスに近いか英英辞典で調べて1つに絞るというもの。word entryは「見出し語」の意味で，ここでは検索して見つかった単語の候補(options)に近い意味。

【5】(1)　1　オ　　2　ア　　3　エ　　(2)　①「血液型は何？」という質問　　③　性格をたった四つのカテゴリーに分類すること
(3)　Few peoples like to talk about blood types as much as the Japanese (do).
(4)　(解答例)　他人との関係を気にしすぎている人々に，血液型は都合のよい言い訳を与えている。　(5)　(解答例)　血液型が人々の性格と関連づけて語られることはめったにない。　(6)　イ
〈解説〉(1)　1　空欄の後の文から，人々が血液占いで4つの性格にわけ

られるとは思っていないことがわかる。　2　次文のfeel relieved「安心する」などから,「O型の女性はB型の男性と相性がいいんだよ」と聞くと, 人は安らいだ気持ちになるとわかる(身近に感じるので)。
3　訳「事実, 4つの血液型で人の性格を分類するのは実際のところ不可能である」　(2)　①　Itは前文の内容を指す。work well「うまくいく」　break the ice「雰囲気をほぐす」　③　itは同文のto不定詞以下を指す。classify (into～)「(～に)分類する」　(3)　as … as ～ の同程度を表す比較表現と, 否定の意味を含む主語(few peoples)を組み合わせて,「～ほど…な人はほとんどいない」の意味。ここのpeopleは「国民」という意味。世界には色々な国があるので複数形になっている。　(4)　provide A for B「BにAを与える」　excuse「言い訳」　obsessed with ～「～を不必要に気にしている」　(5)　否定の意味を含む頻度副詞rarely「めったに～ない」が文頭にきたことで倒置が起こっている。もとの語順はThey are rarely ever discussed ～.である。文脈からtheyはblood typesを指す。in relation to ～で「～に関連付けて」の意味。　(6)　transfusion「輸血」　訳「他の国では血液型は輸血のときだけ考えられる」

【6】①　(解答例)　The distance people keep from each other varies between different cultures.　②　(解答例)　you will feel uncomfortable when someone comes closer than you expect.

〈解説〉①「人と人がお互いの間にとる距離」はthe distance (which) people keep from each otherで表す。「～が異なっている」はvaryで,「文化によって(＝文化間で)」はbetween (different) cultures と表現できる。
②　まず主節となる「人は不快に感じる」を述べる。一般論なので, 主語はyouまたはpeople(＝they)が適当。「近づいてくる」はcome closer (to you)やapproach youで表す。「予想以上に」はthan you expect/than they expectとするのが普通。

【７】(解答例)　Students can learn two things through club activities. First, they can learn that working as a team gives an individual greater power to accomplish something than doing it alone. Second, they are expected to learn that they should do something else than study to be a better person and that they must not judge others based only on their academic ability. (61語)

〈解説〉50語以上なので3～4文くらい書く必要があるだろう。解答例では，人はチームで活動することで独りで何かをするよりもより大きな力を得られること，また人として成長するためには勉学以外も人は行うべきであること，の2点を挙げている。その他，協調性の大切さを学べる，競争社会を生き抜く精神力を養える，努力することの大切さを学べる，などがあろう。

## 【高等学校】

【１】コミュニケーション英語基礎，コミュニケーション英語Ⅰ，コミュニケーション英語Ⅱ，コミュニケーション英語Ⅲ，英語表現Ⅰ，英語表現Ⅱ，英語会話

〈解説〉新学習指導要領の公示により外国語(英語)の従来の科目は廃止され，上記の7科目が設定された。このうち全員必修の科目は「コミュニケーション英語Ⅰ」のみである。それぞれに目的があり，詳細は解説を見ればわかるが，大まかには，「コミュニケーション英語基礎」は，中学校で習った英語の定着とコミュニケーション英語Ⅰへの接続を目的とした科目。「コミュニケーション英語Ⅰ～Ⅲ」は読んだり聞いたりした内容をもとに発表させるなど，4技能の統合を目指した総合科目。「英語表現Ⅰ・Ⅱ」は話すことと書くことの表現の能力を主に養うための科目。「英語会話」は旧来のOCを改編したもので，聞くことと話すことを重視した科目である。

【２】(1)　(解答例)　Make groups of four, and put your desks together.

(2)　(解答例)　Raise your hand if you have any questions.

〈解説〉新学習指導要領のもとでは，英語の授業は原則英語で行うことと

なっている。教室英語は使用頻度が高く，教員だけでなく生徒にとってもとっつきやすい。教室英語を載せた本は多く出ているので，馴染みのない人は1冊持っておくとよい。

【3】(1)　(解答例)　The girl came running to me.　(2)　(解答例)　The old man sat surrounded by children.　(3)　(解答例)　I wonder if you are free today.　(4)　(解答例)　She told me that she had been busy.
(5)　(解答例)　He asked me what I wanted.

〈解説〉(1)　現在分詞が補語になる例は他に，She kept saying that she was right.や，We stood talking until midnight.などがある。文法書の「分詞」の項目を参照するとよい。　(2)　過去分詞が補語になる例は他に，The shop remained closed.や，The treasure lay hidden under the ground.などがある。(1)同様，文法書の「分詞」の項目を参照するとよい。
(3)　3文型で「S＋V＋if節」の場合，目的語となるif節は「もし～」の意味ではなく「～かどうか(whether or not)」の意味。他にはI know if he is married or not.「彼が結婚しているかどうか私は知っている」などもある。辞書でifを調べよう。　(4)　S＋V＋O＋that節の形は他に，He showed me that he was innocent.や，I informed my students that the school would be closed.といった文がある。　(5)　S＋V＋O＋what節の形は他に，I gave him what he had wanted.などがある。解答例は間接疑問文で「彼は私が何がほしいか尋ねた」の意であるが，I gave ～ のほうはwhatが先行詞を含む関係代名詞の文になり「私は彼がほしがっていたものを彼にあげた」という意味である点に注意。文法書の「疑問詞」や「関係代名詞」のwhatのところを見よう。

【4】(1)　①　イ　②　エ　⑨　ウ　(2)　fosters　(3)　④　イ　⑦　ア　(4)　are　(5)　(解答例)　老年期になってもこの精神活動を継続することで，アルツハイマー病という衰えから，年老いた脳が守られるということもありうる。　(6)　Researchers　(7)　B
(8)　イ

〈解説〉(1) ① compulsory「義務的」 obligatory も「義務的，必須の」の意味である。 ② dementia「痴呆などの後天性の知能障害」ここではAlzheimer's diseaseを指す。選択肢で近いのはillnessである。 ⑨ onset「始まり」は，通例，よくないことの始まりの意であるが，選択肢のなかではstart が正解。 (2) nurture「育てる」 第4段落の1文目に foster「育成する」という単語がある。 (3) ④ ここは，教育を受け脳の神経網が発達した人を，教育を受けず神経網が十分発達しなかった人と比較して，彼らが病気になったときに記憶や知識がより簡単に失われるのか(more easily lost)，それともその反対なのか(less easily lost)述べた場面。当然後者である。 ⑦ 文章全体の主旨は受けた教育の年数と病気の関係である。この段落でも脳細胞(brain cells)における神経結合の豊かさ(the richness of connections)と受けた教育の関係を扱っている。異なる教育レベル(different levels of education)の人間を比較実験しないと意味がない。 (4) be likely to Vで「Vする傾向にある」の意味。「The 比較級, the 比較級」の表現によってlikelyは前に出たが，toはそのまま残らなければならない。 (5) 文頭のItは形式主語で真の主語はthat節以下。 ongoing「継続中の」 offer A to B「AをBに提供する」 protection against ～「～に対する保護」 decay「衰え」以上から直訳は「こういった，老年期でも継続した脳の活動は，年老いた脳にアルツハイマー病に対する保護を提供する可能性がある」である。解答例はこれを意訳したもの。 (6) 基本だが，theyは指示対象が複数の名詞に用いる代名詞である。これも踏まえ，「証明する(prove)」のはこの文脈では「研究者(researchers)」だけ。 (7) 入れるべき文の意味は「5年以上の学校教育を受けた者の間では，アルツハイマー病の罹患率は1パーセント以下だった」である。教育年数とアルツハイマー病の罹患率の話をしているのは第2段落である。

(8) 正解のイは第2段落以降をとおして述べられている内容。アについて，第1段落のa substantial number of ～ は「かなりの数の～」という意味。選択肢は本文と全く逆の内容を言っているため×。ウは第2段落に書いてある内容に関連。本文には後者のアルツハイマー病罹患率は前者(＝5年以上教育を受けた者)の14倍だとあるので×。エについて，第3段落の2文目にnot yet clearとあるので×。

【5】(1)　(解答例)　人々の働き方をみると，グローバル化が我々の社会にもたらす影響と同様に人々の価値観がよくわかる。　(2)　A　ア　B　ウ　(3)　(解答例)　質が同じならば，より安くできるところへ仕事は移っていくこと。　(4)　software programmers, call-center employees　(5)　社員が自宅で仕事をすることを選べるようにすること，社員の残業を禁止すること　(6)　globalization

〈解説〉(1)　the way people work「人々の働き方」 S tell(s) a lot about ～「Sは～についてたくさん教えてくれる(→Sから～がよくわかる)」 as well as ～「～と同様に」　(2)　A　文頭のsuch a worldはグローバル化社会のこと。そういった社会ではある場所の出来事や関心事(an incident or an interest in one place)が，離れた(distant)場所の生活にも影響する。　B　次文 That is ～ を読むと，どのようなskillsが労働者に求められているかわかる。すなわち，「職場が変わるので，どこでも働けるように労働者は，専門分野での知識と経験とともに，基本的なコミュニケーションの能力と情報リテラシーを有する必要がある」 この内容に近いのはportable「移動可能の」である。　(3)　This is not just the case with ～ は「このことは～だけの問題ではない」の意味。Thisは前文を指しているので，そこを訳せばよい。whereは場所を表す先行詞(place)を含む関係副詞で，jobsがどんな場所に移っていくか説明している。at a cheaper cost「より安いコストで」　(4)　white-collar jobsとはいわゆる「事務職」のことなので，本文から事務職を2つ探せばよい。どちらも下線部③の次の文にある。　(5)　次の文からwork-life balanceとは「仕事と私生活のバランスをとること」をいう。会社が行っている具体的な取り組みの例は，同段落の最後の2文 Some companies ～. とOthers ～.にある。let＋人＋原形「(人)が～するのを許す」ban A from ～ing「Aが～するのを禁止する」　(6)　eraは「時代」の意味。この文章は一貫してグローバル化(globalization)する社会での生き方・働き方を述べている。訳「よりよく働くために努力をすることは，このグローバリゼーションの時代における私たちの生活をよりよくするプロセスなのである」

【6】(解答例) Some people argue that mastering a foreign language is extremely difficult after a certain age even if it is not impossible, but now this idea is less widely accepted than before.

〈解説〉臨界期仮説に関する英作文問題。まずは全体を「～と主張する人々がいる」と「この考えは～」の2つにわけて文を考え，butで2文をつなげるとよい。前半はさらに「～と主張する人々がいる(Some people argue that ～)」，「外国語を習得することは，ある年齢を過ぎると極端に難しくなる(mastering a foreign language is extremely difficult after a certain age)」，「不可能とは言わないまでも(even if it is not impossible)」の3つにわけられる。後半は「～ほど…でない(less … than ～)」を，比較を使って表すのがポイント。「広く受け入れられている」はwidely acceptedで表せる。

【7】(解答例) I think lying is sometimes necessary especially when telling the truth could hurt someone's feeling. For example, if your child cooks dinner for you and asks you how good her food is, you are not supposed to say it tastes terrible even if you think so. In that case, you might want to say that it is good and give her a tip to cook better. (66語)

〈解説〉50語以上なので3文は必要だろう。最初の1文で自分の立場を端的に述べて，続く文でその根拠となる具体例を示すとよい。どちらの意見を選ぶかは評価に関係ないので，すばやく自分の主張を決めて根拠を考えよう。また，無理に難しい語彙や文法を使う必要はなく，自信のある語彙と文法を使い，簡潔でわかりやすい文章を心がけること。

# 2012年度　実施問題

## 【中高共通】

【 1 】(Words in parentheses should not be read.)

Listening Comprehension Section

There are three parts to this section, with special directions for each part. You may take notes while you are listening.

Now, let's begin Part 1. In this part, you will hear five conversations between two people. After each conversation, a third person will ask a question about what was said. Read the four possible answers on your test paper, choose the best answer to each question, and write it on your answer sheet. You will hear each conversation and question about it just one time.

PART 1 (記号で書け。)

No.1

(M) When do we get to Midtown Station?

(F) Oh, that's two or three stops from here.

Question : Where does this conversation probably take place?

(A) In a taxi.

(B) On the subway.

(C) In an elevator.

(D) At a post office.

No.2

(M) Emily! How long have you been back?

(F) I just got in last night. I'm on my way now to convert my money back to American dollars.

Question : What does Emily mean?

(A) She recently arrived from abroad.

(B) She was in the country.

(C) She came back to earn money.

(D) She's just come from the bank.

No. 3

(F) Laura left long before anyone else.

(M) She must not have been having a very good time.

Question : What does the man mean?

(A) She shouldn't have been late.

(B) Her timing was very poor.

(C) She probably wasn't having fun.

(D) Before long, she was enjoying it.

No. 4

(F) Say, these peaches look ripe to me. Should we get some?

(M) I guess we should while they are still in season.

Question : Where does this conversation probably take place?

(A) At a florist shop.

(B) At a sporting goods store.

(C) At a grocery store.

(D) At a service station.

No. 5

(M) Oh, no. I put my watch right here on the chair and now look.

(F) Check the lost-and-found and see if it was turned in.

Question : What is the man's problem?

(A) His check was lost.

(B) He's unable to find his watch.

(C) He can't put his watch there.

(D) His check didn't arrive.

Now, let's go on to Part 2. In this part, you will hear a conversation. After that, you will be asked five questions. Read the four possible answers on your test paper, decide which one is the best answer to the question you heard, and write it on your answer sheet. You will hear the conversation and the questions about it two times.

(M) We're here. I am really shocked at the water quality of this bay. Look at it there.

(F) Yeah.... Over the years there has been a tremendous amount of development with little thought given to its consequences on the environment.

(M) I can certainly see the effect it's had. I can remember the bay as a child ; it was so clean and full of aquatic life. What do you think the major source of pollution is?

(F) There's no one single source, but I think agricultural runoff causes the most damage.

(M) I remember now. Haven't I heard something about low levels of oxygen in the water?

(F) Precisely. There's too much nitrogen in the water. You see, agricultural runoff contains high amounts of nitrogen. Nitrogen encourages small water plants, called algae, to reproduce rapidly.

(M) Well, what's wrong with that?

(F) When the algae die, the bacteria that consume them use a great deal of oxygen in the process.

(M) Oh, I see. Then, as a result, only small amounts of oxygen remain in the water, and higher forms of aquatic life must move to cleaner water or die.

PART 2 (記号で書け。)

No. 1

Question 1 : What is the main topic of the conversation?

(A) Industrial development.

(B) Declining water quality.

(C) High forms of aquatic life.

(D) Sewage treatment plants.

No. 2

Question 2 : Where does the discussion probably take place?

(A) On a shore.

(B) In a classroom.

(C) On a street.

(D) In a laboratory.

No. 3

Question 3 : According to the woman, what causes most of the damage to the water?

(A) Discharges from industry.

(B) Agricultural runoff.

(C) Storm water runoff.

(D) Hydroelectric dams.

No. 4

Question 4 : What could be done to improve the water?

(A) Reduce levels of oxygen.

(B) Increase plant reproduction.

(C) Reduce levels of nitrogen.

(D) Increase amounts of algae.

No. 5

Question 5 : Why have fish left the bay?

(A) There is insufficient oxygen.

(B) There are not enough small plants.

(C) There is no nitrogen.

(D) There are no bacteria.

Part 3. In this part, you will hear two lectures, both of which will be read two times.

Question 1. You will hear a part of a lecture on vocabulary learning. The lecturer will talk about four useful vocab learning strategies. Write them down briefly in English.

Now, listen.

I believe that teachers should not spend valuable class time focusing on individual low-frequency words. There are too many of them, and it simply takes too much time. Instead of teaching individual words, we need to focus on teaching strategies for coping with and remembering low-frequency words.

Here are the four major strategies, in order of importance :

Guessing from context. This means using clues in written or spoken text to infer the meaning (or at least part of it) of unknown words. To do this successfully, learners need to already know 95-98% of the running words in a text.

Using word cards. This strategy involves deliberately studying words and their translations on small word cards. Usually, the word is on one side with its translation on the other. While this has lately become a rather unfashionable activity, research overwhelmingly shows that it's a worthwhile learning strategy.

Using word part analysis. Here you need to first break complex words into their prefixes, roots, and suffixes. Then you'll have students use the meaning of the parts to help remember the meaning of the whole word. Over 60% of low-frequency words in English come from French, Latin, or Greek, all of which make use of word parts. A small number of very useful prefixes and suffixes occur in many English words.

Using a dictionary. This lets students find meanings and other useful information about words, in addition to giving them independence from the teacher.

When learners encounter a low-frequency word in class, you should use this opportunity to practice one of the four vocabulary strategies. You've got a quick introduction to them above, but we'll really discuss them in more detail in a later lesson.

Listen again.

(1) What are the four useful vocabulary learning strategies? (英語で書け。)

Questions 2 to 4. Read the three questions on the test sheet carefully. You have 20 seconds to read the questions, now.

Listen.

The goal of teaching strategies is to create autonomous learners, learners who can learn by themselves inside and outside the classroom. Research and classroom practices are evolving in many directions to try to better understand and facilitate learning for students of all ages. In general, successful language learners tend to select strategies that work well together, according to the requirements of the language task. These learners can easily explain the strategies they use and why they use them.

Listen again.

(2) What can autonomous learners do? (日本語で書け。)

(3) What do successful language learners often do? (日本語で書け。)

(4) What would YOU do to incorporate this lecture in your future lessons? (日本語で書け。)

Write the answers on your answer sheet in Japanese. You have another 20 seconds.

This is the end of the Listening Comprehension Section

(☆☆☆☆◎◎◎)

【2】次の(1)～(5)のそれぞれについて，下線部の①～④のいずれかに一箇所誤りがある。その箇所を番号で指摘し，正しい表現に直して書け。

(1)　It would be impossible ①for you and ②I ③to do ④such a mean thing.

(2)　Every one ①of us ②has ③a responsibility to the society ④which he is a part.

(3)　After you ①had ②studied a new vocabulary word, you are more likely to ③notice it when you ④hear it spoken.

(4)　I went to Okayama ①by my ②friend's ③new car, a ④bright red sports car.

(5)　She ①wrote to her mother and said she ②was returning to the airport ③next day, two days ④earlier.

(☆☆☆◎◎◎)

【3】次の(1)～(3)の各組において，a)とb)がほぼ同じ意味になるように，b)の(　　)内にそれぞれ適切な一語を書け。

(1)　a)　The Olympic Games are held at intervals of four years.

　　b)　The Olympic Games (　　) place (　　) four years.

(2)　a)　He insists that I should go there on his behalf.

　　b)　He insists (　　) (　　) (　　) there on his behalf.

(3)　a)　When she saw her mother, she leaped for joy.

　　b)　At the (　　) (　　) her mother, she leaped for joy.

(☆☆◎◎◎)

【4】次の(1)～(5)のそれぞれについて，日本文の意味になるように(　　)内に適切な一語を書け。

(1)　今，高松駅に着きました。車で迎えに来てくれませんか。

I've just arrived at Takamatsu Station. Could you (　　) me up?

(2)　彼は事件とはまったく関係ないかのようなそぶりをしている。

He acts as though he had (　　) to do with what happened.

(3)　この町のバス料金はいくらですか？

What's the (　　) on the buses in this town?

(4) 結局は質の良い物を買う方が得をする。

It pays in the long (　　) to buy goods of high quality.

(5) 駅へ着いてみたら，汽車は出たばかりのところだった。

I got to the station only (　　) find that the train had just left.

(☆☆◎◎◎)

【5】次の(1)～(3)のそれぞれについて，下のア～クを並べかえて日本文と同じ意味の英文を作る。その際，( ① )，( ② )内にあてはまる語(句)を，ア～クからそれぞれ選んで，その記号を書け。(文頭に来る語も小文字で表記している。)

(1) 朝どんなに晴れていても，いつ雨が降るかわからないから，万一に備えて傘を持っていったほうがよい。

However fine it looks in the morning, it may start raining at any moment, so you (　　)(　　)( ① )(　　)(　　)( ② )(　　)(　　).

ア an umbrella　イ better　ウ case　エ had
オ in　カ it　キ rains　ク take

(2) 私たちはあなたの発言のおかげで，計画の欠陥に気づき，全事業計画を再検討することにしました。

(　　)(　　)( ① )(　　)(　　)( ② )(　　)(　　) reconsider the whole project.

ア us　イ the fault　ウ and　エ your words
オ the plans　カ made　キ realize　ク in

(3) 税制改革の白熱した議論が国会で行われていた。

A heated debate (　　)(　　)( ① )(　　)(　　)( ② )(　　)(　　) the Diet.

ア under　イ was　ウ in　エ on　オ tax reform
カ way　キ of　ク the problem

(☆☆☆◎◎◎)

【6】次の会話文の①～⑤の(　　)内にあてはまる最も適切なものを，それぞれ下のア～エの中から一つずつ選んで，その記号を書け。

Betty　:　Have you read *Southern Adventure*?

Phyllis :　No. But I read a review of it the other day. It said it was very good. Let me see, (　①　)

Betty　:　Uh...no, Patrick Buxton. You're probably thinking of Philip Burton — you know, the man who wrote *Under the Weather*.

Phyllis :　Oh yes. (　②　) I'm sure that it was *Southern Adventure* I read about. It concerns some people who go off to South America, doesn't it?

Betty　:　Yes, that's right. (　③　) It's extremely well written, and most amusing in parts.

Phyllis :　I must read it. I'll see if I can get Dick to give it to me for my birthday.

Betty　:　My copy is from the library, so I can't lend it to you, I'm afraid.

Phyllis :　Oh, no, of course not. I can easily wait. I've got plenty to do. (　④　)

Betty　:　I know. There's so much to do, isn't there? The only time I get for reading is late at night, when everyone's in bed and asleep.

Phyllis :　That certainly is the quietest time. (　⑤　) I generally fall asleep right away.

①　ア　do you agree with what he says in the book?
　　イ　it's by Patrick Burton, isn't it?
　　ウ　who wrote it, do you know?
　　エ　who's the person I'm thinking of?

②　ア　I always mix those two up.
　　イ　I haven't heard of him before.
　　ウ　I've read those two already.
　　エ　They are confused, aren't they?

③　ア　I hear it's very good.
　　イ　I'll begin to read it one of these days.

ウ　I'm all fed up with reading it.

エ　I'm in the middle of reading it at the moment.

④　ア　I can't read without glasses.

イ　I don't get much time for reading, actually.

ウ　I'm a notoriously slow reader myself.

エ　What is worse, my glasses are being repaired.

⑤　ア　But I can't fall asleep.

イ　But I find I can't keep awake once I get into bed.

ウ　But I have an easy time reading it.

エ　But I suffer terribly from nightmares.

(☆☆◎◎◎)

## 【中学校】

【1】次の文は，中学校学習指導要領(平成20年3月告示)の外国語科の目標を英語で示そうとしたものである。次の①～④の(　　)内にあてはまる英語を書け。

I. OVERALL OBJECTIVES

To develop students' (　①　) communication abilities such as listening, speaking, reading and (　②　), deepening their understanding of language and (　③　) and fostering a positive (　④　) toward communication through foreign languages.

(☆☆☆◎◎◎)

【2】次の(1)～(4)の日本語で説明している活動を表す用語を英語で書け。

(1)　2人1組になって行う言語活動のこと。

(2)　必要な情報のみを素早く見つけ出す読み方のこと。

(3)　現実的な状況の中で，英語を使用する機会を与えるために，学習者に役割を演じさせる活動のこと。

(4)　クラス全体で一斉に音読すること。

(☆☆☆◎◎◎)

【3】英語の授業で次の(1)～(4)のことを生徒に伝えたいとき，英語でどのように話すか。書け。

(1) あなたのカードをだれにも見せてはいけません。

(2) もう2分延長します。

(3) 私たちのお客様に大きな拍手をしましょう。

(4) できるだけたくさんの人に，英語で話しかけなさい。

(☆☆☆◎◎◎)

【4】言語材料として，比較級を導入する際に，JTLとALTが行う対話形式のオーラル・イントロダクションを考え，JTL，ALT(各3項目)に分けて英語で作成せよ。ただし，英文は全部で10文以上とし，追加の部分が必要であれば，付け足してもよい。

(☆☆☆◎◎◎)

【5】1992年に書かれた次の英文を読み，あとの問いに答えよ。

Child labor is a serious and ( ① ) problem in many parts of the world, with as many as 25 percent of all children between the ages of 10 and 14 in some regions estimated to be working. Many are employed illegally or in dangerous conditions that maim and kill them, while others grow up without education and condemned to life-long ( ② ), the International Labor Organization (ILO) says in a study. Statistics on the total number of working children are difficult to estimate because most of these children are unpaid family workers or are working illegally, invisible to the collectors of labor-force statistics.

The dangers that working children face are many and varied. Children laboring in brickyards carry heavy loads that often leave them injured, weakened and deformed. Child carpet weavers work long hours each day under conditions that ( ③ ) their eyesight and lead to deformed backs and limbs. Young pencil-makers, who manufacture the pencils that other children use at school, breathe in hazardous slate dust that condemns them to early disability and death from tuberculosis and other ( ④ ) diseases. Labor in mines and glass or match factories — all places that employ large numbers of children — is also highly dangerous for them.

Youngsters working as household domestic servants may be the most vulnerable and exploited children of all, which is especially true of those who live in the homes of their ( ⑤ ). The majority of such servants are girls, frequently pre-adolescents. Many of these young domestic servants live in enforced isolation with little or no contact with children their own age. Clinical observers have noted a profound stunting of the psychological growth of such children. Others are subjected to sexual abuse by their employers or forced into prostitution, many being infected with the HIV virus through numerous sexual contacts.

Agriculture still accounts for most child workers in the world, but by early in the next century, more children will probably be involved in the urban sector. This is the fastest growing area of child labor partly because so many people are leaving rural areas in search of opportunities in urban areas.

"Child labor is a human rights question. It is just unacceptable that more than a hundred million children are working and that so many children are denied their basic rights," Michel Hansenne, ILO Director General said. "Child labor is the single most important source of child abuse and child exploitation in the world."

(1) 文中の①～⑤の(　　)内にあてはまる最も適当なものを，次のア～エから一つずつ選んで，その記号を書け。

① ア alarming　イ descending　ウ interesting
エ solving

② ア education　イ happiness　ウ insurance
エ poverty

③ ア destroy　イ manage　ウ recover
エ ruin

④ ア heart　イ liver　ウ lung

エ　mental

⑤　ア　employers　　イ　partners　　ウ　siblings

エ　subordinates

(2)　本文の内容と一致するように，次の(a)，(b)の書き出しに続く最も適当なものを，下のア～エから一つずつ選んで，その記号を書け。

(a)　It's hard to guess how many children are working because

ア　helping parents' business is not considered as labor.

イ　it is illegal to collect statistics on the domestic labor.

ウ　most child labor occurs in their own residence or against the law.

エ　there are no children at work in the registered organization.

(b)　One of the serious problems of girls who work as domestic servants is that

ア　becoming adults without education might lead to prostitution.

イ　repeated sexual contacts enable them to mature psychologically.

ウ　sexually abused children have lower levels of self-esteem than nonabused children.

エ　the lack of contacts with their peers causes their mental immaturity.

(3)　本文の内容と一致するものを，次のア～カから二つ選んで，その記号を書け。

ア　One in every four children aged 10 to 14 worldwide is exploited in child labor.

イ　Nearly a quarter of children under 15 are working in hazardous situations.

ウ　Many young workers are often forced into dangerous and unhealthy jobs.

エ　Children living in rural areas are most likely to be engaged in child labor at the beginning of the 21st century.

オ　The fact that youngsters are being exploited through labor is a human rights concern.

カ　The ILO defines "child labor" as a condition where children are deprived of the opportunity for education.

(4) 本文の表題として最もふさわしいものを，次のア～オから一つ選んで，その記号を書け。

ア What is Child Labor　　イ Causes of Child Labor

ウ Child Labor Laws　　エ Costs of Eliminating Child Labor

オ Public Sectors Against Child Labor

(☆☆☆◎◎◎)

【6】次の英文を読み，あとの問いに答えよ。

Many schools in America are cautious about allowing grade skipping even though research shows that it works well both academically and socially for gifted students, and ①<u>that</u> holding them back can lead to isolation and underachievement. A lack of awareness about the benefits of grade skipping indicates a larger problem : most education systems have little idea how to develop their most promising students. ②<u>We take for granted that those with very low IQs require "special" education, but students with extremely high IQs often have trouble learning to interact with average kids and studying at an average pace</u>.

As a culture, Americans feel very ambivalent about genius, and these mixed feelings have led to long debate about what to do with highly gifted children. ③<u>Until the mid-1980s it wasn't difficult for high-ability kids to skip grades, but since that time schools have often forced gifted students to stay in their own age grade</u>. However, research actually shows that if gifted kids are given appropriately ④<u>challenging environments</u> — even when that means being placed in classes of much older students — they usually turn out fine. Moreover, if they are not given special treatment, high-IQ kids can become isolated and may end up as depressed adults who don't have friends or who find it difficult to function in society.

[　　　　　　　　⑤　　　　　　　　]

Davidson Academy rejects ⑥<u>the American belief</u> that if we just try hard enough, we can all be talented. At the academy, the concept of IQ is totally accepted even though it has been challenged by many educators for years. In addition, while many school administrators oppose grouping students by ability because they say it creates social inequalities, Davidson Academy groups the 45 elite students into easier and harder English, math, and science classes. The philosophy of the school asks a tough question about American education : has emphasizing equality over excellence gone too far? ⑦If so, is the only answer to separate the brightest kids from the "average" world?

(1)　下線部①と同じ用法のthatを使用している文を，次のア～エから一つ選んで，その記号を書け。

ア　Our teacher told us yesterday that he had seen it.

イ　She made an announcement to the public that she would get married soon.

ウ　It was her business that the mother left to her son.

エ　He was so impressed by the picture that he decided to be a painter.

(2)　下線部②，③を日本語に直して書け。

(3)　下線部④の例として本文で挙げられているものを，日本語で書け。

(4)　[　⑤　]には，次のア～ウの三つの文が入る。それらを適切な順に並べかえて，その記号を書け。

ア　Some educators argue that a fresh approach to educating very smart children is needed, especially because gifted children are a threatened resource.

イ　The academy started with 45 of America's smartest children aged 11 to 16 who took classes at least three years beyond their grade level.

ウ　That's the idea behind the Davidson Academy of Reno, Nevada, which was established as a public school in 2007.

(5)　下線部⑥は具体的にはどのようなことか。日本語で書け。

(6)　下線部⑦を，soの指す内容を明らかにして，日本語に直して書け。

(☆☆☆◎◎◎)

【7】次の日本文を読み，下の問いに答えよ。

①*We Are The World*は，約25年前アフリカの飢餓救済運動のテーマソングとして作られた。その中で「私たち一人ひとりが手を差し伸べて，一緒に明るい明日を作ろう。」と呼びかける45人のアーティストたちの歌声は，現代を生きる私たちをも勇気づけてくれる。

②地球温暖化や環境汚染，貧困など，世界は今，数多くの問題に直面している。私たちの身の回りにも解決すべき問題がたくさんある。ある調査によると，日本では4人に1人が何らかのボランティア活動を経験している。私たちの小さなやさしさが人々の心に灯をともし，少しずつ世の中を変えてゆく。さあ，今日からできることを始めよう。

(1) 文中の下線部①，②を英語に直して書け。

(2) あなたが今までに取り組んだボランティア活動について，その活動を通して学んだことも含め，50語以上の英語で書け。

(☆☆☆◎◎◎)

## 【高等学校】

【1】次の各文は，高等学校学習指導要領(平成21年3月告示)の外国語科の一部を示そうとしたものである。①～⑦の(　　)内にあてはまる語句を書け。

○　「コミュニケーション英語Ⅰ」においては次に掲げるすべての事項を適切に取り扱うものとする。

(ア)　不定詞の用法，(イ)　関係代名詞の用法，(ウ)　関係副詞の用法，(エ)　(　①　)の用法，(オ)　代名詞のうち，itが名詞用法の句及び節を指すもの，(カ)　動詞の(　②　)など，(キ)　(　③　)，(ク)　分詞構文

○　(　④　)については，コミュニケーションを支えるものであることを踏まえ，言語活動と効果的に関連付けて指導すること。

○　英語に関する各科目については，その特質にかんがみ，生徒が(　⑤　)を充実するとともに，授業を(　⑥　)の場面とするため，授業は英語で行うことを基本とする。その際，(　⑦　)に応じた英

語を用いるよう十分配慮するものとする。

(☆☆☆◎◎◎)

【2】次の英文は，授業におけるJTLとALTの役割について述べようとしたものである。①～⑫の(　　)内にあてはまる最も適切な語を，あとのア～シから一つずつ選び，その記号を書け。ただし，同じ選択肢を2回以上選ぶことはできない。

The ( ① ) of communicative activities is for students to learn to communicate in the target language. Through communicative activities, students are expected to learn to listen to, speak, read, and write the language for the ( ② ) of communication. In order to learn to communicate in a foreign language, both learning activities and communicative activities should be treated as steps toward ( ③ ) communication.

Learning activities are activities in which students focus on the ( ④ ) of language, such as ( ⑤ ) the rules of sentence structures, ( ⑥ ) words and phrases, or reading sentences out loud. On the other hand, communicative activities are any activities in which students ( ⑦ ) communicating through role-play dialogs, speeches, reading, writing, etc., or actually communicate with the JTL and the ALT or with each other. Judging by students' ( ⑧ ), the JTL can alternate or ( ⑨ ) learning activities and communicative activities so that the students attain the goals set for listening, speaking, reading, and writing abilities.

Through communicative activities, students can practice listening, speaking, reading and writing, and may often make mistakes in ( ⑩ ) and understanding English. This is, however, a necessary step to communicate effectively. Though learners are eventually expected to acquire all of the abilities (listening, speaking, reading and writing), they should be given ( ⑪ ) opportunity to listen to and speak the language before or at the same time that they learn to read and write it. Therefore, the JTL and the ALT should ( ⑫ ) much more time to communicating with students and to giving them frequent opportunities to talk with each other.

| | | | |
|---|---|---|---|
| ア real | イ feedback | ウ dedicate | エ mechanics |
| オ using | カ ample | キ integrate | ク pronouncing |
| ケ goal | コ understanding | サ purpose | シ practice |

(☆☆☆◎◎◎)

【3】代名詞itを形式的に主語として用いるもののうち，itが名詞用法の句を指すものを1文，節を指すものを1文書け。また，代名詞itを形式的に目的語として用いるもののうち，itが名詞用法の句を指すものを1文，節を指すものを1文書け。

(☆☆◎◎◎)

【4】次の英文を読み，あとの問いに答えよ。

A personal computer that was sold in the early 1980s probably included a keyboard as the only input device. Today, most new PCs include a pointing device as standard equipment. If the computer is a desktop or tower model, the pointing device is usually a mouse. [ ① ] Another type of mouse is the optical mouse. This non-mechanical mouse emits a beam of light from its underside and uses the light's reflection to judge the distance, direction, and speed of its travel.

The mouse's history actually goes back to the early 1960s when a group of scientists and engineers at the Stanford Research Institute (SRI) in California were charged with the task to develop ways to "increase human intellect." Specifically, Dough Engelbart's group was looking for ways to use computers to help people complex problems. In his vision of this problem-solving system, Engelbart saw the need for a device that would enable the computer user to input data more efficiently than could be done using other standard input devices of the time, such as keyboards, light pens, and joysticks. With funding from NASA, Engelbart's team developed a series of simple tests to determine which input device would enable users to move a cursor around the screen in the amount of time and with the least effort. Engelbart and a fellow scientist, Bill English, created a simple ②gadget that became a prototype for the mouse we know today.

The first mouse was a small wooden box with a button on the upper right corner. (　A　) the hard rubber ball used in modern mice, Engelbart's mouse actually used two small wheels that were positioned at an angle of 90 degrees to each other on the mouse's underside. With this device, the user could move the mouse only up and down or side to side. (　B　)moving it diagonally was a problem, the prototype worked well. On December 9, 1968, Engelbart and his co-researchers demonstrated their first mouse at a conference held in San Francisco.

The mouse was not noticed immediately by people in the industry. Many people did not see much of a future for computers in general, except for military and large business use. This lack of vision, however, did not stop or even slow ③the visionary Engelbart. ④Through his career in computer science, he has described or developed technology that was considered to be ahead of its time. His discoveries and inventions in the fields of networking, user interface technologies, and other computing disciplines continue to affect everyday computer users. Although inventing the mouse did not make him rich as his patent ran out before the mouse became widely used in personal computers, it helped launch one of the most innovative pursuits in the history of computer science.

(1) [　①　]には，次のア～オの五つの文が入る。それらを適切な順に並べかえて，その記号を書け。

ア　The ball rolls inside the case when you move the mouse around on a flat surface.

イ　The computer uses this data to position the mouse pointer on the screen.

ウ　Most mice are mechanical.

エ　Inside the mouse, rollers and sensors send signals to the computer, telling it the distance, direction, and speed of the ball's motions.

オ　They contain a small rubber ball that protrudes through a hole in the bottom of the mouse's case.

(2) 次のア，イの語は，第二段落から抜き出したものである。それぞれの語を本来の位置に戻したとき，その次の語を書け。

ア　solve　　イ　least

(3) 文中のA，Bの(　　)内にあてはまる最も適切な語(句)を，次のア～エから一つずつ選んで，その記号を書け。

A　ア　When　　イ　As soon as　　ウ　Unless　　エ　Rather than

B　ア　Thus　　イ　But　　ウ　Although　　エ　However

(4) 下線部②，③について，次の説明文の(　　)内にあてはまる最も適切な語(句)を，それぞれのア～エから一つずつ選んで，その記号を書け。

② The word "gadget" can be replaced by (　　).

ア　screen　　イ　device　　ウ　input　　エ　button

③ The phrase "the visionary Engelbart" means (　　).

ア　Engelbart was foresighted　　イ　Engelbart was practical

ウ　Engelbart had good eyesight　　エ　Engelbart had fuzzy visions

(5) 下線部④を日本語に直して書け。

(6) 本文の内容と一致しないものを，次のア～カから二つ選んで，その記号を書け。

ア　Most personal computers marketed in the early 1980s were not equipped with a mouse.

イ　Nowadays, a desktop computer usually comes with a mouse as its pointing device.

ウ　Engelbart's first mouse consisted of a wooden case and two wheels placed parallel to each other.

エ　In the 1960s, computer systems were considered by many people to be useful for only military and large business purposes.

オ　Engelbart contributed to the field of computer science with his inventions not only in user interface technologies but also in networking.

カ　Engelbart did not earn a lot of money from inventing his mouse because he never held a patent on it.

(☆☆☆☆◎◎◎)

【5】次の英文は，雲の形成や降水における，ある微生物の役割について述べたものである。英文を読み，あとの問いに答えよ。

Scientists have been probing the role of microbes in cloud formation and precipitation, something discussed in a session at the American Society for Microbiology meeting, in New Orleans. But ①this type of precipitation may not be an accident of chemistry so much as an evolutionary adaptation by certain bacteria, argues Brent Christner of Louisiana State University.

He's referring to the ability of certain one-celled organisms to foster the nucleation of ice crystals.

Even an airborne dust mote can serve as the surface on which water vapor condenses and freezes. But he notes that the most efficient ice nucleators — micro-particles that can catalyze freezing at the highest temperatures — are microbes. Some bacteria, like Pseudomonas syringae, for instance, can serve as nuclei for ice formation at temperatures as warm as -2 degrees Celsius, more than 10 degrees warmer than the ice-forming limit for dust motes.

Christner now thinks it's probably no accident that “the most active ice nucleators are biological.” As part of a (　A　) strategy, he contends, many microbes may have evolved “to essentially piggyback on the hydrological cycle.”

The plant pathogen P. syringae “can probably be found on any plant in your back yard,” Christner says. But if winds fling this germ high enough into the air, it can be entrained by currents for up to a week or more. ②During that time, the fragile microbe faces a risk of deadly drying or irradiation by damaging solar ultraviolet rays. Safety, from its perspective, is a moist leaf back on the ground.

This bacterium can return to Earth, he says, by fostering the nucleation of moisture that will eventually rain out as liquid or ③frozen precipitation. And don't worry about their getting cold along the way. Christner and other biologists have isolated live germs from precipitation — including the heart of a fallen hailstone.

I can even picture the graphic novel story line the LSU scientist might offer students: wind-kidnapped microbes that turn on the synthesis of ice-nucleating proteins in hopes of skydiving back ④home.

(1) 下線部①を日本語に直して書け。

(2) 空気中のほこりより微生物の方が氷の結晶の核になることにおいて効率的である点を日本語で書け。

(3) 文中のAの(　　)内にあてはまる最も適切な語を，次のア～エから一つ選んで，その記号を書け。

ア harmful　イ negative　ウ mischievous　エ survival

(4) 下線部②はどのようなときか，日本語で書け。

(5) 下線部③の例を同じ段落中の一語で書け。

(6) 下線部④は何を意味しているか。文意に即して，日本語で書け。

(☆☆☆☆◎◎◎)

【6】次の日本文を読み，下の問いに答えよ。

70代の母は時々終戦後の日本の貧しい生活について話す。①台所も風呂もない間借りで新婚生活を始めた話をする母の表情は，なぜか明るい。当時の日本は，貧しいながら，明るい将来を思い描くことのできる時代だったのであろう。

今の日本は，戦後ほど貧しくはないが，地球温暖化や少子高齢社会など，新たな課題が立ちはだかっている。また，私たちの身の回りにも解決すべき課題がたくさんある。②今の教育に求められるのは，若者に，今後直面するであろういかなる困難にも負けないたくましさを身につけさせることである。

(1) 文中の下線部①，②を英語に直して書け。

(2) 困難な状況に立ち向かうことのできる生徒を育てるために，あなたは教師としてどのような取り組みをしようと考えるか。50語以上の英語で具体的に書け。

(☆☆☆◎◎◎)

# 解答・解説

## 【中高共通】

【1】(Part1)　No.1　(B)　No.2　(A)　No.3　(C)　No.4　(C)　No.5　(B)　(Part2)　No.1　(B)　No.2　(A)　No.3　(B)　No.4　(C)　No.5　(A)　(Part3)　(1)　Guessing from context.　Using word cards.　Using word part analysis.　Using a dictionary.

(2) 教室の内外において自分で学ぶことができる。　(3) 言語課題の要求に従って，組み合わせることでうまく機能する方略(ストラテジー)を選択する。　(4) 英語だけでなく，その学び方を指導する機会を授業ごとに取り入れるようにする。

〈解説〉(Part1)　インストラクションも英語で流される場合に備え，「メモを取って良い」「最後に質問が読まれる」などの指示は間違いなく聞き取れるよう，表現を頭に入れておくこと。また，問題を解いた後，次の問題が読まれるまでの間に，できる限り次の選択肢に眼を通すようにしておく。前もって選択肢を読んでおくことで聞き取りも楽になるはずである。　(Part2)　会話が比較的長く，内容もリスニングテストとしては難しい。したがって，比較的出題されやすい環境，福祉，人口問題等近年の社会問題に多く使用される語彙は，長文問題対策としてもよく頭に入れておく必要がある。問題文が読まれる間，キーワード，話の流れなど必ずメモを取ること。　(Part3)　この設問は教職の専門分野がテーマになっており，聞き取れさえすれば解答はできるはずである。専門分野に関する文はメディア等による練習でカバーし切れない面があるが，専門書を読む際に自身で音読するだけでも，音声として聞き取るときのリズムや文の構成をつかむ際の助けになるので，試してみると良い。

【2】(1) ② me (2) ④ of which (3) ① have
(4) ① in (5) ③ the next day

〈解説〉(1) It is ～ for (人) to do「(人)にとって…することは～だ」という意味の表現で，Itはto以下を置き換えた形式主語。(人)の部分には固有名詞または代名詞の目的格が置かれる。 (2) which以下の従属節の元の文を考えると，“He is a part of the society.” という文なので，前置詞 “of” が必要である。設問は下線部④を書き換える問題なので “of which” が解答となるが，文全体の自由な書き換えであれば，“the society which he is a part of” でも良い。 (3) 「～したあと，こうなるだろう」という文であるから，前半部分は後半より1段階時制が遡っていなければならない。“had studied” とする①は2段階遡っているので不適切。また，前半を生かして過去完了とすると，後半を事実に基づく結果の表現としなければならず，more likely「さらに～だろう，～しそうである」の表現自体不適切になる。 (4) 「(人)の車で」は，“in one's car” で表現する。ただし，文中に “my friend's” がなく，交通手段としての「車で」であれば，“by car” となる。 (5) “next” は「次の」という意味の形容詞だが，「次」とは常に特定の何かの「次」であるから，それ自体特定のものとなり，“the” が必要となる。一方，名詞で「次の人」という意味で使う場合には，“Next, please.(次の方どうぞ)” のように “the” なしで使用する。

【3】(1) take, every (2) on, my／me, going (3) sight, of

〈解説〉(1) 「オリンピックは4年ごとに開催される」の意味の文。「開催される」は “take place”，「～年ごとに」は “every ～ years” と表現できる。 (2) 「彼は，自分の代わりに私がそこに行くことを主張した」という文。「私が～することを主張する」は，慣用句 “insist on my(またはme) ～ing” で表現できる。この場合，「～すること」は動名詞で表し，その意味上の主語を前に置く。意味上の主語の形は，所有格または目的格となる。　(3)「母親の姿を見たとき，彼女は喜びのあまり飛び上がった。」という文。"at the sight of ～" で，「～を見て」の意味の成句。

【4】(1)　pick　　(2)　nothing　　(3)　fare　　(4)　run　　(5)　to

〈解説〉(1)　"pick (人) up" で，「(車などで)人を迎えに行く」という意味の熟語。　(2)　"have nothing to do with ～" で，「～と関係がない」の意味。表現のバリエーションとして，nothingの代わりにsomethingを置くと「～と関係がある」，疑問・否定文ではanythingで「～と何か関係がありますか」「～と何の関係もない」という意味になる。　(3)　バス，地下鉄などの料金(運賃)は "fare"，「料金」に当てる表現は他に，service charge／service fee「サービス料金」，tollage／toll「有料道路の料金」などがある。　(4)　"in the long run" で「結局は，長い目で見れば」の意味の熟語。逆に，in the short run「さしあたりは，短期的に見れば」という表現もある。　(5)　only to find that ～「結局～した，～しただけだった」という表現。that節でなく名詞(句)であれば，「～があっただけだった」となる。

【5】(1)　①　ク　　②　ウ　　(2)　①　ア　　②　ク　　(3)　①　キ　②　ア

〈解説〉(1)　had better do「～した方が良いですよ(かなり強いアドバイス)」，in case ～「万が一～の場合に備えて」の意味。so以下の空欄部分を埋めると，"so you had better take an umbrella in case it rains." となる。　(2)　"made" と "us" が選択肢にあるので，「～が私達に…させた」という構文を想定し，「あなたのアドバイスが私達に気付かせた」という英文を組み立てる。空欄を埋めると，"Your words made us realize the fault in the plans and (reconsider ～.)"　(3)　"under way" で「(計画や作業などが)進行中」という意味を表し，「(議論が)行われていた」の部分を占めると判断できる。tax form「税制改革」。"on" と "in"

の使い分けだが，原則として「議論，話合い，計画」などのテーマには“on”,「場」の前には“in”と考えれば良い。空欄を埋めると，“(A heated debate) on the problem of tax reform was under way in (the Diet).”となる。

【6】① イ　② ア　③ エ　④ イ　⑤ イ

〈解説〉① 問いかけに対する返答に“Patric Buxton”とあるので,「Patrick Burtonの作ですよね？」と問いかけているイがあてはまる。返答が“no”なので，疑問詞を含むウとエは除外できる。また，アは「著者の意見に賛成か」との問いかけであり，返答と対応しない。
② mix up「混同する」。名前の似た作家2人を混同して，いつも間違えてしまう，と言っている。ウは「その2つをすでに読んだ」で，名前を話題にしている文脈にそぐわない。エは“confusing(間違えやすい)”ならば可能だが，選択肢では「彼らは混乱している」なので話題が逸れている。 ③「南米に出かける人達のことを書いた本でしょ？」との問に「そうそう」と答えたあとのコメント。空欄の後に,「非常によく書かれているし，部分的にも楽しめる」と言っているので，ア「面白いと聞いている」，イ「そのうち読み始めるつもり」，ウ「読み続けるのにうんざり」はあてはまらない。 ④ 話が進み，Bettyが「悪いけど図書館の本なので貸せないの」と言ったことに対し，Phyllisが「もちろんいいの。待っていられるから。やる事いっぱいあるし」と答え，続けて「実際，読書のための時間はあまりないの」とするイが適切。ア「眼鏡なしでは読めない」，ウ「私も読むのが遅くて有名なの」，エ「さらに悪いことに眼鏡が修理中で」は全て論点がずれている。 ⑤ Bettyが「みんなが寝静まった時間にしか読書できない」と言ったのに対し，Phyllisが「確かにそれが一番静かな時ね」と答え，最後に「すぐに眠ってしまう」と言っているので，イ「いったんベッドに入ったら起きていられない」があてはまる。ア「寝付けない」，ウ「本を読んで気楽に過ごす」は文脈に矛盾，エ「悪夢にうなされる」も意味が通らない。

## 【中学校】

【１】① basic　② writing　③ culture　④ attitude

〈解説〉元の文は，「外国語を通じて，言語や文化に対する理解を深め，積極的にコミュニケーションを図ろうとする態度の育成を図り，聞くこと，話すこと，読むこと，書くことなどのコミュニケーション能力の基礎を養う。」となっている。下線部分(設問空欄部分)を英訳して行けば良いわけであるが，文部科学省による英語訳も同省のHP上に掲載されているので参考にできる。

【２】(1) pair work　(2) scanning　(3) role play　(4) chorus reading

〈解説〉教室活動に関連した語彙は，当設問のように用語を直接問う問題以外にも，具体的な指導方法について，英語で自分の意見を述べるような問題にも必要となる。また，教育現場でのALTとのコミュニケーションや，指導においても必要となるので，ぜひワーキングボキャブラリーに入れておきたい。

【３】(1) Don't show your card to anyone.　(2) I'll give you two more minutes.　(3) Let's give our guest a big hand.　(4) Talk to as many people as possible in English.

〈解説〉解答は例であり，文法的間違いさえなければ表現は多少変わっても差し支えない。但し，授業において生徒に伝える指示であることを踏まえ，平易で理解しやすい表現を心がける必要がある。非常に簡略化された表現や俗語的表現等は避けるべきである。

【４】JTL : I'll go around some *udon* shops next Sunday. Would you like to come with me?

ALT : Sure. That sounds like fun. I love noodles.

JTL : Really? Which do you like better, *udon* or *soba*?

ALT : I like *udon* better than *soba*. Actually, I like *udon* the best. How about you?

JTL : Of course, I love *udon* better than *soba*. Every day I have *udon* for lunch.

ALT : Oh, you love *udon* so much!

〈解説〉あくまでも解答は例であり，比較級がわかりやすく盛り込まれていれば，どのようなテーマの会話でも良い。解答では，香川県の中学生を指導するという状況を踏まえて，特産品のうどんがテーマにあがっているが，このような発想は教室で常に必要とされるものである。想像力や機転は日頃の練習で十分身につくものなので，日頃からいろいろなケースを思い巡らし，将来の教職現場に備えてもらいたい。

【5】(1) ① ア　② エ　③ エ　④ ウ　⑤ ア

(2) (a) ウ　(b) エ　(3) ウ，オ　(4) ア

〈解説〉(1) ①「児童就労は深刻で憂慮すべき問題である」で，ア。② while以下は「一方，他(の子供達)は教育を受けずに育ち，一生続く貧困を運命づけられる(condemned to)」で，エ。 ③「児童のカーペット織工は視力を損ない，(中略)な環境で長時間就労している」で，エ。④「結核やその他の肺疾患」で，ウのlung「肺」を選ぶ。 ⑤ 家事を行う使用人についての記述。「雇い主の家に住み込みの場合，特にこれがあてはまる」で，ア。ウのsiblingsは「兄弟」，エのsubordinatesは「部下」の意。 (2) (a) 第1パラグラフ最後の文が設問に対応する。“child labor in their own residence” は “family workers” と同義。(b) 第3パラグラフの第3～5行目に「同年代の子供とのコンタクトがない，或いは非常に少なく，精神発達における成長阻害(stunting)が見られる」とあり，エに対応する。 (3) ウは，本文第2パラグラフに，危険で不健康な児童就労の例が記述されている。オは，最後のパラグラフ冒頭に「児童就労は人権問題である」との記述がある。 (4) 選択肢すべてが「児童就労」に関連したものではあるが，イ～オについては本文に言及がない。

【6】(1)　ア　　(2)　②　私たちは，非常に知能指数の低い生徒に「特別な」教育が必要なことは当然のことだと思っているが，極端に知能指数が高い生徒は，平均的な子どもたちとふつうに接する事や，平均的なペースで勉強するのにしばしば苦労している。　③　1980年代の半ばまでは，能力の高い子どもが飛び級をするのは難しいことではなかったが，それ以降，学校は才能のある生徒を，しばしばその年齢の学年にとどめてきた。　(3)　はるか年上の生徒のクラスに入れられること。　(4)　(ア)　→　(ウ)　→　(イ)　　(5)　十分に努力しさえすれば，みんな優秀になれるということ。　(6)　もし，優秀であることよりも平等であることを重視しすぎているとすれば，最も優秀なこどもたちを「平均的な」世界から引き離すことが唯一の解決策なのだろうか。

〈解説〉(1)　問題箇所の文は，"research shows that holding them back can ～." という形で，「researchはthat以下のことを示している」という文。この場合のthatは接続詞のthatであり，「先生はthat以下のことを私たちに告げた」という構文のアと同じ用法である。イのthatも接続詞ではあるが「～という声明を発した」とする「同格」のthatであり，that以下はannouncementとイコールの内容となっている。ウは "business" を強調するために前に出したIt is ～ thatの強調構文。エは，so ～ that …「あまりにも～なので…だ」の構文である。　(2)　②　take ～ for granted「～を当然のことと受け止める」の意。問題文は目的語がthat節で長いので後ろに持って行った形。have trouble ～ing「～するのに苦労する」。　③　skip grades「飛び級をする」。現在完了の意味が伝わるよう注意して訳す。　(3)　下線部④に続く文 "even when that means ～" の "that" は "challenging environments" が置き換えられた代名詞であり，"that means ～" で④が説明されていると考えられる。(4)　イ・ウはそれぞれ "The academy", "That's the idea ～" と，定冠詞・代名詞で始まっており，先行する文には，それらについての記述があるはずと考えられる。したがって，いずれもパラグラフの第1文目にはならない。アの全体をウの代名詞Thatで受け，ウの文中の

“Davidson Academy of ～” をイの “The academy” で置き換えた，という順序が推察できる。 (5) 下線部⑥の後に同格のthatが続き，以下の文が “the American belief” と同義であると判断できるので，that以下を訳出すれば良い。 (6) 問題のポイントは，soの指す内容を明示できているかどうかであり，soは先行する文 “has emphasizing ～ gone too far?” を受けているので，その内容を具体的に解答に盛り込む。

【7】(1) ① *We Are The World* was composed about 25 years ago as a theme song for a campaign to help save Africa from starvation. ② The world is now faced with various problems such as global warming, environmental pollution, and poverty. (2) (略)

〈解説〉(1) ① 解答中 “save” は原形不定詞。helpは後ろにto不定詞，原形不定詞の両方を置くことができ，この場合「救済を助ける」の意味となる。歌のタイトルは “The song *We Are The World*” とするのが一般的だが，設問の場合あまりにも有名な曲なのでタイトルを斜体にするにとどめた。「作られた」は “written” でも可。「飢餓救済運動～」は，“to support famine relief in Africa” 等としても良い。 ② “global warming”，“environmental pollution”，“poverty”，“$CO_2$ emission” など世界的な問題についての表現は，新聞等で用語をおさえておくこと。(2) 50語は文章としてそれほど長くないので，数行～10行以内で考えをまとめれば良いが，何を書くか考え込んでいれば時間切れになってしまう。貧困，人口問題，気候変動，環境保護／汚染，教育など，出題されがちなテーマについては日頃から自分なりの姿勢や考え方をすぐまとめることができるよう，問題意識を持っておくことが大事である。平易な内容で良いが，文法的間違いは絶対に犯さないよう注意すること。

## 【高等学校】

【1】① 助動詞 ② 時制 ③ 仮定法 ④ 文法 ⑤ 英語に触れる機会 ⑥ 実際のコミュニケーション ⑦ 生徒の理解

の程度

〈解説〉高等学校学習指導要領＞第8節外国語＞第3款英語に関する各科目に共通する内容等＞2ウ，3イ，4をそのまま引用した問題である。学習指導要領に関する問題は，この設問のように，具体的な語句で空欄補充をさせる場合が多い。外国語科に関する記述は指導要領中の数ページにすぎないので，よく読みこなして完全に頭に入れておくこと。

【2】① ケ　② サ　③ ア　④ エ　⑤ コ　⑥ ク
⑦ シ　⑧ イ　⑨ キ　⑩ オ　⑪ カ　⑫ ウ

〈解説〉①「生徒にとっての伝達活動の目標は，目標言語での意思疎通を学ぶことである」で，後半に出てくるtarget(目標)という語と対を成すgoalが適切。　② for the purpose of ～「～の目的で」　③ 空欄を含む文意は，「外国語でコミュニケーションを取ることを学ぶために，言語学習活動と伝達活動の両方は，実際の(real)意思疎通へのステップとして取り扱われるべき」となる。学習の場と，実際の(real)場という2つの場を軸に，言語学習について論じている。　④⑤⑥ 問題箇所の文は「学習活動は，文構造の理解(understanding)，単語やフレーズの発音練習(pronouncing)，あるいは文の音読など，その中で生徒が言語の仕組み(mechanics)に重点的に取り組むための活動である」となる。　⑦ throughの前までの文意は，「一方，伝達活動とはその中で生徒がコミュニケーションを取ること(communicating)を練習する(practice)あらゆる活動である」ということ。　⑧⑨ 空欄を含む文は，「生徒からの反応(feedback)によって判断しつつ，JTLは生徒が聴く，話す，読む，書く能力の獲得に向けて定めた目標を達成できるよう，学習活動と伝達活動を，交互に行ったり(alternate)，あるいは統合したり(integrate)することができる」という意味。　⑩ 問題箇所の文意は，「伝達活動を通じ，生徒は，聴き，話し，書き，読む練習ができ，また英語を使い(using)，理解する上で誤りを犯すかもしれない」ということ。　⑪ 問題箇所they ～ languageまでの文は「彼らはその言語を聞いて話す十分な(ample)機会を与えられるべきである」という意味。

⑫　空欄を含む文意は「したがって，JTLとALTは，生徒とコミュニケーションをとるために，そして生徒に対し彼らが相互に話す機会を頻繁に与えるために，より多くの時間を割く(dedicate)べきである」ということ。

【3】[主語・句]　It is fun to travel to new places.　[主語・節]　It is a pity (that) you can't come.　[目的語・句]　I thought it wrong to tell her about it.　[目的語・節]　Let's keep it a secret that they got married.

〈解説〉作業としては単純な英文作成であるが，文法的事項を説明するための例文を作成するのは教育現場で頻繁に要求されることであり，実践的な能力を問われていると考えるべきである。したがって，生徒に理解できないような難解な例文は必要なく，与えられた文法的事項が明確に把握でき，理解しやすい文を作成する必要がある。内容は何でも良いが，条件を読み違えないよう丁寧にこなしてほしい。

【4】(1)　ウ→オ→ア→エ→イ　(2)　ア　complex　イ　amount　(3)　A　エ　B　ウ　(4)　②　イ　③　ア　(5)　彼(エンゲルバート)は，コンピュータ・サイエンスにおける自身の仕事を通じて，時代の先を行くと考えられていた技術を説明したり開発したりしてきた。　(6)　ウ，カ

〈解説〉(1)　パラグラフ内の文の順序は，指示語や定冠詞theのついた名詞を手がかりに判断する。ア文頭のThe ballは，オのa small rubber ballを表し，イのthis dataはエのthe distance, direction and speedを表していることから，オ→ア，エ→イという順序が推察できる。さらに，オの主語Theyが複数であることからmiceを受けているとわかれば，ウ→オ→アという順番が判断でき，ウ「殆どのマウスは」から，イ「コンピュータはこのデータを利用して～」に至る文章の繋がりを把握することができる。　(2)　この設問は，それぞれの語が抜けていて違和感のある箇所を探して行くほかない。アは“help people (solve) complex problems(人々が複雑な問題を解く助けとなる)”で，原形不定詞の

「help＋人＋動詞原形」の形，イはin the (least) amount of timeとwith the least effortの2つのフレーズが対となっている。　(3)　A　空欄を含む文前半が「現代のマウス」，後半が「Engelbartのマウス(初期のマウス)」についての叙述であり，空欄にア・イ・ウが入るのは時系列的に成り立たない。rather thanは必ずしも「むしろ」という意味合いではなく，対立的に「～ではなく」という意味で使われている。　B　“was a problem”と“worked well”は意味の上で対立しているので順接的なアは除外。対立的な2文の間に入るのであればイ・エも可能だが，トップに位置するのでalthoughまたはthoughが入ると判断できる。

(4)　②　that以下「私達が今日知っているマウスの原形となった」から，「道具」の意味のdevice。　③「しかしながら，この展望(vision)のなさもEngelbartをとどめることはおろか，減速させることすらなかった」から，物理的視力・視界について表現しているウ・エは除外。foresightedは「先見の明のある」，practicalは「実際的・実用的」で，前者が適切。　(5)　特に複雑な構文ではなく，“He has described or developed technology. (彼は技術を説明，あるいは開発してきた)”というSVOに，文頭からカンマまでの修飾部分「コンピュータ・サイエンスにおける自身の仕事を通じて」と，technologyにかかるthat以下「時代の先を行くと考えられていた」を加えて文をまとめる。　(6)　ウ　選択肢の「互いに平行に位置づけられた2つのホイール」に対し，本文の第3パラグラフの第2文に「90度の角度で位置づけられた」とある。カ　選択肢の「特許を取っていなかった」に対し，本文最後の文に「マウスがパソコンに広く使われる前に特許が切れた」とある。

【5】(1)　この種の降水は，化学的な偶然性というより，ある種のバクテリアが進化の過程で適応したという面が大きいかもしれない。

(2)　より高い温度で氷の結晶の核になることができる点。　(3)　エ

(4)　微生物が風によって巻き上げられ，1週間もしくはそれ以上空中にあるとき。　(5)　hailstone　(6)　地上

〈解説〉(1)　not A so much as B「Aではなく，むしろB」という意味。

bacteriaは「細菌」としても良い。また文後半は英文に忠実に，「ある種のバクテリアによる進化的適応かもしれない」としてもかまわないが，解答では日本語として意味がより伝わりやすい形で訳されている。
(2)　第3パラグラフの2行目に「彼は最も効率的な氷の結晶の核は(中略)微生物であると指摘している」とあり，3行目に「ある種のバクテリアは(中略)，粉塵が氷の結晶を生成できる限界よりも10度も暖かい摂氏マイナス2度の暖かさで氷の結晶の核として作用できる」と例示がある。　(3)　空欄箇所以下に「(Christnerは)多くの微生物が“主として水循環に便乗する方向で”進化した，と考えている。」とある。piggybackは「おんぶ・肩車される」から「便乗する」という意味。
(4)　文頭が指示語を含む“During that time ～”であることから，「そのとき(that time)」は直前の文に記述があると推察できるので，その箇所を引用する。　(5)　下線部③を含むフレーズに「液体あるいは凍った降雨として」とあり，すなわち「雨またはあられ，ひょうなど」を意味するとわかるのでそれに当たる語をさがす。同じ段落の最後の部分に「落ちてきたhailstoneを含む降水から生きた菌を取り出した」とあることからもこの語と推察できる。　(6)　コロン以下の「風に連れ去られた微生物」，「故郷へ戻るスカイダイビング」から，地上にあった微生物が風に巻き上げられ，戻ってくるという流れがつかめる。

【6】(1)　①　When she tells the story of her newly married life living in a rented room without a kitchen and a bathroom, she somehow looks happy.
②　What is expected of today's education is to equip the youth with the mental strength to survive any difficulties that they might face in the future.
(2)　(略)
〈解説〉(1)　解答は例であり，表現が異なっても差し支えない。原文の意味が伝わることが第一であるから難しい言い回しは避け，自信の持てる平易な語彙を使い，文法的な誤りを犯さないよう注意を払って書く事が望ましい。英作文の問題は何らかの形式で出題されるので，短文から200語程度の文まで，日頃から書きなれておく必要がある。

(2)　自分の考えを自由に記述する問題であり，模範解答はない。このような設問のテーマとして何が出題されるかを予測するのは難しいが，教育現場での取り組みばかりでなく，現代の社会問題についても，自分なりの姿勢や考え方をすぐまとめることができるよう，日頃から問題意識を持っておくことが大事である。平易な内容で良いが文法的間違いは絶対に犯さないよう注意すること。

# 2011年度　実施問題

## 【中高共通】

【1】(Words in parentheses should not be read.)

Listening Comprehension Section

There are three parts to this section, with special directions for each part. You may take notes while you are listening.

Now, let's begin Part 1. In this part, you will hear five conversations between two people. After each conversation, a third person will ask a question about what was said. Read the four possible answers on your test paper, choose the best answer to each question, and write it on your answer sheet. You will hear each conversation and question about it just one time.

PART1(記号で答えよ。)

No.1

(M) Did Alice show any interest in going to Montreal with us?

(F) As a matter of fact she did, but decided against it because we'll be getting back so late.

Question: What are the man and woman going to do?

(A) Return from Montreal early.

(B) Leave Alice in Montreal.

(C) Go to Montreal without Alice.

(D) Go back to Montreal later.

No.2

(F) Would you push four for me, please?

(M) Sure. I'm getting off there, too.

Question: What does the man mean?

(A) I'm going to the fourth floor.

(B) I'm getting off at two o'clock.

(C) I'm going to Room 44.

(D) I'm getting off the train.

No.3

(M) Haven't you gotten in touch with Marie yet?

(F) I keep trying, but all I get is a busy signal.

Question: What does the woman want to do?

(A) Keep busy.

(B) Talk to Marie.

(C) Remember to call.

(D) Touch Marie.

No.4

(F) I know how much ice cream to get, but what kind?

(M) Oh, I'll leave that up to you.

Question: What does the man mean?

(A) I'll see you later.

(B) I'll be up soon.

(C) You can leave it with me.

(D) You can decide that.

No.5

(M) Where was this one taken?

(F) Oh, that must have been in New York. Look how tall the buildings in the background are.

Question: What are the man and woman probably looking at?

(A) The backyard.

(B) A map.

(C) Stolen property.

(D) A photograph.

Now, let's go on to Part 2. In this part, you will hear two conversations.

After each of them, you will be asked some questions. Read the four possible answers on your test paper, decide which one is the best answer to the question you heard, and write it on your answer sheet. You will hear the conversations and the questions about them two times.

PART2(記号で答えよ。)

Questions 1 to 4 refer to the following dialog.

(F) These two rooms contain postwar American paintings from New York in the 1950s.

(M) You know, I've never really understood modern art.

(F) Well, it helps to know a little about the artists and their ideas.

(M) Tell me about the one on that wall—to me it just looks like splashes of paint.

(F) Well, it *is*, and that's just what the artist intended. He put the canvas on his studio floor and poured the paint on it very quickly.

(M) [*Chuckle.*] I can see that. But *why*!

(F) Many artists in the fifties were very interested in psychological theories. They felt their accelerated method of painting was really quite directed—but not by the conscious mind. They thought that when they painted quickly the subconscious mind made instant, intuitive choices about color and shape. They didn't want logical, deliberate decisions to interfere with the free flow of images. The artists actually believed their work was more honest that way, and they cared more about honesty than anything else.

(M) I always wondered why they painted like this. I guess modern art makes a little more sense when you hear the ideas behind it.

No.1

Question 1: Where does this conversation probably take place?

(A) In a movie studio.

(B) In a gallery.

(C) In a PC supplies shop.

(D) In a psychologist's clinic.

No.2

Question 2: Which of these words most accurately describes the artists' working method?

(A) Spontaneous.

(B) Tedious.

(C) Uninteresting.

(D) Painstaking.

No.3

Question 3: Which of these words probably best describes the paintings?

(A) Realistic.

(B) Disproportionate.

(C) Abstract.

(D) Unfinished.

No.4

Question 4: What is the man's attitude in this conversation?

(A) He hates modern art.

(B) He wants to understand the art.

(C) He doesn't trust psychologists.

(D) He isn't interested in the explanations.

Questions 5 to 9 refer to the following dialog.

(F) Wasn't that lecture interesting? Of all sea animals, the jellyfish, with its clear plastic membrane and strange bell-shaped body, has always intrigued me.

(M) Professor Smith sure knows what he's talking about, but I don't understand why he said that jellyfish can't really swim. He carefully explained its distinctive method of locomotion.

(F) Yes, and it's fascinating. When the jellyfish expands its bell, water rushes in. When it contracts its bell, the water is expelled in one direction, and the jellyfish moves in the other.

(M) It's really unique in the way it uses the principle of jet propulsion to move. But isn't that swimming?

(F) Perhaps, but I suppose not in the same sense as fish do. Fish propel themselves with their tails to go wherever they want. You see, a jellyfish can only move upward. Then, as it begins to sink again, it poisons the tiny creatures it uses for food with its long string like tentacles that dangle beneath it.

(M) Oh, so it can't swim just anywhere it wants.

(F) Not at all. A jellyfish is taken wherever tides and currents carry it.

No.5

Question 5: What is the main topic of this conversation?

(A) What jellyfish look like.

(B) How jellyfish move.

(C) What jellyfish eat.

(D) Where jellyfish live.

No.6

Question 6: Where did this conversation probably take place?

(A) Below the boat.

(B) At the reception desk.

(C) In a school.

(D) In the air.

No.7

Question 7: How is a jellyfish shaped?

(A) Like a bell.

(B) Like a long stick.

(C) Like a small locomotive.

(D) Like a flat tire.

No.8

Question 8: How does a jellyfish go up?

(A) By dangling its tentacles.

(B) By using tiny jets.

(C) By waving its tail.

(D) By expelling water.

No.9

Question 9: When does a jellyfish catch its food?

(A) When contracting its string.

(B) When surrounded by fish.

(C) When near the shore.

(D) When sinking downward.

Part 3. In this part, you will hear about the results of a study on snoring two times. Before listening, you should read the four questions carefully so that you can write the answers in Japanese on the answer sheet. You have 20 seconds to read.

Now, listen.

PART3(日本語で答えよ。)

Children who always snore when they sleep are four times more likely to get bad grades in school than are students who never snore, according to a new study.

A group of German scientists asked the parents of 1,129 third-graders whether their children snored always, frequently, occasionally, or never. The researchers also collected information about how well the students did in school.

Frequent and constant snorers did worse in math, science, and spelling than did occasional snorers and non-snorers, the data showed.

Questions

(1) What is the problem with children's snoring?

(2) Who carried out this research?

(3) What did the scientists ask the parents?

(4) Name the three fields in which the scientists found significant differences.

This is the end of the Listening Comprehension Section.

(☆☆☆◎◎◎◎◎)

【2】次の1～5のそれぞれについて，下線部のいずれかに誤りがある。誤りのある箇所を番号で指摘し，正しい表現に直せ。

1 He asked me ①how I thought of ②his decision about going ③overseas to ④study drama.

2 I wonder if you ①were aware that ②because of his work he had to ③give up ④to study.

3 She is not, ①proper speaking, ②a British citizen, but she ③has lived in Britain for ④nearly twenty years.

4 I ①came down with ②the flu, and the doctor suggested ③to take a few days off ④to rest at home.

5 ①I'm sorry to bother you, ②but ③could you please tell me where ④is the post office?

(☆☆☆◎◎◎)

【3】次の1～3の各組において，a)とb)がほぼ同じ意味になるように，b)の(　　)内にそれぞれ適切な一語を書け。

1 a) If I had had a little more money, I could have bought the bag.

b) A little more money would have (　　)(　　) to buy the bag.

2 a) You had better not go out until the weather is better.

b) I advise (　　)(　　)(　　) go out until the weather is better.

3 a) He failed repeatedly, but he never gave up.

b)　(　　)(　　) of repeated failures, he never gave up.

(☆☆◎◎◎◎)

【4】次の1～5のそれぞれについて，日本文の意味になるように(　　)内に適切な一語を書け。

1　それを今日しようが，明日しようが，たいして変わりない。

It makes no (　　) whether you do it today or tomorrow.

2　今の私があるのは母のおかげである。

My mother has made me (　　) I am today.

3　仕事を中途半端なままにしてはいけない。

Don't (　　) your work unfinished.

4　出発が遅かったら，夕立にあっていただろう。

(　　) you started later, you would have been caught in a shower.

5　いつまでにそれを直してもらえますか?

How (　　) can I get it mended?

(☆☆◎◎◎◎)

【5】次の1～3のそれぞれについて，与えられた語(句)を並べかえて日本文と同じ意味の英文を作るとき，(　①　)，(　②　)内にあてはまる語(句)を，下のア～クからそれぞれ選んで，その記号を書け。(文頭に来る語も小文字で表記している。)

1　彼の家は駅から非常に離れたところにあるので，通学にとても不便を感じている。

His house is located (　　)(　　)(　①　)(　　)(　　)(　②　)(　　)(　　) great inconvenience in going to school.

ア　away　　イ　far　　ウ　from　　エ　he

オ　so　　カ　suffers　　キ　that　　ク　the station

2　彼女がヘビを非常に嫌っていたことは疑いがないようだ。

(　　)(　　)(　①　)(　　)(　　)(　②　)(　　)(　　) very much.

ア　that　　イ　snakes　　ウ　seems　　エ　no

オ there　カ doubt　キ disliked　ク she

3 彼にはそのことについて話し合える友達がいなかった。

He (　)(　)(　①　)(　)(　)(　②　)(　)(　) matter.

ア with　イ friends　ウ the　エ talk

オ no　カ about　キ to　ク had

(☆☆☆◎◎◎◎)

【6】次の会話文の1～5の(　)内にあてはまる最も適切なものを，それぞれあとのア～エの中から一つずつ選んで，その記号を書け。

*Kenji, an exchange student, is sitting at a table in a restaurant. A waiter comes to serve him.*

Waiter : Good evening. Have you decided what you'd like to order,(　1　)

Kenji : I think I'm ready. I'd like the grilled halibut dinner with potato, please.

Waiter : (　2　) You can have boiled, mashed, baked, or French fries.

Kenji : I'd like the baked potato. And I'd like to order the Caesar salad, too.

Waiter : Oh. Are you sure? That salad is a main dish. You know that a salad comes with the halibut?

Kenji : No, I didn't know that. In that case, forget the Caesar salad.

Waiter : OK. The meal also comes with soup. There's a choice of cream of mushroom or tomato.

Kenji : Hmm.... I'm not very keen on mushrooms. I think I'll have the tomato.

Waiter : Fine. What kind of dressing would you like with your salad? We have Italian, French, and Thousand Island.

Kenji : Italian sounds good.

Waiter : All right then. (　3　) Anything to drink with that?

Kenji : Just water, please.

Waiter : (　4　) Anything else?

Kenji : Just one thing: what is halibut?

Waiter : A fish, sir.

Kenji　: I see. (　5　) Can I see the menu again?

1　ア　or can I get you anything else?

　イ　or do you need more time to think?

　ウ　or would you like the halibut dinner?

　エ　or are you ready to pay?

2　ア　Can I get you anything else?

　イ　Wouldn't you like a salad with that?

　ウ　What kind of potato would you like?

　エ　We're out of halibut, but we have plenty of potatoes.

3　ア　One grilled halibut dinner with a baked potato and Caesar salad.

　イ　One grilled halibut dinner with a baked potato, tomato soup, and a salad with Italian dressing.

　ウ　A tomato salad with Italian dressing and soup. No mushrooms.

　エ　A halibut dinner with a baked potato, mushroom soup, and a tomato salad with no dressing.

4　ア　Right.　イ　Please.　ウ　Pardon me?　エ　I'm sorry.

5　ア　That sounds delicious.　イ　What kind of fish is it?

　ウ　Could you bring my salad first?　エ　Actually, I don't like fish.

(☆☆◎◎◎◎)

## 【中学校】

【1】次の文は，中学校学習指導要領(平成20年3月告示)の「言語材料の取扱い」の一部を示そうとしたものである。次の①～③の(　　)内にあてはまる語句を書け。

1　発音と(　①　)とを関連付けて指導すること。

2　文法については，(　②　)を支えるものであることを踏まえ，(　③　)と効果的に関連付けて指導すること。

(☆☆☆◎◎◎◎)

【2】次の1～3の日本語を英語に直せ。

1　指導案　　2　復習　　3　まとめ

(☆☆◎◎◎◎)

【3】英語の授業で次の1～4のことを生徒に伝えたいとき，英語でどのように話すか。書け。

1　3人のグループを作りなさい。

2　一人が質問して，もう一人が答えなさい。

3　正しい答えを丸で囲みなさい。

4　すべてのものを机の中に入れなさい。

(☆☆◎◎)

【4】言語材料として，動名詞を導入する際に，JTLとALTが行う対話形式のオーラル・イントロダクションを考え，それぞれの書き出しを「JTL: 」「ALT: 」という形にして英語で作成せよ。ただし，英文は10文以上とする。

(☆☆☆☆◎◎◎)

【5】次の英文を読み，あとの問いに答えよ。

Research has shown that heart attack victims who have pets live longer. Even watching a tank full of tropical fish may lower blood pressure, at least temporarily. A study of 92 heart disease patients found that a year later those who owned pets were more likely to be ( 1 ) than those who did not. The study found that only six patients who owned pets died within one year compared with 28 percent of those who did not own pets.

The therapeutic use of pets as companions has gained increasing attention in recent years for a wide variety of patients—people with AIDS or cancer, the elderly, and the mentally ill. ( 2 ) people, with whom our interactions may be quite complex and unpredictable, animals provide a constant source of comfort and focus for attention. Animals bring out our nurturing instinct.

They also make us feel safe and unconditionally accepted. We can just be ourselves around our pets.

Research has found that pet ownership can reduce stress-induced symptoms. In a study, people undergoing oral surgery spent a few minutes watching tropical fish in an aquarium. Their relaxation level was measured by their blood pressure, muscle tension, and behavior. It was found that the subjects who watched the fish were much more relaxed than those who did not watch the fish (　3　) to surgery. Other researchers have found that petting a dog has been shown to lower blood pressure, and that bringing a pet into a nursing home or hospital can uplift people's moods and enhance their social interaction.

We should point out here that pets can be a source of (　4　) to some people. They may worry who will take care of their pets when they die. In most cases, however, the need to take care of the pets gives a (　5　) for living to many terminally ill patients, prolonging their life span.

It is surprising that it does not matter what the pet is in order to get the therapeutic benefit. It could be a dog, a cat, a parakeet, a goldfish, or anything else. The only thing that matters is that the animal is of interest to you. However, it is important that the pet you have selected fits your temperament, living space, and lifestyle. Otherwise, it will be an additional source of stress. So, have a good look at the pet and see whether it is a perfect match for you.

問1　文中の1～5の(　　)内にあてはまる最も適切な語を，次のア～エから一つずつ選んで，その記号を書け。

| | | | | | | | | |
|---|---|---|---|---|---|---|---|---|
| 1 | ア | alive | イ | dead | ウ | dying | エ | living |
| 2 | ア | Likely | イ | Not | ウ | Similar | エ | Unlike |
| 3 | ア | ahead | イ | before | ウ | prior | エ | superior |
| 4 | ア | care | イ | stress | ウ | comfort | エ | symptoms |
| 5 | ア | hand | イ | reply | ウ | reason | エ | question |

問2　本文の内容と一致するように，次の(1)～(3)の書き出しに続く最も適切なものを，あとのア～エから一つずつ選んで，その記号を書け。

(1) The presence of pets

ア is reported to be useful for oral surgery because it lowers surgeons' relaxation level.

イ always causes pet owners to feel anxious about what happens after their death.

ウ can help people feel relaxed and can decrease their heart rate and blood pressure.

エ evokes the patients' responsibility to take care of them.

(2) A study showed that

ア 28 among 92 heart disease patients with pets died within one year.

イ when the participants watched fish for a few minutes they felt less stressed.

ウ bringing a pet into a nursery encouraged people's socialization.

エ all the pet owners had lower blood pressure than the people who did not own a pet.

(3) When you want to have a pet,

ア you must consider how well you can get along with it.

イ you should examine the temperament of the animal.

ウ you must depend on the therapeutic benefit of it.

エ you should be careful of the breed of the animal.

問3 本文の内容と一致するものを，次のア～カから2つ選んで，その記号を書け。

ア Pets give a positive effect on both people's physical and emotional aspects.

イ A study found that taking care of pets improves the cognitive functioning of patients.

ウ The author expects that animal-assisted therapy will become more popular in 10 years.

エ How much you are interested in animals is the predictor of long life.

オ Any pet is available for the therapeutic benefit if chosen carefully.

カ　It is said that animals stimulate the patients' survival incentive because they are safe.

(☆☆☆◎◎◎◎)

【6】次の英文を読み，あとの問いに答えよ。

The early settlers went to the North American continent to establish colonies which were free from the controls that existed in European societies. They wanted to escape the controls ( 1 ) on their lives by kings and governments, priests and churches, noblemen and aristocrats. To a great ( A ), they succeeded. In 1776 the British colonial settlers declared their independence from England and established a new nation, the United States of America. ①In so doing, they rejected the control of the king of England and declared that the power to govern would lie in the hands of the people. They were now free from the power of the kings. In 1789, when they wrote the Constitution for their new nation, they separated church and state so that there would never be a government-supported church. This greatly limited the power of the church. Also, in writing the Constitution they expressly prohibited titles of nobility to ensure that an aristocratic society would not develop. There would be no ruling ( B ) of noblemen in the new nation.

②The historic decisions made by those early Americans have had a profound effect on the shaping of the American character. By limiting the power of the government and the churches and ( 2 ) a formal aristocracy, they created a climate of freedom where the ( C ) was on the individual. The United States came to be associated in their minds with the concept of individual freedom. This is probably the most basic of all the American values. Scholars and outside observers often call this value "individualism," but many Americans use the word "freedom." Perhaps the word "freedom" is one of the most ( 3 ) words in the United States today.

By "freedom," Americans mean the desire and the ability of all individuals to control their own destiny without outside ( D ) from the government, a ruling noble class, the churches, or any other organized authority. The desire to be free from controls was a basic value of the new nation in 1776, and it has continued to attract immigrants to this country.

There is, however, a price to be ( 4 ) for this individual freedom: self-reliance. Americans believe that individuals must learn to rely on themselves or risk losing freedom. This means ( 5 ) both financial and emotional independence from their parents as early as possible, usually by age 18 or 21. It means that Americans believe they should take care of themselves, solve their own problems, and "stand on their own feet."

問1 文中の1～5の( )内には，次の[ ]内の語を適切な形に直したものが入る。それぞれ適切な形に直した一語を書け。

[pay eliminate achieve place generate respect]

問2 文中のA～Dの( )内にあてはまる最も適切な語を，次のア～オから一つずつ選んで，その記号を書け。

ア interference イ extent ウ independence エ class
オ emphasis

問3 下線部①，②を日本語に直せ。

問4 本文の内容と一致するように，次の(1)～(3)の書き出しに続く最も適切なものを，下のア～エから一つずつ選んで，その記号を書け。

(1) The early settlers went to the North American continent and established colonies because they wanted to be free from

ア the control of British colonists.
イ the power to give orders to them.
ウ the influence of their families.
エ the problems of poverty and hunger.

(2) There are no titles of nobility in the United States today because

ア no one likes aristocrats.
イ very few of them are from the aristocracy.
ウ the churches don't allow it.
エ they are forbidden by the Constitution.

(3) The American belief in self-reliance means that

ア　receiving money from charity, family, or the government is never allowed.

イ　a person will be respected by others if he or she is very dependent on them.

ウ　people must take care of themselves and be independent, or they risk losing their freedom.

エ　students must pay all the fees for themselves when they go to college.

(☆☆☆☆◎◎◎◎◎)

【7】次の日本文を読み，下の問いに答えよ。

①今の世の中は我々が育った頃と大きく異なっているということは否定できない。個人主義が浸透した結果，地域社会の結束力が弱まり，人間関係も希薄になってきている。その反面，インターネットなどの普及により，地域を越えた人間関係が新たに生まれつつある。こうした社会の変化に伴い，教師の役割も変わってきている。②教師はもはや英語や数学といった教科を教えることだけを期待されているのではなく，生徒のあらゆるニーズに対応していかなくてはならないのだ。

問1　文中の下線部①，②を英語に直せ。

問2　昔と比較して中学生が変わったと思われる点を一つ挙げ，それについて50語以上の英語で書け。

(☆☆☆☆◎◎◎)

## 【高等学校】

【1】次の1～6の各文は，高等学校学習指導要領(平成21年3月告示)の外国語科について述べたものである。内容の正しいものには○印を，間違っているものには×印をつけよ。

1　「コミュニケーション英語基礎」及び「コミュニケーション英語Ⅰ」をすべての生徒に履修させなければならない。

2　「コミュニケーション英語Ⅰ」の標準単位数は3単位であるが，2単位とすることができる。

3　「コミュニケーション英語基礎」の目標は，「英語を通じて，積極的にコミュニケーションを図ろうとする態度を育成するとともに，情報や考えなどを的確に理解したり適切に伝えたりする基礎的な能力を養う。」である。

4　「英語表現Ⅰ」は，「コミュニケーション英語Ⅰ」を履修した後に履修させなければならない。

5　「英語会話」は，1年次に履修させてもよい。

6　「コミュニケーション英語Ⅰ」，「コミュニケーション英語Ⅱ」及び「コミュニケーション英語Ⅲ」をすべて履修した場合，高等学校で1,300語，中学校・高等学校で2,200語を指導することとなる。

(☆☆☆☆◎◎◎)

【2】次の英文は，高等学校の授業でJTLとALTがティーム・ティーチングを行う際の利点を，動機付けの観点から述べようとしたものである。①～⑩の(　　)内にあてはまる最も適切な語を，あとのア～コから一つずつ選んで，その記号を書け。ただし，同じ選択肢を2回以上選ぶことはできない。

The mere ( ① ) of the ALT in class can be motivating to students because he / she is a native speaker of the language. Students look very happy when they talk to the ALT and find themselves understood. It is in this way that they are motivated to study the language.

At a certain stage students may be willing to study simply out of( ② ), but the JTL and the ALT should constantly try to think of how to ( ③ ) students' motivation. In other words, ( ④ ) should be created to keep students studying the language in an enjoyable and effective way. The ALT is expected to speak as often as possible to students on an individual basis not only in class but out of class as well. The more ( ⑤ ) there is between the ALT and students, the more motivated the students will feel in their studies.

Most students want to express in the language what they feel or think while studying it in an interesting and stimulating way.

Games and game-like activities are effective for motivating students to study the language in an enjoyable manner. These activities can be all the more effective if developed so that students have to express themselves in order to ( ⑥ ) part in them.

As for reading comprehension, if ( ⑦ ) from a book or a magazine seem too difficult, the JTL can ask the ALT to ( ⑧ ) it or have a group of students read it together, helping each other. These are sure ways to motivate students to read more. And as for writing, students should not only ( ⑨ ) some given Japanese into a target language, but they should write about their own ( ⑩ ) regarding different topics.

| | | | | | | | |
|---|---|---|---|---|---|---|---|
| ア | translate | イ | materials | ウ | take | エ | presence |
| オ | rewrite | カ | thoughts | キ | maintain | ク | curiosity |
| ケ | interaction | コ | methods | | | | |

(☆☆☆◎◎)

【3】関係副詞where, when, why, howを含む英文をそれぞれ1文書け。ただし，where, when, whyについては先行詞のある用法とする。

(☆☆◎◎)

【4】ロサンゼルスの小学校で学級担任をしているレイフ・エスキス氏の取組みについて述べた次の英文を読み，あとの問いに答えよ。

The teacher is afraid: afraid of looking bad, of not being liked, of not being listened to, of losing control. The students are even more afraid: afraid of being scolded and ( A ), of looking foolish in front of peers, of getting bad grades, of facing their parents' wrath.

* * * * *

( B ) though it was, I had to admit that many children in my class were behaving the way they were because they were afraid. Oh, lots of kids liked the class and quite a few learned all sorts of wonderful lessons. But I wanted more. We spend so much time trying to raise reading and math scores. We push our kids to run faster and jump higher. Shouldn't we also try to help them become better human beings? In fact, all these years later, I've recognized that by improving the culture of my classroom, ①the ordinary challenges are navigated far more easily. It's not easy to create a classroom without fear. It can take years. But it's worth it. The following is what I do to ensure the class remains a place of academic excellence ( ② ) resorting to fear to keep the kids in line.

On the first day of school, within the first two minutes, I discuss this issue with the children. ③White most classrooms are based on ( a ), our classroom is based on ( b ). The children hear the words and like them, but they are only words. It is ( ④ ) that will help the children see that I not only talk the talk but walk the walk.

I use the following example with the students on their first day. Most of us have participated in the trust exercise in which one person falls back and is caught by a peer. Even if the catch is made a hundred times in a row, the trust is ( C ) forever if the friend lets you fall the next time as a joke. Even if he swears he is sorry and will never let you fall again, you can never fall back without a seed of ( ⑤ ). My students learn the first day that a broken trust is ( D ). Everything else can be fixed. Miss your homework assignment? Just tell me, accept the fact that you messed up, and we move on. Did you break something? It happens; we can take care of it. But break my trust and the rules change. Our relationship will be okay, but it will never, ever be what it once was. Of course ⑥( trust / break / kids / do ), and they should be given an opportunity to earn it back. But it takes a long time. The kids are proud of the trust I give them, and they do not want to lose it. ⑦They rarely do, and I make sure on a daily basis that I deserve the trust I ask of them.

問1　文中のA～Dの(　　)内にあてはまる最も適切な語を，次のア～

オから一つずつ選んで，その記号を書け。(文頭に来る語も小文字で表記している。)

ア painful イ broken ウ humiliated エ irreparable
オ brilliant

問2 下線部①の具体的内容を本文から見つけ，日本語で書け。

問3 文中の②，④，⑤の( )内にあてはまる最も適切な語を，次のア～エから一つずつ選んで，その記号を書け。

② ア by イ in ウ without エ besides

④ ア words イ facts ウ thoughts エ deeds

⑤ ア doubt イ anger ウ trust エ interest

問4 下線部③のa，bの( )内にあてはまる最も適切な一語を，本文から探し出して書け。

問5 下線部⑥の( )内の語を正しく並べかえよ。

問6 下線部⑦に関して，doが指す内容を明らかにした和訳となるように，解答欄の( )内に適切な日本語を書け。

問7 本文の内容と一致するものを，次のア～オから一つ選んで，その記号を書け。

ア The author's class has always been free of fear.

イ Trust works better than fear in achieving academic excellence.

ウ Academic achievement cannot be overrated.

エ Students cannot regain teachers' trust once they lose it.

オ Once trusted, students would not betray teachers.

(☆☆☆◎◎◎)

【5】ニューヨーク州における少年法について述べた次の英文記事を読み，あとの問いに答えよ。

Governor David Paterson of New York has sent the Legislature a juvenile justice bill that would achieve two urgently important goals. It would improve the quality of the leadership and care in the state's often dangerous and inhumane juvenile facilities. And it would ensure that only children who need to be institutionalized—because they present a risk to the public—end up in the facilities.

*Albany's lawmakers must finally stand up to ①unions that are more interested in preserving jobs than in doing what is best for children.

②The argument for closing down the worst facilities and treating low-risk children in their home communities is irrefutable. In a report last year, the Justice Department found that young people in state detention facilities were frequently hit and abused; emotionally disturbed children rarely got the help they needed. Governor Paterson's juvenile justice task force found that more than half the children sent to these facilities were guilty of minor, nonviolent infractions.

In addition to the emotional toll on young people, the cost of institutionalization is prohibitive: as much as $200,000 per child, per year. That is more than 10 times the cost of successful local programs that provide monitoring, guidance and help to troubled families.

Governor Paterson's bill seeks to fix this broken system. It would create an independent office to investigate the state's facilities and recommend ways to improve residential care. It would allow the state to seek out and hire the best qualified directors for juvenile facilities. Current law requires that ③they be chosen from the ranks of people who already work within the system.

Perhaps most important, it would seek to limit the number of children who are sent away. ④It would bar family court judges from placing young people in state facilities unless they have been convicted of violent crimes, sex offenses or are found to present a public safety risk.

Gladys Carrion, Governor Paterson's commissioner of the Office of Children and Family Services, is rightly committed to closing empty, unneeded ( ⑤ ) and is a strong advocate of community-based programs. More than a dozen have been closed in the last three years, for an estimated savings of about $30 million. There are still another 26 facilities that hold about 730 young people. They employ around 1,900 people at an estimated annual cost of about $190 million.

By rights, the state should have used ⑥the $30 million it has already saved by closing facilities to help finance new community-based programs. It passed on only about $5 million, while the rest went into the general fund. It will have to put a lot more money into community programs for this new system to work.

*Albany:　ニューヨーク州の州都

問1　下線部①は，どのような施設で働く人たちの組合か，具体的に日本語で書け。

問2　下線部②の理由のうち3つを日本語で書け。

問3　下線部③が指すものを日本語で書け。

問4　下線部④を日本語に直せ。

問5　文中の⑤の(　　)内にあてはまる最も適切な一語を，本文から探し出して書け。

問6　下線部⑥は，どのように使われたか日本語で書け。

(☆☆☆◎◎◎◎◎)

【6】次の日本文を読み，下の問いに答えよ。

①研究によれば，人がいっぱいの部屋にいれば笑うようなユーモアでも，自分ひとりだけのときにはめったに笑わないことが分かっている。人がユーモアに反応する仕方には強い社会的側面がある。②お気に入りのコメディも，真顔を崩さない人がまわりにいると，あまり面白くなくなってしまう。

問1　文中の下線部①，②を英語に直せ。

問2　人と接するときにあなたが心がけていることを一つ挙げ，それについて50語以上の英語で書け。

(☆☆☆☆◎◎◎◎◎)

# 解答・解説

## 【中高共通】

【1】PART 1　No.1　(C)　No.2　(A)　No.3　(B)　No.4　(D)　No.5　(D)　PART 2　No.1　(B)　No.2　(A)　No.3　(C)　No.4　(B)　No.5　(B)　No.6　(C)　No.7　(A)　No.8　(D)　No.9　(D)　PART 3　(1)　学校の成績が悪くなる傾向がある。　(2)　ドイツ人科学者のグループ。　(3)　自分の子どもがいびきをかく頻度。　(4)　数学，理科，つづり。

〈解説〉PART 1　No.2　エレベーターでの会話。　No.3　get in touch with ～「～と連絡をとる」　No.4　up to ～「～の義務で」
PART 2　1つ目の会話は，美術館での近代美術に関するもの。2つ目の会話は，クラゲの移動に関する講義についてのもの。　PART 3「子どものいびき」について説明した英文を聞き，その内容についての質問を読み日本語で答える。

【2】1　①，what　2　④，studying　3　①，properly speaking　4　③，that I should take　5　④，the post office is

〈解説〉文中にある文法・語法上の誤りを正す問題。　1　間違えやすいがWhat do you think of [about]～? が正しい表現である。　2　give upの後には動名詞のみが続く。　3　分詞speakingを修飾するのは副詞である。　4　suggestは後に「that＋主語＋(should)＋動詞の原型」が続く。　5　間接疑問文では主語と助動詞の倒置は起こらない。

【3】1　enabled，me　2　you，not，to　3　In，spite

〈解説〉空欄補充問題。2つの文章が同じ意味になるように空欄に当てはまる語句を答える。語彙，語法，熟語の基本的な知識が問われる。　1　enableの意味，語法の知識が必要。「もう少しお金があれば，そのバッグを買うことができたのに。」　2　adviseの語法，不定詞を否定するnotの位置に注意。「天気が良くなるまでは外出しないほうがよい。」　3　in spite of～「～にも関わらず」の熟語の知識が問われる。「何度も失敗しているのだが，彼は決してあきらめない。」

【4】1　difference　2　what　3　leave　4　Had　5　soon

〈解説〉空欄補充問題。与えられた日本語に合うように空欄に当てはまる語句を答える。語彙，熟語の知識が問われる。　1　make no difference の熟語　2　what I am (now)「今の私」を知っているかが問われる。3　leave O Cの語法と意味の知識が問われる。　4　仮定法のifの省略表現　5　how soon「どれくらいすぐに，あとどのくらいで」

【5】1　①　ア　②　キ　2　①　エ　②　ク　3　①　イ　②　ア

〈解説〉整序英作文。与えられた日本語に合うように選択肢を並び替える。1　so ～ that…構文。　2　there is(seems) no doubt that～　の熟語　3　不定詞の前置詞を伴う形容詞的用法。talk with friendsの関係性でto talk withがfriendsを後置修飾する点に注意。

【6】1　イ　2　ウ　3　イ　4　ア　5　エ

〈解説〉空欄補充問題。空欄前後の会話の流れを把握すれば，それほど難しい問題ではない。3の場合，KenjiとWaiterのやりとりから，Kenjiが最終的に注文するものを選択する。5ではhalibutが魚であることを知ったKenjiが，メニューをもう一度見せてほしいと願い出た理由として合致するものを選ぶ。エが正解。

**【中学校】**

【1】①　綴り　②　コミュニケーション　③　言語活動

〈解説〉平成20年3月告示の新中学校学習指導要領より出題。出題された項目は，小学校で外国語活動が導入されたことに伴い示された。学習指導要領は改訂に伴う変更点とともに，空欄補充問題に対応できるよう使用されている表現などもチェックしておくとよい。

【2】1　teaching plan　　2　review　　3　consolidation

〈解説〉学校や英語教育に関する英単語は，ALT(外国語指導助手：Assistant Language Teacher)との授業の打ち合わせのためにも覚えておこう。他には，JTE(Japanese Teacher of English)「日本人英語教師」や，evaluation「評価」，read aloud「音読する」などがあげられる。

【3】1　Make groups of three.　　2　One person asks questions and the other person answers.　　3　Circle the right answer.　　4　Put everything in your desks.

〈解説〉クラスルームイングリッシュの表現を答える問題。生徒に指示を与える簡潔な表現を用意しておきたい。

【4】解答例

JTL　: Mr. Brown, what do you usually do on Sundays?

ALT : Well, I enjoy swimming. Swimming is a lot of fun. How about you?

JTL　: I love playing tennis. Playing tennis is a lot of fun, too.

ALT : Really? I also like playing tennis.

JTL　: Great. Are you free this Sunday?

ALT : Yes.

JTL　: Let's play tennis in the park.

ALT : Sure. What time shall we meet?

JTL　: How about two o'clock?

ALT : OK.

〈解説〉JTLとALTが行うオーラル・イントロダクションを考える問題。新出表現を多く用いながらも，何について話しているのか生徒が予想できる内容が望ましい。

【5】問1　1　ア　　2　エ　　3　ウ　　4　イ　　5　ウ
問2　(1)　エ　　(2)　イ　　(3)　ア　　問3　ア，オ
〈解説〉人間とペットに関する読解問題。問1は文法知識や文脈の流れを掴む力が問われる。5では前置詞forを後続できる名詞はウ以外ないことにも気付きたい。問2では各段落の要点を押さえることが解答につながる。(2)は第3段落，(3)は最終段落を参照。問3のような内容一致選択問題は，解答の根拠となる部分を見つけることが大切である。第2段落1文目，最終段落1～3文目より，アとオが正解となる。

【6】問1　1　placed　　2　eliminating　　3　respected　　4　paid
5　achieving　　問2　A　イ　　B　エ　　C　オ　　D　ア
問3　①　そうする際に，彼らは英国王の支配を拒否して，統治権は人民の手にあるのだと宣言した。　②　あの初期のアメリカ人たちによってなされた歴史的決定は，アメリカ人の特性を形成するのに強い影響を与えてきた。　問4　(1)　イ　　(2)　エ　　(3)　ウ
〈解説〉問1は文脈の流れや文法的な特性を考えて解答する。1は名詞直後に空欄があるため，分詞の後置修飾だと判断でき，かつ前置詞onを後続できるものを選ぶ。問2のAにはextentが入り，to a great extentで“大部分は”という意味になる。問3の英文和訳問題はとりわけ難しい英単語もないので，文型にさえ気をつければ容易に解答できる。問4の解答の根拠は，(1)第1段落前半部分，(2)第1段落後半部分，(3)最終段落である。

【7】問1　①　There is no denying that today's world is vastly different from the world in which we grew up.　②　Teachers are no longer expected only to teach their subjects such as English or math, but they must meet any needs of their students.　問2　Most junior high school students in the old days said only "hello" even though teachers encouraged them to talk with ALTs. On the other hand, a lot of students talk to ALTs even during a break today. They are less embarrassed to speak English. Present students have a more positive attitude toward communication in English than before.

〈解説〉問1は和文英訳問題。 ①「我々が育った世界」はthe world in which (where) we grew upのように前置詞＋関係代名詞，もしくは関係副詞を用いて表すことに注意。「～ことは否定できない」は客観的な事実を言っているのでThere is no denying that ～.が望ましい。 ②「もはや～ない」はno longer ～.「対応する」はmeetである。 問2は自由英作文問題。模範解答では近年の中学生が英語を活用するようになったことを述べているが，設問にもあるように，昔の事実と今の事実を対比させて書かなければならない。昔の事実と今の事実をon the other handやhoweverなどでつなぐとよい。

## 【高等学校】

【1】1 ×　2 ○　3 ×　4 ×　5 ○　6 ×

〈解説〉3「情報や考えなどを的確に理解したり適切に伝えたりする」ではなく「聞くこと，話すこと，読むこと，書くことなどの」が正しい。 6 正しくは，高等学校で1,800語，中高で3,000語である。

【2】① エ　② ク　③ キ　④ コ　⑤ ケ　⑥ ウ　⑦ イ　⑧ オ　⑨ ア　⑩ カ

〈解説〉① ALTが単にクラスにいることが　② 好奇心から　③ 生徒の動機を維持する　④ 生徒が勉強し続ける方法を生み出すべきである　⑤ ALTと生徒との交流が多くなれば　⑥ 参加するために　⑦ 本や雑誌からの教材　⑧ ALTに書き直してもらうよう頼む　⑨ 与えられた日本語を目標言語に翻訳する　⑩ 異なった話題に関する自分の考え

【3】[where] I remember the house where I was born.

[when] I will never forget the day when we first met.

[why] He will not tell me the reason why he gave up painting.

[how] This is how I trained my dog.

〈解説〉下線部が先行詞である。関係代名詞は，関係詞節中で主語や目的語や補語といった名詞の役割を果たすが，関係副詞は関係詞節中で副詞の役割を果たす。例えば，関係副詞のwhereは「その場所で～する」という意味の節を作り副詞の働きをする。ちなみに，I remember the house where I was born.は I remember the house in which I was born.に書き換えができる。

【4】1　A　ウ　　B　ア　　C　イ　　D　エ　　2　読解や数学の試験の点数を上げること。より速く走り，より高く跳べるようにすること。
3　②　ウ　　④　エ　　⑤　ア　　4　a　fear　　b　trust
5　kids do break trust　　6　子どもたちはめったに(私からの信頼を失うことはない)。だから私は，自分が(彼らに求めている信頼)に値する人間であるということを日々確認するようにしている。　7　イ

〈解説〉怖さでクラスを成り立たせるのではなく，生徒と教師の信頼を基に学級経営をしていこうとするレイフ先生の取組みについての文章である。一度失ってしまった信頼を取り戻すのは難しいということをアクティビティを通して学ばせたり，教師自身も生徒に求めている信頼に値する人間であることを日々確認したりするといった実践例が述べてある。

【5】1　違法少年の収容施設　　2　①鑑別所の少年はよく虐待を受けているから。　②情緒不安定な少年が必要な支援をめったに受けられないから。　③鑑別所に送致される半分以上の少年の違法行為は軽微で非暴力的なものだから。　④少年を収容するための経費が法外なものだから(※3つ書けば可)　　3　少年収容施設に最も適任の管理職
4　法案が通れば，少年が凶悪犯罪や性犯罪で有罪になるか公共の安全に危険を及ぼすことが明らかでない限り，家裁判事が少年を州の施設に送致することができなくなるだろう。　5　facilities　　6　500万ドルは，地域に基づいたプログラムの財政支援に使われたが，残りは一般財源に回った。

〈解説〉1　dangerous and inhumane juvenile facilitiesのことである

2　第3段落に書かれている　3　直前の文の“the best qualified directors for juvenile facilities”のこと　6　一番最後の文が該当する。

【6】解答例

1　①　Research has shown that when people are alone they rarely laugh, even though the same kind of humor makes them do so in a room full of people.　②　If you watch your favorite comedy with people who remain straight-faced, it can stop you from finding it so funny.

2　Smiles are powerful as well as universal. For example, a baby's smile has a greater power than anything else. In an instant, it makes us relaxed and refreshed. Even when we are sad or depressed, we can be happy if others smile at you. So I always try to keep on smiling.

〈解説〉1　①　研究によれば「Research has shown that」，めったに笑わない「rarely laugh」，人がいっぱいの部屋「in a room full of people」

②　笑顔を崩さない人「people who remain straight-faced」

## ●書籍内容の訂正等について

弊社では教員採用試験対策シリーズ（参考書，過去問，全国まるごと過去問題集），公務員試験対策シリーズ，公立幼稚園・保育士試験対策シリーズ，会社別就職試験対策シリーズについて，正誤表をホームページ（https://www.kyodo-s.jp）に掲載いたします。内容に訂正等，疑問点がございましたら，まずホームページをご確認ください。もし，正誤表に掲載されていない訂正等，疑問点がございましたら，下記項目をご記入の上，以下の送付先までお送りいただくようお願いいたします。

> ① **書籍名，都道府県（学校）名，年度**
> （例：教員採用試験過去問シリーズ　小学校教諭 過去問　2025年度版）
> ② **ページ数**（書籍に記載されているページ数をご記入ください。）
> ③ **訂正等，疑問点**（内容は具体的にご記入ください。）
> （例:問題文では"ア〜オの中から選べ"とあるが，選択肢はエまでしかない）

〔ご注意〕

○ 電話での質問や相談等につきましては，受付けておりません。ご注意ください。

○ 正誤表の更新は適宜行います。

○ いただいた疑問点につきましては，当社編集制作部で検討の上，正誤表への反映を決定させていただきます（個別回答は，原則行いませんのであしからずご了承ください）。

## ●情報提供のお願い

協同教育研究会では，これから教員採用試験を受験される方々に，より正確な問題を，より多くご提供できるよう情報の収集を行っております。つきましては，教員採用試験に関する次の項目の情報を，以下の送付先までお送りいただけますと幸いでございます。お送りいただきました方には謝礼を差し上げます。

（情報量があまりに少ない場合は，謝礼をご用意できかねる場合があります）。

◆あなたの受験された面接試験，論作文試験の実施方法や質問内容

◆教員採用試験の受験体験記

---


| 送付先 | | |
|---|---|---|
| | ○電子メール：edit@kyodo-s.jp<br>○FAX：03-3233-1233（協同出版株式会社　編集制作部 行）<br>○郵送：〒101-0054　東京都千代田区神田錦町2-5<br>協同出版株式会社　編集制作部 行<br>○HP：https://kyodo-s.jp/provision（右記のQRコードからもアクセスできます） |  |


※謝礼をお送りする関係から，いずれの方法でお送りいただく際にも，「お名前」「ご住所」は，必ず明記いただきますよう，よろしくお願い申し上げます。

教員採用試験「過去問」シリーズ

**香川県の**

**英語科 過去問**

編　集　© 協同教育研究会

発　行　令和5年11月25日

発行者　小貫　輝雄

発行所　協同出版株式会社

〒101-0054　東京都千代田区神田錦町2 - 5

電話　03－3295－1341

振替　東京00190－4－94061

印刷所　協同出版・POD工場

落丁・乱丁はお取り替えいたします。